Dedication

I dedicate this book to my wife, who has been the greatest support and encouragement in my life, especially towards realizing my dream of conveying my knowledge through this book to the greater good of aviation and to other professionals, not only in this magnificent industry, but also from other related industries or fields of study. I also dedicate this work to all the professionals who taught me, guided me and accompanied me in my continuous quest for perfection, satisfaction and achievement of goals (academically, professionally and personally).

Subash S Narayanan

Aircraft Ground Handling

Austin Macauley Publishers™

LONDON · CAMBRIDGE · NEW YORK · SHARJAH

Copyright © Subash S Narayanan (2019)

The right of Subash S Narayanan to be identified as author of this work has been asserted by him in accordance with Federal Law No. (7) of UAE, Year 2002, Concerning Copyrights and Neighboring Rights.

All rights reserved. No part of this publication may be reproduced, stored in a retrieval system, or transmitted in any form or by any means, electronic, mechanical, photocopying, recording, or otherwise, without the prior permission of the publishers.

Any person who commits any unauthorized act in relation to this publication may be liable to legal prosecution and civil claims for damages.

ISBN 9789948373711 (Paperback)
ISBN 9789948373704 (E-Book)

Application Number: MC-02-01-9498469
Age Classification: E

The age group that matches the content of the books has been classified according to the age classification system issued by the National Media Council.

Printer Name:
iPrint Global Ltd.
Printer Address:
Witchford, England.

First Published (2019)
AUSTIN MACAULEY PUBLISHERS FZE
Sharjah Publishing City
P.O Box [519201]
Sharjah, UAE
www.austinmacauley.ae
+971 655 95 202

Acknowledgements

I would like to acknowledge the great contribution played by Emirates Group and Dubai International Airport in giving me the opportunity to excel in my chosen field.

Foreword

An airport can be a city within a city. There are many activities taking place both by internal and external organizations, governmental agencies, commercial, etc. at an airport. My intention here is to provide an insight into the professional knowledge, activity, and the customer service orientation required by one of the core areas of any airport ground handling operation. The main subject for study in this book relates to the most critical branch of airport ground operations services. Their activities and services to customer airlines will be examined and studied in detail. In addition there is a certain basic understanding and knowledge required for all entrants or existing airport employees that is also included.

This is not a manual, nor is there any intention to replace or correct any existing manual, processes, regulations, etc. These are purely based on knowledge and experience gained through active participation in aircraft handling activities, over the past 26 years in this highly motivating and extraordinary industry. Knowledge gained through academic pursuits, exposure to related manuals and specific programs. Hands on experience gained through both personnel endeavors and active deployment, in a variety of roles under truly professional, multi-cultural, and multi-lingual environments.

A major part of my professional amelioration was due to the ideal opportunity provided at Dubai International airport, where two major aviation industry leaders operate. One is a world pioneer in airport ground handling and another is one of the top airlines in the world. I am fortunate to work for both these exemplary and prestigious organizations. This gave me ample exposure to truly professional interactions, ability to be at the forefront of cutting-edge technological knowledge and to gain understanding of the best industrial practices. The multi-cultural society and the cosmopolitan attitude were instrumental in creating a universal outlook. I take this as an opportunity to thank the Dubai government for encouraging and supporting the advancements that has made Dubai a world pioneer in the aviation industry.

The intention has been to focus on explaining the specific and complicated area of airport handling operations in an easy to understand process. Thus, several related subjects were included and explained. So it becomes a tool for both the existing and potential aviation professionals. Over the years, I noticed a need for new aspirants and existing professionals in related aviation fields for a source point to get the most critical understanding. This book is aimed at those new aspirants and professionals. There are manuals, course materials, and trainings being conducted. They are employee specific or direct job related or pertain to a main area of study. However, here the aim is to create the awareness, at the same time explain the basics, and finally touch base with ground handling core activity.

I hope this becomes a tool to all those who are eager or are fascinated to learn about a not so known branch of a fabulous industry.

Table of Contents

Introduction	**11**
Ramp Staff	**42**
Communication	**63**
Basic Aviation Knowledge	**85**
Aircraft Documentation (Ramp Operations)	**154**
Unit Load Devices	**167**
Passenger Baggage Handling	**196**
Aircraft Unloading and Loading	**220**
Aircraft Weight and Balance (Load Control)	**322**
Aircraft Ground Dispatch	**379**
Aviation Safety and Security	**401**

Introduction

An airport is the final point to begin a journey by air or for the culmination of it. For some it is a place to send off or receive loved ones, hold business meetings, eat lunch, do shopping, etc. The whole process of travel and commercialization has been simplified by the result of countless complex and complicated planning and actions of a multitude of qualified and experienced professionals, using equipment worth billions of dollars. Air travel has been made simple and safe by the rules and regulations formulated by the two world airline governing bodies known as International Air Travel Organization (IATA) and International Civil Aviation Organization (ICAO) and executed by the local government civil aviation authorities. The members of IATA are the airlines and the members of ICAO are the governments of the various countries and it is composed of a committee of experts. Although most airlines are members of IATA, there are non-IATA member airlines also.

A busy international airport is a city by itself, with government organizations, commercial enterprises, airport operators, handlers, the various airlines, etc.

Fig. 1.1: Airport terminal interior.

All of these have the common goal of making sure that travel is economical, safe, convenient, and enjoyable, so that a passenger arrives at an airport with a smile. All the functions in an airport of a country are the under preview or responsibility of the civil aviation authority of that country, which is a government organization. The basic aim of this body is the enforcement of regulatory matters governing the safe conduct of aviation operations. It is known with different names in different countries, e.g. in the US it is called the Federal Aviation Administration (FAA), for others as General Civil Aviation Authority (GCAA), etc.

Although the scope of this authority tends to vary all over the world, the core function remains the same, which is to regulate operations and supporting infrastructure of the air transport industry of their own country through the enforcement of standards. It makes sure that the national aviation system is consistent with international obligations as promulgated by ICAO and sets rules, which reflect national objectives and standards that are specific to the prevailing national socio-political climate. Its other duties include investigative duties. This is to investigate incidents and accidents to determine causes and contributing factors to make recommendations for and amendments to any shortcomings in the system.

Some governments may not have the economic power to develop or sustain the growth of an airport and in some cases the government may decide to make money out of the whole set-up. In these cases, it may give some or all of the operations to specialized commercial entities to develop the infrastructure, maintain, and run the operations at an airport, but retain itself as an overseer, enforcer, a rent collector, etc. The civil aviation authority of the government may decide to perform some of the airport functions/services e.g. airport terminal management, ramp and runway maintenance, aircraft stand /parking planning, flight operations, etc. In this age of increased commercialization, governments have turned over complete airports' concepts to businesses on a build and operate basis, with itself performing services that can have a direct implication on its territorial or judicial integrity etc. Some of these services provided by a country's government agencies at an airport are e.g.

- Security
- Immigration
- Health (medical facility)
- Fire services
- Meteorology

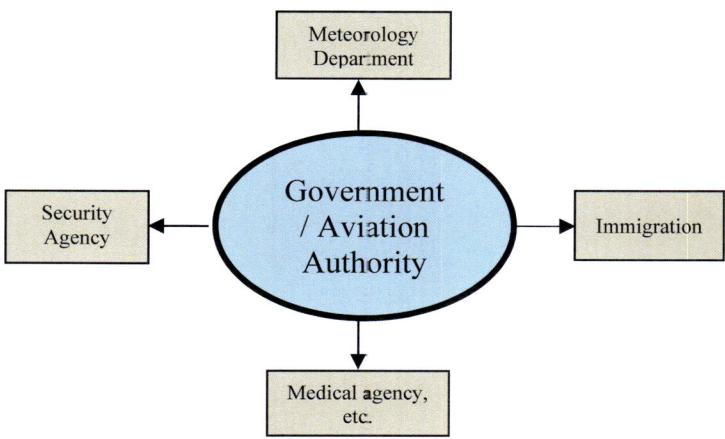

Fig. 1.2: Government agencies operating in an airport.

Introduction

It may not be possible for the civil aviation authority to provide all the services or perform all the functions at an airport due to the following:

a) The vastness of the airport; if it covers acres of land, many equipment, buildings, and personnel
b) Huge investments, maintenance, and management required for the specialized infrastructure and manpower
c) Local government business interests
d) Its own business interest for profitability
e) Airline requirements

These services are outsourced to non-governmental, private, and specialized organizations, within the legal (both local and international) parameters set and monitored by the country's civil aviation authority. These organizations can be as follows:

a) Ground handling agents
b) Airline companies
c) Catering agents
d) Maintenance companies
e) Duty-free shopping centers, etc.

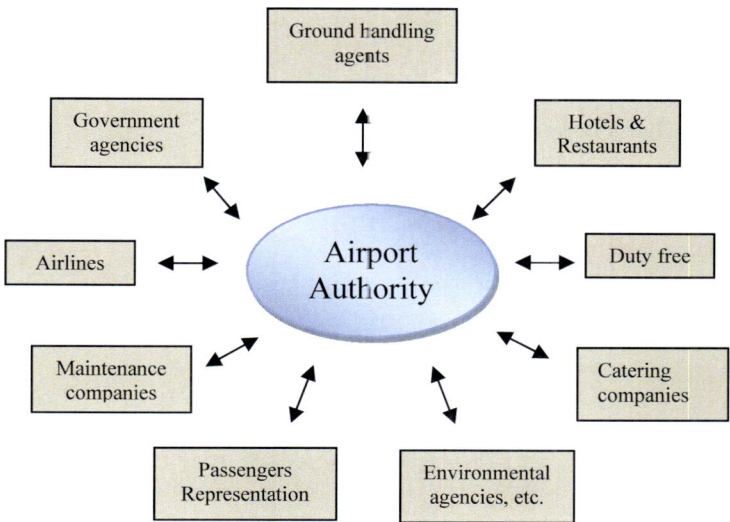

Fig. 1.3: Examples of other external service providers operating at an airport.

The latest trend is to privatize the airport to commercial entities, on a build, operate, and transfer basis. In this concept the government's main aim is to develop infrastructure through external investments of capital and expertise, thus reaping maximum economic benefits, but at the same time have an overseer approach to its operations.

We will concentrate on the ramp activities of a ground handling agent of an airport, which can be interesting, complicated, and diverse among the activities of the various organizations at an airport.

Ground Handling Company/Agents (Ground Handler)

The ground handling company or agent can be wholly private, state-owned, or a division of an airline. It is an organization or division that provides specialized service for handling the aircraft, passengers, cargo, etc. for an airline while it is on ground at an airport. Even if the ground handling services are provided by another airline's ground handling wing at an airport, this airline will be called as the ground handling company or agent for handling the aircrafts of an airline operating to that airport once agreed. For example, if an airline Y is planning to operate flights to a particular airport in India, and the ground handling services at that airport are provided by the ground handling division of another airline called X, established there and once agreed, that airline ground handling division will provide the services to the flights of the airline Y when it starts operating to that airport. Here that airline X will be called the ground handling agent or company of airline Y at that airport. The services may not be limited but would depend on the infrastructure or knowhow available with it or that it is able to procure for agreed services or level of agreed service required by the airline and finalized (contracted) for a fee. For example, the ground handling company may provide staff to function as an airline's own staff, complete with uniform and limited authority, etc. When an airline decides to operate to an airport and has received the necessary approvals from the authorities, it will need fuel for its aircrafts, food for its passengers, equipment, and trained staff to handle its passengers, baggage, other loads, etc.

Agreements are made with fuel suppliers, catering companies, ground handling companies etc., who are operating at the airport to service its needs. That is if the airline finds it commercially not viable to do it by itself or if it is not authorized to do so by the authorities. If permitted to provide ground handling services or any other services at an airport, an airline will find it commercially viable only if it is providing the services to the required number of its own operations or of other airlines also. Here commercial viability is of paramount importance, due to the large amount of investment for qualified staff, with continuous training requirements and specialized equipment, with maintenance facilities and its periodic upgrading. And of course, the technical knowhow in that particular field is also a necessity. Ground handling is essential, because without it air transportation simply cannot take place. Airports can have ground handling services provided by private companies, a consortium of companies, airlines, the aviation authority, etc. This is based on the government legislation for the country. Hence, if an airline decides not to ground handle at an airport, then it will then select a ground handling company based several factors, some of which are,

a) Cost,
b) Expertise in the area of service requirement,
c) Approved handling practice from governing bodies,
d) Meeting its standards and requirements,
e) Infrastructure available to meet its needs,
f) Quality of service, etc.

The ground handling company in turn will take into account if it can provide the services required by an airline; again, this is based on several factors, similar to the above factors considered by the airline. Basically speaking, a ground handling agent at an airport is a government (aviation authority) approved and authorized company that provides the services required to handle the aircraft, passengers, baggage, cargo, etc. as per the agreement between an airline and itself. So, as specified in the ground handling agreement between the airline and itself, the ground handling agent provides the agreed services. Sometimes an airline may decide to do some of the handling by its own staff. For example, guide arriving passengers using own airport staff. This may be due to reducing the cost by not giving it to the handling agent, to maintain the airline's profile and standards, or to meet certain airline requirements, etc. The ground handler agrees to provide those services for which it has necessary trained staff and infrastructure. Some of the services normally required by an airline at an airport are,

a) Passenger handling (check-in and boarding, disembarkation, and special services).
b) Baggage handling, build-up, etc.,
c) Aircraft cleaning,
d) Aircraft unloading and loading,
e) Aircraft weight and balance,
f) Operations Communications center,
g) Cargo acceptance, build-up, necessary documentation, etc.

Introduction

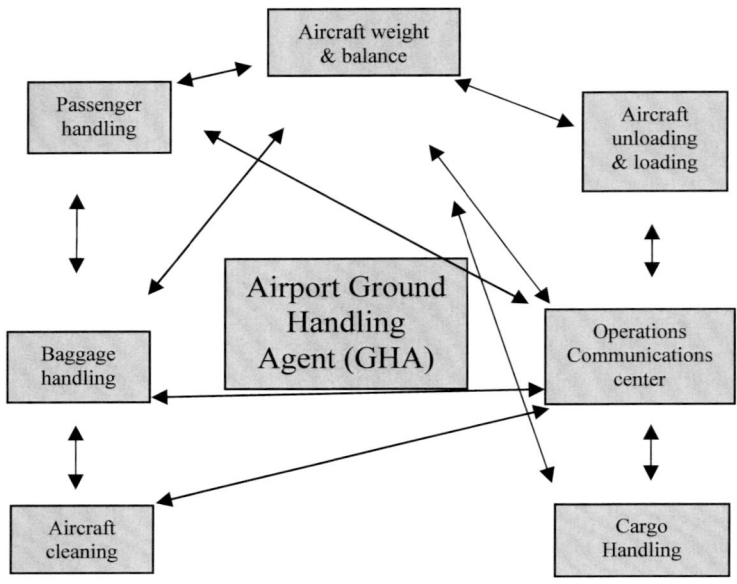

Fig. 1.4: Examples of various components of an airport ground handling agent's activities.

Now these services or activities are very broad or general terms that are the sum result of several activities together, requiring specially trained staff, the necessary area, sophisticated and specialized equipment, etc. For example, aircraft unloading and loading would mean the special equipment needed to unload the incoming load from an aircraft hold, the staff having knowledge and experience of different aircraft holds (layout and operation), segregation of the unloaded load as per category and its transportation to the respective dismantling areas, its handover to customers, etc. Also, there are backstage or support sections that provide crucial support to frontline sections, like IT, human resources, planning, etc. Another example is passenger handling, which would mean

- Guiding passengers from an arriving aircraft,
- Checking in outgoing passengers,
- Tagging the bags correctly,

- Segregating the bags as per priority or routing,
- Transporting it to the aircraft,
- Loading it correctly at a predetermined hold in the aircraft,
- The personnel and specialized equipment required for these processes, etc.

Ground handling has become a major cost item in the operation of an airline, approximately 15% of the operating cost. It actually forms a tool which helps airlines to gain and keep customers. Ground handling becomes a very important part of the total airline product.

Standard Ground Handling Agreement (SGHA)

Once a ground handling company or the ground handling by another established airline has been identified by the airline planning operation to handle its aircrafts, then there should be a legally binding agreement between the operating airline and the ground handler. Now, if each airline made legal agreements with the various handling companies across its network, it would be a very lengthy process and a legal nightmare. This is because the civil aviation handling services are quite similar, interconnected, and should complement each other.

The first attempt to standardize handling contracts took place in Europe in 1958, with a proposal to IATA for worldwide implementation. Thus, the first SGHA came into being in 1964 and was used initially by a few European carriers and then was taken over by IATA for worldwide use. The airport handling agreements sub-committee (AHASC) of the airports handling committee (AHC) ensures that the SGHA keeps pace with developments in the airline industry. The AHASC is composed of representatives of IATA member airlines working in cooperation with other airlines and non-airline handling companies. Standard IATA handling procedures have helped airlines wishing to negotiate handling agreements. These procedures were designed for two reasons, such as to specify all functions of the handling services required and to standardize the format of the ground handling agreements. The standard ground handling agreement (SGHA) fulfills these two requirements. The SGHA is made up of 3 parts:

- The main agreement,
- Annex A and
- Annex b.

The main agreement and annex A cannot be altered, but annex B can be amended and adapted to suit the needs of the parties involved. The handling agreement is of the utmost importance as it specifies, in great detail, the services which are to be provided, the legal aspects such as duration, termination of agreement, standards, and liability. The primary aim of all handling companies/ground handlers is to ensure complete customer airline satisfaction in the services provided, and the agreement acts as a guideline. The airline and handling company staff must therefore ensure to adhere to the agreement, as it would be in their best interest. Basically, the agreement contains the list of required services, handling procedures, responsibilities, etc. Annex B is used by the airline to include the specifics of the handling requirements.

Continuous training of staff and equipment upgrades are major concerns, as the aviation industry is a technology-hungry industry. The existence and profitability of any ground handling company lies in its ability to acquire and assimilate the latest technology for providing cutting-edge quality service. Today it is important to provide the best of quality service to the customer, as the customer has become more educated to quality of service, to stay above the rest. For this it is necessary to be at the forefront of technological advancements and its incorporation into the infrastructure of the ground handling services at an airport.

The ground handler's main areas of operations are at the terminal buildings and the ramp. The ramp/apron means the area within the airport, consisting of aircraft parking stands, aircraft taxi-ways/runways, and the general service roads for airport vehicles, and this area is off limits to the general public. The taxi-ways are only for the movement of aircraft to and fro from the parking stand and the runway before departure or after arrival. Both the taxi-ways and runways are prohibited to the ground handling agent employees, unless trained, carrying the necessary equipment, and only if required by authorities. The ramp of a busy and big airport is an extremely interesting place to work, where you work alongside a lot of people and equipment and come across different scenarios and problems. Handling no two aircraft on the ramp is the same. Each will have its own challenges for you to conquer. The first challenge on the ramp is the time limit to handle an aircraft, which needs to be within the airline safety and schedule requirements, at same time maximizing the load. Also, each airline and each type of aircraft will have different requirements and procedure of handling. A very important aspect of all the work done at the airport is the staff motivation and a proactive approach to the task at hand. Unlike work at other organizations, no two days or handling an aircraft is the same. The requirements for each airline are different and the problems to solve and to take corrective steps are also different. The solutions are also different, with the major consideration given to safety, economic viability, and punctuality of airline schedule. A ground handling agent can have many departments such as IT, administration, ticketing, reservations, etc. The services provided normally by a ground handling agent at an airport can be categorized into three main departments, but not restricted to the same. They are as follows:

1. Passenger Services
   a) Passenger check-in
   b) Passenger special handling
   c) Passenger guidance
   d) Acceptance and boarding passengers into an aircraft at the boarding gate
   e) Check-in of transfer passengers from other stations
   f) Provide assistance to passengers in case of lost or mishandled baggage
   g) Passenger services information and coordination section
   h) Coaching/bus services.
   i) Computer systems updates, monitoring, and support.

The various sections of passenger services provide different services to the airline passengers. The passenger for a flight is checked in at the specified time, at the check-in counters. The bags are tagged and send to the baggage make-up area for sorting, build-up, and subsequent dispatch to the aircraft for loading. At check-in passengers may be checked for any restricted items for carriage on board an aircraft, visa or other requirements are met etc. Physically challenged passengers/ un-accompanied minor passengers are provided with assistance, be it for departure or arrival. Passengers are guided to and from an aircraft. Passengers are accepted at the waiting lounge before boarding them onto an aircraft based on their boarding cards given at check-in counters. Transfer passengers from other flights, who are at the transfer area awaiting acceptance or check-in to their connecting flights, are also handled. Inbound passengers who have lost or received their baggage are assisted. Flights parking away from the terminal building with no aerobridges are provided with passenger coaches and boarding staff to transport passengers to and from the aircraft and the terminal building. These categories of services are the passenger's first contact with the airport staff, and his experience forms a factor that decides if his travel was enjoyable and if that airport is customer-friendly, with quality service.

2. Technical Services

    a) Aircraft technical services
    b) Technical equipment maintenance section
    c) Aircraft cleaning services
    d) Airline interior stores.

These categories of services are based on the ramp side of the airport. They maintain all the specialized equipment used to service and unload/load an aircraft.

Common examples of technical equipment are:

The aircraft may be parked with its nose facing the terminal building, and then it needs to be pushed back onto the taxi-way for departure. This is done by a pushback tractor. The older version of these tractors cannot be connected directly to the nose wheels of the aircraft, so a tow bar is connected in between. The tow bar for different aircrafts is different. The newer versions of the pushback tractors do not need a tow bar.

An aircraft may not have its own electric power for lights or for its on board systems i.e. its auxiliary power unit (APU) (for a common man the generator) may be unserviceable. Then a ground power unit (GPU), again a generator for the common man, is provided as a supplement to the APU. Sometimes if the aircraft will be on ground for a long period of time, the APU is switched off and the GPU is connected, to reduce the wear and tear of the APU components, as the spare parts and the repair of an APU are more costly than paying for using a GPU.

The aircraft may not be able to start its engines on its own for departure, for this an air start unit (ACU) is provided.

The aircraft air conditioning may not be sufficient or functional or APU inoperative, in this case, an air conditioning unit is connected to the aircraft. An aircraft's wheel assembly may get over-heated while landing, although it has its own cooling system (fans). In this case the hose of an ACU or sometimes, although not advisable as per aircraft engineers, the water servicing truck (normally used for replenishing the on board water tanks) are directed at the wheel assembly to cool them off. This is done only as per the instruction of the aircraft engineer/cockpit crew.

Some airlines (usually cargo) connect a tail jack unit to the tail jack mount found at near the aircraft tail, to avoid any backward tipping of the aircraft in case there is no load (weight) in the forward of the wing and heavy load in aft of the wing. This also depends on the availability of a mounting on the aircraft. The use of this unit is warranted by the load master or the safety precaution policy. *Refer to figure 1.5.*

Fig. 1.5: An aircraft tail jack (for preventing the tail section of the aircraft from tilting to the ground due to load imbalance on board).

Fuel for an aircraft is brought to the aircraft by fuel tankers or is available on the parking stand from underground pipelines. Specialized pump trucks called fuel bowsers are connected to the trucks or the stand fuel hydrants and the fuel inlet found on the wings of the aircraft. These fuel bowsers have lifts on them to reach the wing heights. There are meters or gauges to show the amount of fuel pumped and the density of the fuel, both of which are required

Introduction

by the captain. These fuel bowsers are used to de-fuel an aircraft if the fuel pumped is more than what the aircraft can take during take-off. These equipment are provided and operated by the fueling companies operating at an airport.

These are some of the main and commonly used technical equipment on the aircraft. The use of any new equipment not specified in the handling agreement on an aircraft needs the approval of the airline concerned.

Refer to figures for some of the commonly used or noticed technical equipment on the ramp.

Fig. 1.6.a.

Introduction

Fig. 1.6.b.

Fig. 1.6: An aircraft pushback tug (for pushing the aircraft onto the taxiway/runway or positioning of the aircraft at the desired position/parking on the ramp or for towing the aircraft from one point to another, without starting the aircraft engines).

Introduction

Fig. 1.7.a.

Fig. 1.7.b.

Fig. 1.7: Aircraft tow bar (for connecting the pushback tractor / tug to the docking mechanism on the aircraft nose wheel). It has safety pins which shear off in case of excess load or incorrect docking, to prevent damage to the expensive aircraft nose wheel structure.

Fig. 1.8.a.

Fig. 1.8.b.

Fig. 1.8: Aircraft tow-bar-less tug (functions similar to a pushback tractor / tug, but does not require a tow bar)

Introduction

Fig. 1.9: Aircraft Power Unit (APU), an inbuilt generator that generates electricity on board the aircraft by using the fuel for running all aircraft systems and components on board.

Fig. 1.10: Ground Power Unit (GPU), an external generator that has its own power source or fuel to generate electricity for running aircraft components when connected. Used when APU is unserviceable or not desired.

Fig. 1.11.

Fig. 1.11: Aircraft Air Start Unit (ASU), an external unit used for starting or shutting down the aircraft engines, when not possible by the inbuilt component in the aircraft.

Introduction

Fig. 1.12: Aircraft Air Conditioning Unit (ACU), an external unit used for cooling aircraft interiors when its own air conditioning unit is unserviceable.

Fig. 1.13: Aircraft technical steps, used by engineers or qualified servicing staff to reach inaccessible areas on the aircraft (for maintenance purposes).

Aircraft handling equipment are as follows:

Air-Bridges – The passengers can board from the terminal into the aircraft through a bridge positioned between them. These bridges are fixed to the terminal on one side and the other side is moveable. This moveable side is positioned at the aircraft door. Although these bridges are fitted with sensors as a safety feature, extreme care is required while positioning them.

Introduction

Fig. 1.14.a.

Fig. 1.14.b.
Fig. 1.14: Air-Bridge, for boarding or disembarking from an aircraft.

Passenger Step – Airports where air-bridges are not available or if the aircraft is parked at a remote parking stand away from the terminal building, a passenger step is required to disembark or board passengers, due to the height of the aircraft door from the ground.

Introduction

These steps may be manually or motor driven, built with certain necessary safety features e.g. each step lighting and locking systems in case of hydraulic failures.

Fig. 1.15: Passenger step (for boarding or disembarking from an aircraft).

Refer to figures of some other additionally used aircraft handling equipment on the ramp. (Low floor passenger coach, Hi-loader, tractor, dollies, trolleys, transporter, conveyor).

Fig. 1.16.a.

Fig. 1.16.b.

Fig. 1.16: Low floor passenger coach (For transporting passengers between terminals or from aircrafts to terminal and vice versa).

Introduction

Fig. 1.17.a.

Fig. 1.17.b.
Fig. 1.17: Aircraft high loader (for lifting, positioning and moving ULDs into the aircraft holds, similarly for unloading and shifting the ULDs to dollies on the ramp).

Introduction

Fig. 1.18: Tractors / Tugs (for towing / transporting ULDs on the ramp).

Fig. 1.19.a.

Introduction

Fig.1.19.b.

Fig.1.19.c.

Introduction

Fig.1.19.d.

Fig. 1.20: Dollies (for transporting Unit Load devices [ULDs] and airline pallets).

Fig. 1.20: Trolley (for transporting loose loads).

Fig. 1.21: Transporter (for positioning ULDs between dollies to high loader and vice versa).

Fig. 1.22: Conveyor belt (for loading loose loads up to the aircraft bulk hold and vice versa from bulk hold to the ground level and onto the trolleys).

Introduction

Safety Notes

All operators must perform safety and serviceability checks before and after every use of all equipment. If an equipment does not meet any of its operational or safety requirements, however minute, it must be taken out of service and send for the necessary repairs. Any leaks, whether hydraulic or oil, must be cleaned appropriately immediately and reported. One staff should be available to give directions while maneuvering heavy or high vehicles near an aircraft. All equipment must have yellow colored beacons switched on during night or during low visibility operations. All equipment servicing an aircraft must have reflectors around them. Never approach or drive behind an aircraft when its beacons (red lights), found at top and bottom of the fuselage (body of the aircraft), are flashing. This indicates that the aircraft has just arrived, its engines are still running or if it is ready to depart and its engines will be started soon or is running, so all staff and equipment must keep away from the aircraft.

Safety cones must be placed after an aircraft has come to a stop, its engine and beacons are switched off, under the tip of every wing, in front of engines and under tail section to alert/prohibit drivers of vehicles of low height or vulnerability to prevent the aircraft from getting damaged. All equipment must be fitted with portable fire extinguishers. Only trained and qualified staff should operate these equipment at the ramp. Never leave running equipment unattended. When not in use, all equipment must be removed and parked in its parking position away from the aircraft. Always try to drive a vehicle near an aircraft with the driver's side facing the aircraft.

3. Ground Operation Services

a) Aircraft documentations section
b) Aircraft unit load devices (ULD) handling section
c) Passenger baggage handling section
d) The aircraft unloading and loading section
e) The load control or aircraft weight and balance planning section
f) The ramp information and coordination center
g) The ramp coordinators or aircraft ground dispatchers.

Almost all sections of this department are located at the airport ramp side and may be restricted to general public. Our main area of study and the subsequent chapters will be dedicated for

Introduction

understanding of the various functions and roles played by a typical ground operations department. The basic sections under our study that would normally come under the ground operations department's umbrella are: Documentation, Unit load devices, Passenger baggage handling, Aircraft unloading and loading, Load control and Aircraft Ground Dispatch. Although these may vary from airport to airport, ground handling agent to agent, we will use these basics for our study.

Depending on the vastness of operations and expansion plans of a ground handling agent, the sections may be enlarged or reorganized into a departmental category. For example, the baggage services can be a department with various sections such as baggage build-up, baggage arrival, baggage transfer area, mishandled baggage section etc. Some ground handling companies also offer limited security services as well, such as guards for aircraft access control, passenger or crew escort, baggage, cargo, and other special load escort, passenger document checks, etc. So the services offered by the ground handling company vary and will depend on the requirements and availability, based on local conditions, legislation, and customer demands.

****

Chapter I
Ramp Staff

Introduction

It important to look at the most important ingredient for a quality ground handling service before we begin the actual study of the various sections of the ground operations department – staff. For any operation or work it is necessary to have the right person to do it. The right personnel are not just qualified but have the right attitude and positive outlook. Before examining and studying the different sections of ground operations services department, there are a few very crucial personal aspects and general ramp knowledge required by ramp staff, which will become apparent as we move along through various chapters. It will form the basis for good service to customer airlines, indirectly affecting passengers and directly affecting other departments' functions also. As mentioned earlier, there are a lot of people from different organizations, capacities, and backgrounds working on the ramp, so this chapter is to introduce to you the frame of mind or attitude desirable for a true professional when interacting with other co-workers and organizational colleagues.

At an airport with 24 hours' operations, in the ground handling organization, unlike most other organizations, work goes on 24 hours a day, 365 days an year, whatever the weather, with constant interaction between the medium level management to the lowest level of the organization during this time. No matter how much technology, latest equipment, or technical training is provided to staff, the important attributes mentioned in this chapter will make the difference and take the organization that extra mile in terms of quality ground handling at an airport. Although desirable behavior or attitude or habits cannot be taught, suggestions can be made and the individual should make an effort towards gaining them. Please note, just like you can draw indefinite lines through a dot, so are opinions of each individual concerning behavior/attitude of a person. What one feels appropriate may not be the case for another. The following lines of personnel behavior and attitudes are compiled from experiences gained and interpreted over many years, working on the ramp in a multi-cultural, multi-lingual, multi-religious workforce or environment. A "can do" and "will do" attitude is to be cultivated, always required, and desirable.

Chapter Contents

The ramp staff attitude and behavior
Personal grooming
Health
Performance feedback; managing conflicts and negotiations.
Performance review and promotions.

****

Ramp Staff Attitude and Behavior

Nowadays it is more correct to say that the staff comes first for an organization. An ideal organization is not where a few at the top do all the thinking and decision making while those at the lower level follow the instructions. Employees are encouraged to stimulate their initiative, and self-reliance and accountability at all levels is cultivated. Everyone must contribute to the success of the organization; it is the fruit of their achievement and both will benefit mutually.

Organizations have corporate goals and aims and so department objectives, goals/aims are formulated to complement the corporate goal/aim. It is important to align individual professional goals/aims with the departmental objectives as well. The ability to shape our future lies in our hands at the present. There is a tendency for some to blame fate, internal policies, internal politics, organizational set up, etc. for their inadequacies or failures. This is professionally fatal or reduces the person to a vegetative state with no development or contribution or negative growth. It robs them of the power to reason, to have a dream, to choose a plan to realize that dream, and aggressively pursue that dream till it becomes a reality. Blaming superiors, policies, wrong perceptions, and internal politics for lack of progress up the organization ladder can be a common trend among some staff, and all new employees should also understand that just completing their job is not enough. They should ask a few questions, like,

a) What additional qualification/experience have I got/gained (or would like to gain going forward) during the time I have been in the job? Since there are new procedures, technologies, and curricula coming into the aviation industry, it is the necessity of the staff to keep themselves educated. As the organization may only train you for you to be in the job due to the costs involved and give options for developmental education, it is your responsibility to ameliorate your professional and academic qualifications continuously.

b) Have I shown more than the required level of sustained enthusiasm, innovation, and motivation in my current job? Here enthusiasm is other than doing the assigned job quickly and correctly, rather your willingness to take on additional work or responsibilities with fervor. Innovation is to find a new and better method of doing something or to find a better solution to a problem. Motivation is a person's inner drive and desire to obtain the next higher satisfaction.

c) How well do I adapt to change? Change is constant in our environment, people must learn how to change as well if they hope to adapt successfully to an unpredictable future. Here change means in practical terms, your ability to accept and adapt to a new and better procedure or set of tasks to accomplish your job, whether the change is enforced or suggested by your superiors or junior staff.

d) Can I guarantee complete satisfaction to my superiors or customer airlines when it comes to my work or any assignment put forward? You must be able to take your responsibilities seriously and if required, at times put it above everything else.

e) Do I have the support of my colleagues / junior staff and is there mutual motivation?

The answers to all of the above will automatically tell you if you are capable, and for new employees it will provide the mindset for their way forward in the company. Today more and more organizations are taking a friendly and considerate approach towards their employees, but there is another common tendency to find fault and be critical of the policies of the company. As an employee, you should exercise positive thinking and acting. This will increase your contribution and the feedback from your surroundings will also be positive. You will receive positive or negative feedback in direct proportion to how well you satisfy the departmental objectives/goals. What you must understand is that it is in your best interest, for both the present and long term, to perform appropriately and create an edge over others to offer the best service. Another important action required is to empower yourself with additional knowledge and experience, which will enable your superiors to move you to higher responsibilities. Thus, our thoughts and actions shape our future, and the interesting point is that we can fully control both. Now you must understand that the only limiting factor in your life is your present thinking, which involves purposeful use of your imagination and accepting responsibility for everything that happens to you. A classic example of positive thinking is that of the half-filled glass. There are two answers to it, one person may say the glass is only half full and another might say that it is half empty. Here the person saying the first statement is thinking positively.

Interactions

To be successful in any field, it is important to have the appropriate knowledge, behavior, its skillful application, together with success in human relations. At an airport operations service, there is always someone working over you and below you and the ideal working environment is where people mutually motivate one another. Here our direct customer is the airline and the indirect customers are the passengers. So as a staff you will have to interact with your superiors, the airline managers, airline staff, passengers, your junior staff, and other departments or organization employees. In some airports each will be from various backgrounds, cultures, follow other traditions, languages, etc. So the frame of mind to approach them and interacting with each will be different, but you must portray a true professional attitude at all time. You should not expect to get a favorable or professional response always from any of the people mentioned. It will be in the best interest of your organization and above all yourself that you do not reciprocate with a negative response.

For example, due to a shortfall in the service provided, you are faced with a shouting or angry customer, with only minutes to complete your job strictly as per the manuals and instructions, the weather being humid and several people calling for an update on the status of your on-ground flight, the pressure inside your head maybe a thousand times more than what you can handle. It is easy to lose control, but very difficult to remain calm and objective-oriented. In this case you have to attentively listen to him, calm the customer, make him feel that you fully understand the situation, you are genuinely eager to do whatever is possible to control the damage caused and complete your job satisfactorily. Inform him of the facts and the steps being taken for service recovery and steps that will be taken to make sure to avoid recurrence. This form of calm and professional approach will foster good relations and will be suitable in the long run, as you may have to work closely in the future.

The factors on the ramp that have a negative influence on the performance and attitude of a ramp staff, in increasing order of importance, are,

1) Climatic conditions. Hot, humid, rain etc…
2) Lack of proper infrastructure or tools to do his work.
3) Customers lacking professional knowledge but questioning that of the staff and getting no support from superiors.
4) Lack of understanding (personal, empathy, sympathy) from superiors.
5) Lack of proper intervals/rest between flights and not being able to leave on time for home after the shift due multiple flights or busy ramp conditions.
6) Reduced ground times, when a flight comes delayed and staff are pressured to do the normal amount of work in less time. This is done by some airlines to gain some time to offset the effect of the delay to its schedule.
7) Duty call-up at short notice and compulsion to work extra hours.

So, before leaving home for work, you must program your mind to expect some of the above factors and build immunity to any negative effects these might have on your performance, work, and attitude. It should not affect your relationship or interaction with your superiors, colleagues, and customer airlines. Above all, it must not have any negative effect on your work as it has a direct impact on the safety of others working on the ramp and the safety of the passengers and aircraft crew. Hence, at any time if you feel any of the factors mentioned above are overwhelming and will affect your performance or work, stop and talk to your superiors. Escalate the matter if necessary. But do not get pressurized. The risk you take is not worth it because remember, you are responsible for what you do. Although your work is part of a long chain of planning and actions of many people, safety is the paramount consideration here. So, if an error is committed by someone along the line, ultimately, it may be possible for you to detect it in time. Take corrective steps while performing your functions correctly and take actions that will make the difference, ensuring the flight departs and reaches its destination safely, profitably, and punctually. The final responsibility is yours. Some ways to prepare a mental blockade or fighting off these de-motivating factors can be,

a) By taking it as a challenge to perform even better. Sometimes, over time, when you are faced with the same problem day after day or flight after flight, your mental resolve might be worn out. If this happens, you can draw inspiration from past successful experiences, where your efforts had made a difference. It does not matter whether you received appreciation for it or not, but above everything, the personal high feeling, the mental happiness and satisfaction you had felt is more than enough. Take it as an opportunity to give a plus point to yourself in your mental score board.

b) Imagine all the days when you went home after work with a feeling of complete satisfaction and the smile you had on your face for facing up to the challenges faced during the shift and performing your job better than anybody else.

c) The understanding between you and your superiors, that he can count on you to do the job, no matter what, and if required, go that extra mile is also a motivator.

d) Personal gains or recognition such as rewards, promotions, recognition from colleagues, letters of appreciation etc.

e) Job satisfaction and love for it should be sufficient.

f) Finally, never take work worries or tensions home. You must exercise, especially through outdoor activities, and spent quality time with friends and family.

When you are assigned a task by your superior, ask as many questions as possible, don't be put off if he is unapproachable, because you might get some information which is important and can help you in completing the task. If he gets irritated, talk to him calmly, making him understand that it would be mutually beneficial if the task is completed quickly and perfectly. As per the procedures, if you think you are right, you have all the right to put your foot down. Always avoid escalating a disagreement or argument into becoming a confrontation. You as a professional in the field can fully control and steer any conversation or argument to a mutually agreeable settlement. For this avoid the stumbling blocks in any professional talks such as personal remarks, pre-conceived liking or disliking of the person or his background, lack of knowledge or information on the situation/matter and of course, wrong body language. As per the various researches done on the subject of body language, it has shown that the other person you are speaking to is affected over ninety percent by your tone of voice, facial expressions, movements of the hands, and only less than 10 percent by the actual words spoken. So your body language will first show your sincerity and the truth in your statement. Do your research on the problem or task at hand, believe in your formulation and solution because then your body language will transmit your true feelings. Keep an open mind, your statements should be matter of fact, and always suggest remedial steps or solutions that are practical.

A Friend, Guide, Motivator, and Leader

Increasing productivity and job satisfaction will depend on your man-management skills. It is not necessary that you like every one you work with, but it is in your best interest to cultivate a cordial or good understanding between you and your staff. Their success will be your success. Trying to force your seniority on someone is not fruitful; instead, your interaction with them should be such that they look at you as a friend, guide, and leader. Here are some of the ways of building up a good working relation with your staff and cultivating a winning team atmosphere.

a) Do not look down upon them, either professionally or socially. There are many instances where loading team members or assistant staff on aircrafts have solved problems very smoothly and efficiently, which their team leaders or supervisor could not do. This they did because of the understanding they had with their superiors and the superiors' acknowledgment and acceptance of their ability and reliability. You might be a supervisor or a team leader, but you must work like a team with others under you, like the five fingers to make a fist. Treat them as you would like them to treat you. If giving comes first, then getting will be automatic. Respect their point of view. This will encourage them to talk to you more. When there is free flow of communication, there is less chance of misunderstanding, mutual learning takes place, less chance of not reporting on errors, possibility of getting new and better ideas etc. Their trust and confidence in you will increase. Start by greeting them and using their first names, instead of going straight to what you want from them. Don't get so preoccupied with the task that you become insensitive to the people, who will be actually performing them under your supervision. If you are not sensitive to them, they may not give their full cooperation or use their full potential. You might get away the first day, but remember you need them constantly. In an atmosphere of understanding and mutual self-respect, you can accomplish even the most difficult tasks, with your team. Remember, two heads are better than one. Give praise, goodwill, and empathy when applicable.
b) Keep an open mind to listen to your staff more effectively. Show that you are interested, understand, and care.
c) Constantly teach them and make them understand new procedures at work and policies of the company. No one is born master at anything. They may not understand the far reaching implications of their opinions, criticisms, or actions. In this case it is your duty to channel or counsel thoughts in the right direction.
d) You have to be firm on instructions and do it by positive assertiveness and not by being aggressive. For this, be open, direct, and honest in your communication with them. When considering all possibilities, be sensitive and objective to your staff's reactions. Formulate an action

plan in detail. Then discuss it with your staff openly, honestly, and with tact and humor. If you succeed, well and good, but if you didn't, then accept and admit it. If your staff makes a mistake or does not come up to your expectations, do not ridicule him. Coach him and understand that only through trail, error, and practice does a person improve his performance. A smart person learns from his mistakes, a wise person learns from the mistakes of others, and a coward never even tries.

e) You are the leader and so lead by example. You must be confident and believe in your abilities; assert a positive leadership skill in problem solving and setting objectives.

The benefits of the above points are many. You can mutually rely on each other, whatever the challenge; your staff will give you that extra effort when you need it the most, etc.

Your success and, in turn, the success of your organization will be in getting extraordinary effort from ordinary employees. It does not take much to make your staff do mediocre work, but to get peak performance, you must get them to have an internal force or desire. Everyone is motivated to act in their self-interest. And it is your duty to show them that their self-interest is being served because of their cooperation in setting and achieving organizational goals. It is difficult and sometimes impossible for some employees to separate their personal feelings, and effects of social and professional lives. You must understand this and if possible, coach them to gain self-respect, feel good, and cultivate a feeling of sincerity in their work.

Management staff must show particular care when it comes to formulating operating procedures, staff performance reviews, promotions, and staff well-being. It is easy to take on an authoritarian or a no-care attitude. Sometimes it is easy to overlook or think of certain concerns as unimportant or irrelevant. E.g. developing the work hours/duty timings of ramp staff based on the operational peaks. This can lead to a 12 hours duty pattern to cover several peak operations, with little or no rest periods, under severe climatic conditions. Here the emphasis is to cover the operations, but the greater negative impact is ignored. The ramp staff has to deal with numerous pressures, some are:

a) Time limits – The need to complete certain functions may be counted in minutes, e.g. some aircrafts have to turn around in 45 minutes, i.e. passengers disembarking, aircraft cleaning, fueling, unloading, loading, load planning, security checks, passenger security checks, and boarding, etc.

b) Overbearing or critical customers/supervisors – Sometimes staff during the process of performing their allocated task simultaneously have to deal with people who tend to ignore or have limited knowledge of the functions, rules, regulations, etc. that the staff must do or follow. They take a narrow view and will only give importance to what they want. Here they have to be appropriately handled by first listening to them and then assertively and professionally make them understand the process and allay their worries.

c) Lack of sufficient rest periods – It can be so busy that there may not be sufficient gaps between handling flights, with little or no rest periods.

d) Staff shortage – This can lead to doing additional duty hours, sometimes on days off, or perform the same amount of work within the same time limit using insufficient staff.

e) Climatic conditions – Staff has to work in uncomfortable weather conditions such as hot, cold, windy, during sandstorms, humid, rainy, etc. to keep the operations moving, etc.

These are just a few of the occupational pressures that a ramp staff has to deal with, but they can vary depending on the rules, regulations, and conditions in each country. The negative impact can be:

a) Low motivation
b) Mood swings (volatile, aggressive)
c) Disobedience
d) Lack of interest
e) High sickness rates, etc.

It must be understood that a ramp staff should not be compared with a staff working indoors or in a controlled environment. It may be possible to do continuous 12 hours in an office and the local rules may allow it, but on the ramp the physical and mental alertness diminishes over long hours due to various pressure factors mentioned above. This is when fatigue sets in, which can result in a no care or less care state of mind. This should completely be avoided at all times because it is necessary for ramp staff to be active and alert at all times for the safety and efficiency of passengers, crew, airline assets, other airport users, services, etc. All functions performed on an airport ramp must be accurate and precise. This was an example to show the implications to be considered when formulating a policy or procedure.

Standard operating procedures must not be amended or implemented only because it suits the company or it is seen to be working elsewhere or due to the whims of a certain people wielding power. Before amending or formulating any operating procedure, it is necessary to get whole-hearted and sincere feedback and dedication of all the staff that will get affected directly and indirectly due it. To do this it is necessary to do the following:

a) Understand the requirement or changes and the need for it thoroughly.
b) Study the current layout and functions that will be affected directly and indirectly.
c) Formulate your own procedures that will satisfy the requirement, make sure it is user friendly, and avoid too much deviations.
d) Discuss the matter with supervisors and officers for their inputs and suggestions.
e) Put the requirements and the preliminary conclusions in the form of a simple questionnaire with the critical points to all the staff (or a majority number), who will be affected and ask for their feedback. Some procedural requirements e.g. in cases of safety may be necessary and are thus not negotiable, but the ways to implement them effectively can be many, and it is wise to get feedback from all concerned.
f) All their concerns, queries, and suggestions must be given due importance and their active participation sought.
g) Where applicable hold meetings if necessary to discuss further and finalize. In case of any extreme feedbacks, a one-to-one meeting to clear and satisfy both parties must be arranged.

Grooming

The impression a person has of another can last a long time and will directly have an impact on his interactions and decision he may have to make regarding that person. This is applicable not just between staff and the customer but also is applicable between colleagues. The first factor that a person notices or that forms the building blocks of an impression of another person is the way he is dressed and talks. After this come all the other factors such as tone, language, behavior, humor etc. It is often said that how you are dressed is what you are. At an airport the majority of staff, except higher level of management, wear uniforms. It is not just to show to which organization you belong or what your position is in the company. There is deeper meaning or use to it. How its employees are dressed has a direct impact on the professional image of the company, in addition to security requirements. Here are some of the points to be noted:

a) It should give you a sense of pride and belonging every time you wear it. Do not ridicule it, especially in front of others.
b) It goes without saying that your uniform should be clean and neatly ironed, avoid heavy perfumes.
c) In countries with high humidity and heat, it is advisable to change into a new uniform after every shift.
d) Wear uniforms the way they are intended to be worn and do not make unnecessary or stylish alterations, because it may be styled or made so as to meet certain safety and precautionary requirements. This is so designed for your safety.
e) Always wear the necessary safety and protective clothing and gear, if applicable, such as gloves, safety vests etc. because even though it might seem unimportant, during an emergency it may save your life or protect your body. Always have the necessary protective clothing against adverse climatic conditions in store and well stocked.
f) Avoid wearing loose clothing such as tie, scarf with loose ends etc., especially near moving equipment or machinery such as conveyor belts etc. In case a tie is must, then use only clip-on ties, which are safe.
g) Polish your shoes every time before you go on duty.
h) Hair length for men should be short and for ladies, recommend shoulder-length, but neatly pinned down. This is also a safety precaution. Hair-style must be very formal.
i) Nails must be short and kept snipped.
j) Always make sure your desk, office, and surrounding areas are clean and orderly. You might not know who might

suddenly come to see you. The way you keep your surrounding also reflects on how responsible a person you are. This will also help you get space and find something quickly; the benefits are endless. This also includes making sure that your company car, computer systems, communication equipment such as radios, cell phones etc. are in good working order, serviced periodically, and are parked, placed, or stored correctly.

k) Do not eat or drink while working. Smoking and alcoholic beverages are strictly prohibited on the ramp.

l) Conversations should be relevant and intelligent. A little humor is also fine to relieve the pressure sometimes, but strictly avoid horseplay and jokes on work-related information or procedures, however small.

Health

Sometimes we come across colleagues with bad breath. Even though it would be awkward to tell them, you must do it discreetly, as the person may not know that a problem exists and that it is affecting the people around him. It will give him the opportunity to correct the problem. There are different causes to bad breath; the main causes are as follows:

a. Lack of dental care. Bruṣh twice a day and check with the dentist regarding the correct way to brush your teeth. A dental check and cleaning every six months is a must, during which any plaque, tartar, or dental deposits are removed.

b. Gastric problems e.g. indigestion is another cause, which require specialized medical treatment.

c. Dry mouth causes bad breath and is due to some systemic condition of the body. Drinking sufficient water may fix his or in extreme cases it may need medical attention.

Some other important points to prevent bad odor from the mouth or stomach discomfort are as follows:

i) Avoid garlic or onions in food before going for work.
ii) Avoid spicy or too oily food.
iii) Avoid heavy or large meals.
iv) Avoid taking meals at irregular times.

Most importantly, a periodic health check is necessary. Some of the other major health issues on the ramp are as follows:

a) Back injuries are a major avoidable health problem on the ramp. This is avoidable to a higher extent if staff are given training or are taken through an industrial injuries awareness programs. Back injuries occur due to incorrect posture during lifting, lowering, carrying, pushing, or pulling objects, or excessive repetition of movements, such as twisting and overreaching. The lifting process, for example, involves a combination of moving body segments, joints, several muscles etc. The major injuries are sprains, fractures, sprains, and back aches, which never seem to go away. The key to avoid these injuries is the use of correct posture and the maximum use of the legs or thigh muscles as much as possible. *Refer to figures* I.1.a & b.

Always check the object or surrounding area for any danger or sharp objects, which can injure you or your colleagues. Always keep your back straight, do not use your back muscle to take the strain in case you are bending or straightening up, and put the strain on the muscles of the legs. Stand close to the object, bend your knees to lower yourself comfortably to the level required in relation to the object, get a good grip, lift yourself with the object, keeping your back straight, using your leg muscles.

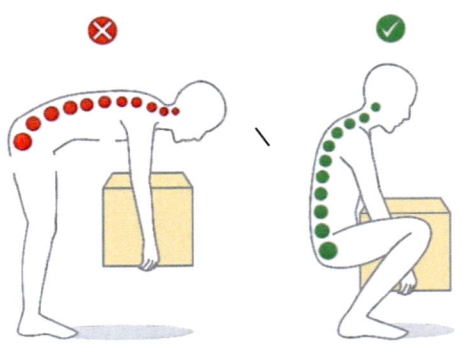

Fig. I.1.a

Fig. I.1.b
Fig. I.1: Lifting postures.

a. Again in case of pushing, place your back straight against the object and move back using your legs.
b) There is the danger of heatstroke or over-exertion in countries where the temperature is hot and humid. The daytime temperatures can cross 40 degrees centigrade or at night 100 per cent humidity. The temperature near the aircraft can rise more than the surrounding areas as the tarmac gets heated and the aircraft ventilation/exhaust also gives out a lot of heat, constantly throughout the time it is on ground also. So, with these conditions, the work involved and the restricted time to complete it lead to excessive perspiration and if not controlled, lead to heatstroke or physical exhaustion. The best precaution is to take a lot of water and keep it in supply. Whenever possible, rest for sufficient intervals and avoid wearing tight-fitting clothing.
c) Heart diseases or heart attacks are a major health issue in an organization. The only precautions are proper eating habits and periodic health checks. Consult a doctor or dietician for dietary recommendations that best suits you.
d) Long-term stomach ailments (ulcers or gastric issues) are other possible health issues. During long hours on the ramp, staff may forget to have their meals or have irregular food intake habits with long gaps. These can cause stomach ailments over time. It is absolutely necessary that meals are taken at the correct times, if not possible, at least a small amount of food must be taken. Consult a doctor or dietician for recommendations that best suit your body.
e) Bruising, cuts, falls, ankle twists, etc. are accidents which can only be avoided by being extra vigilant, following safety guidelines, and wearing the protective clothing. These accidents can occur while working near an aircraft, inside an aircraft cargo compartment, or while operating equipment unsafely.

The treatment of each is different, but providing quick and effective first-aid can mean the saving of a life or lives. You must be a qualified and authorized first-aider to give first aid to a casualty. In all major airports, normally some staff members are trained and have the added responsibility to provide this noble service.

If you are qualified to give first aid, you will know the symptoms and the steps to be taken at the site of an accident or on seeing a casualty. If not, then please adhere to some of the common actions to be followed:

1) Check for danger to yourself and the casualty. Do not move the casualty if there is no immediate danger.
2) Immediately inform the emergency medical service and locate or inform the nearby first aider.
3) If requested to do so, provide assistance to the first aider; otherwise, keep the area clear and avoid crowding.
4) Inform your superiors.

When first in a new job it is advisable to check the local rules of the authorities and the policy of your company also, in cases such as those mentioned above. As the rules and policies vary from country to country and company to company.

Managing Conflict and Negotiation

It may not be easy at times to see the difference between a discussion and an argument. It is how we see it or for the person putting forth the subject, it may be a discussion, while the other person may see it as an argument. This situation develops to a conflict stage when one person loses control, followed by the other. The causes of conflict can be:

1. Interests
2. Understanding each other
3. Personal values
4. Method of performing a task
5. Conflict of opinion
6. Different background (communication blocks, linguistic, accents, cultural, etc.).

Managing conflict is a complex process, involving proper communication, assertiveness, and keeping out emotions, to have clear thinking, as it may lead to self-pity or anger. The factors that form an obstacle in this process are the other person's interest in resolving the conflict; he may respond passively or aggressively opt out of the problem-solving process. The three main ways to dealing with conflicts are to aggressively fight it, passively duck it, and assertively negotiate it. Here the most preferable would be to negotiate for a win-win situation as far as possible. Again, this may depend on many situational or conditional factors as well. The skills of negotiation are as follows:

1. Foresee it and stop it. A conflict becomes more difficult to manage as it progresses, so stop it before that. On the ramp, conflicts are caused mainly due to a clash of ego, poor communication, and misunderstanding. Clear the causes earlier on.
2. Identify the causes, history behind it, and understand the other person's point of view.
3. Formulate a win-win situation, which is possible in most conflicts, by cool thinking, collaboration, and calm.
4. The right time to act. For this first check if it matters to you or the task, if it is in the best interest/image of your staff/department/company, do you have the time for it, and does the situation warrant your intervention.
5. After the conflict has been resolved, check it by going over it and asking if the other person is comfortable with the solution.

Performance Reviews and Promotions

Performance reviews and promotions are again of high importance as it can have a direct impact on the motivation, sincerity, punctuality, efficiency, and self-development of each and every staff member. A favorable impact can have a marked impact on the quality of the service provided by the company and thus the reputation of the company. It can also have a positive impact on maintaining a cost-effective operation also. It is said that the true value of a tree is identified by the good fruit it produces. Similarly, it is important to have performance reviews to focus on the true human inside an employee and not the number of flights he handled, the number of days he was sick, etc. Also, it is superficial to only concentrate on only his leadership qualities, communications skills, attention to details, etc. It is important to go deeper and chart the basic foundation qualities that make up a person's true nature, such as his sincerity, loyalty, punctuality, cleanliness, efficiency, motivating factors, thirst for knowledge, etc. Because it is from these basic foundation qualities that come leadership, need to achieve, satisfy, customer orientation, etc. These basic qualities are the branches from which the fruits or secondary qualities such as customer orientation skills, leadership skills, etc. come forth.

Organizations have recognized the superficial qualities and have come up with numerous ways to measure them. The basic foundation qualities are either ignored or do not have mechanisms in place to measure and promote them. Some organizations give cash awards to employees who give favorable suggestions or cost-effective solutions. Unfortunately, it stops there, both for that employee and the performance of the rest. In a large organization with thousands of staff, only a minute percentage get this short-lived award/recognition. It is necessary to recognize and reward on the basic foundation qualities and the superficial qualities together, thus have a much higher positive impact on an individual in addition to financial awards. Both the qualities will form the merit list of an employee, all others like job knowledge can be gained or taught over a fixed period of time. Thus, this merit list should be the basis for all awards and the next crucial step for an employee's need, which is promotion. Hence, accurate and unbiased performance reviews records should form the first step to the promotion shortlisting process. A promotion for an employee is the ultimate recognition for his performance and self-development. It showcases himself as an achiever to his colleagues and to his relations, acting as an emotional boost to his self-confidence and self-respect. So all promotions must be merit-based. Bearing all of the above in mind, all managers and selectors must be careful to avoid:

a) Favoritism based on culture, religion, color of skin, acquaintances, etc.
b) Recommendations, irrespective from whom
c) Pretentious staff, etc.
d) Prior or preconceived like and dislike of a person
e) Personal distastes of certain behavior, personality traits, etc.

All promotions must be merit-based and must be done with total integrity, impartiality, and sincerity.

Any wrongdoing by the manager can cause tensions, loss of respect, etc. It can de-motivate staff, increase operating costs, refrain from giving valuable inputs or solutions, lead to loss of quality, reduced loyalty, etc.

It is recommended to have a panel to review every promotion on each level and not leave it to the discretion of a single manager. There should be a confidential mechanism to raise concerns of anomaly to an independent internal body, and this practice must be encouraged. It must be emphasized that promoting the right staff is in the best interest of the manager and the company as a whole in the long run.

Performance Feedback

It is quiet natural to receive or give feedback on a variety of subjects, at any place of work. If your superior tells you about how he feels about how you do your work or your attitude towards it, etc., this is called feedback. The skill in giving or receiving feedback on performance constructively is of particular importance. It increases self-awareness, encourages personal development, teaches you the effect of your behavior on others etc. You may know more about yourself that you did not know about. How you give or receive feedbacks makes a difference to your creditability and has an effect on the aim of this process. Not all feedbacks may be positive; negative feedback when given constructively and skillfully can lead to self-amelioration or betterment. The points to remember when giving feedback are:

1) Think about what you want to say in advance. Lay it out clearly with his/her plus points at the start.
2) Be specific. Avoid general remarks like you are excellent or lazy etc., but tell what he/she did which made you to come to that conclusion.
3) Give suggestions to change, for which he/she has control over like his/her behavior and not is lack of hair, skin color etc.
4) Alternatives. When giving negative feedback, instead of only criticizing, give suggestions to perform differently.
5) Describe but don't evaluate. Tell what effect his/her actions had on you and not just it was good or bad.
6) Own responsibility to the feedback and don't make it look like it is from the group managers above you. Maintain integrity.
7) Give the feedback as soon you can after his action, otherwise its relevance may be lost. Leave him/her with a choice, whether to act on it or not. There should be periodic private sessions for performance reviews and feedbacks. Here find out your staff's aspirations, level of job satisfaction, factors affecting better performance, and offer suggestions or solutions.

Some of the points to be noted when receiving feedbacks are:

1) Hear the person completely rather than quickly rejecting or arguing. If you think the feedback is incorrect, choose to ignore it.
2) Understand the feedback completely; avoid jumping to conclusions and becoming defensive.
3) Check if the feedback is consistent with that formed by others about you.
4) Update your performance periodically through feedbacks and seek it if not provided.
5) Choose a line of action to perform, based on the feedback. Access the value of the feedback, think about the consequence of ignoring it or using it for your development, and finally appreciate the person giving it, as it may not have been easy for him/her.

Staff and their positive attitude and a constant thirst to ameliorate their professional standing are necessary for both the organization and the staff. Positive attitude should also translate to positive steps or actions in that direction. Then every staff in that direction will be a valuable asset for his company and thus the staff will in turn make his company a valuable asset to the industry that it belongs.

****

Chapter II
Communication

Introduction

An important attribute for all employees in the aviation industry, particularly in ground handling, is excellent communication abilities. This is first and foremost tool required for the trade. Good communication is beneficial, as we can influence others, understand or make others understand what we intend to convey, learn more, get more of what we want, settle differences, achieve our ambitions etc. Communication on the ramp involves different systems, methods, and skills. It is important to know and have a good understanding of aviation communication, as it is the first tool with which most critical functions are carried out. Communication on the ramp above all has a direct impact on lives, both on the ground and in the air. After this come all other considerations such as equipment, punctuality, and profitability.

Chapter Contents:

    Verbal communication systems
    Aviation communication terms
    Word spelling in Radiotelephony
    Non-verbal communications systems/methods
    Information for record or for action

****

Verbal Communication Systems

There are essentially two methods of direct verbal communication on the ramp, they are:
1) Face-to-face communication.
2) Communication using telephone, radios/walkie-talkies, etc.

Communication

1. Face-to-Face Communication

It is of greater relevance than any industry, that good communication is the cornerstone of a successful enterprise. It is a known factor that people do more communication, compared to other activities in the airline industry. When communication breaks down, then the chain of activities stop. All communications consists of,

A Need → Sender → Receiver → Purpose/Fulfillment

So during a conversation the arrows change directions, with the sender becoming receiver and receiver becoming sender and vice versa continuously. The qualities of a good communicator are to make the other person feel valued and important i.e. respect, no pretense, honesty and trying to see things from the other person's point of view i.e. empathy. This will help in getting the correct meaning to the receiver and him understanding it faster. A bad communicator feels frustrated, de-motivated, and confuses others. The factors that influence or change the meaning of the message communicated along the chain of senders and receivers are as follows:

a) Distortion: When we are listening to a person, we might think we are concentrating, but our level of concentration depends on whether the subject is interesting, our like or dislike of the sender, whether the message is of some personal value/beneficial, or if it is convenient etc. Then it is then transmitted to the next person or is stored in memory (if required), based on the concentration during the receiving process. The facial expression and the body language of a person have a big impact on our intake of what he is saying, as well as our ability to understand or decipher the meaning and transform it into reactions, actions, or reply. So distortion can be mild to substantial.

b) Self-talk: Our brain is constantly talking to us about our surroundings, pictures, sounds, sensations etc. The list is endless. This is called self-talk and it has an influence on what is said to us, what meaning we make of it. Our thoughts or state of mind can have an impact on what is the message being conveyed to us. When this self-talk is positive, you will feel good about yourself and your outlook will be positive. But when it is negative, such as you think today is going to be a bad day, it is likely you will feel negative and defensive. Your reactions are likely to then be unfriendly and you will have a grumpy attitude, the end result being negative reactions from your receiver.

c) Gossip and popularity of the sender: We all form a picture of most of the people we work with. They are in the good list, the bad list, or the okay list. When someone gives his opinion of another person, it will be based on his experience with that person. When they tell you of that person whom they approve or disapprove, it can have an influence on how you take a message from the first person.

Methods/Skills:

The Dos for a speaker are,

- Think about what you want to say and do it clearly.
- Look at the person you are speaking to. Not making eye contact will mean you are uninterested, are being evasive, and are not truthful.
- Consider the feelings of the person you are speaking to.
- Your words should match your tone and body language.
- Check if the other person understood what you are saying. For this summarize in between and ask questions to make sure.
- Vary your tone and pace of speech to make it interesting.
- Giving nods and comments encourages them.

The Don'ts for a speaker are,

- Don't use difficult language and go into too much detail.
- Give the other person a chance to comment or give feedback on the subject from time to time.
- Stick to facts.
- Don't pretend, ridicule, and put down, use ideas that can irritate the other person, ignore signs of confusion/disinterest or resentment.
- Avoid rapid body movements, which can be a suggestion of anger, irritation, or frustration. This will cause the receiver to become defensive, respond in the same manner, or be humiliated if anyone else is watching. All these

reactions can lead to a breakdown in communication and a blockage of problem-solving thoughts and ideal team spirit.

The Dos for a listener are,
- Look at the person and understand how much importance the subject holds for the speaker.
- Find matters to agree, rather than to argue on and summarize in between to make sure you heard correctly. Concentrate on the subject.

The Don'ts for a listener are,

- Avoid the factors which hinder concentration such as distortion, self-talk etc.
- Any previous undesirable characteristic of the person should not affect you, because he might say something important for you.
- Avoid prejudices getting in the way. Don't be negative or belittle what is said. Don't change the subject or distract the speaker.

2. Communication using telephones, radios etc.

Some of the systems used for communication due to long distances and convenience in the airline industry are,

a) Telephone
b) Walkie-talkies or handheld radio receiver/transmitter
c) VHF (very high frequency) radios or ground-to-air radios
d) ACARS (aircraft communication and reporting system)

The above communication network forms the backbone of all communication on the ramp. It is like air to the human body. Unlike face-to-face communication, where the speaker is in front of you and it is easier to see the importance of the matter, seek clarification and it does not cost money, the above form of communication requires knowledge, extra care, attention, and is costly.

Methods/Skills:

Some of the main points to remember before and while using the above equipment are as follows:
- These are expensive equipment, requiring special care in handling, proper storage, and knowledge of operating it.
- First compose and be sure in your mind what needs to be said, especially while using a radio. It is advisable for each written message to be read prior to commencement of transmission in order to eliminate unnecessary delays in communications.
- Conversations must be brief, without losing the importance, meaning, or urgency of the subject. Avoid irrelevant information, be specific and to the point. This is preferred even in the case of telephone conversations, as there can be someone trying to reach you urgently, probably due to some emergency which you may not be aware of it.
- In ground-to air-radios, before transmitting listen out on the frequency to ensure that there will be no interference with a transmission from another station or aircraft.
- When attending to a telephone call, always greet the person, then follow with the name of the section/office and your name. If making a telephone call, always greet the person on the other end, then follow with your name and name of your office/section/department, based on which name will be familiar to the person you are calling.
- In case of radios, since you cannot see the other person, pass on the information/matter in short sentences.
- When using cell phones or radios, avoid running or any over-exertion as shortness of breath will make conversation difficult, may cause loss of concentration, the other person may not understand, and it can be a safety hazard, as you may not be aware of your surroundings.
- Transmissions should be conducted concisely in a normal conversational tone; full use should be made of standard phrases. Also maintain an even rate of speech not exceeding 100 words per minute. When a message is transmitted and its contents need to be noted by the receiver, the speaking rate should be slower, to allow the receiver to write it down.
- Maintain the speaking volume at a constant level.

Communication

- When you are the listener during a telephone conversation, say a yes or understood every time the speaker stops. This will let him know that you are listening, have understood what he said, and he can continue. If you have not understood, never assume but ask for clarification and repeat what you have understood. This will remove any ambiguities, misunderstandings, and errors in copying what he said.
- In case a list of actions, long messages, or numbers are given to you over the phone or radio, it is advisable to write them down in short understandable points, however good your memory is.
- Your voice should be clear. Usually people from different parts of the world have different accents even when speaking a common language. This is natural and is based on their mother tongue. Now, in airports where people from different parts of the world work and communicate with each other, the different accents can be stumbling blocks and frustrating, especially if the conversations are through telephone or radios. You may come across a situation where although the messages are clear, the speaker's accent is making it difficult for you to understand, or if you are speaking on the radio or phone, the other person keep asking you to repeat. This may be because he cannot understand what you are saying because of your accent. In both cases, do not get irritated, understand that it is not anybody's fault. A practical solution will be to say each sentence slowly or in extreme cases, say each word in a sentence with short intervals in between.
- In case of a lot of static or frequency disturbance, it may not be possible to hear what message is given by another person on the radio. Or if you are passing the message, the other person may respond with "message not clear" or "repeat". In any case, don't leave it at that, assuming that everything is fine or he must have got your message. Try again, if the response is same, use a landline such as an intercom or telephone, next call someone else to check, but tell him you are waiting for his reply till you do anything further, and if none of it is possible, then go meet the person physically. Please note only you will know the seriousness of what you are doing, depending on the

Communication

urgency or importance or seriousness of the job at hand or being performed will directly correspond to the importance of message being transmitted or received on the ramp.

So the nature of your work and the knowledge of the consequence of a miscommunication will tell you how importance it is for you to get messages clearly, correctly and in time.

Radio Test Procedure

Sometimes it is necessary to check the serviceability or transmission of a radio, normally after installation or following a complaint. Then the form of test transmission should be as follows:

The tester should say the following-
  a) The name or identification of the radio/station/aircraft being called,
  b) The name or identification of the aircraft/station/radio calling from,
  c) The words, "RADIO CHECK".
  d) In case of ground-to-air, the frequency being used.

The reply from the receiver should be as follows-
  a) The identification of the radio/station/aircraft of the tester or sender,
  b) Identification of the aeronautical station/radio/aircraft replying,
  c) Information regarding the readability of the transmission.

The above procedure is to be followed in case of ground-to-air or individual radio to radio transmissions.

Please note, all forms of communication must start with the first two points ('a' and 'b') of the sender and receiver in radio communications.

Readability Scale has these levels:

1. Unreadable
2. Readable now and then
3. Readable but with difficulty
4. Readable
5. Perfectly readable.

Communication

Aviation Communication Terms

Now let us examine some common accepted phrases used in radio communications. In the case of radio or ground-to-air communications, press the transmit switch, say the name of the person or section or flight number you are calling, followed by your name or section/office you are working in. As explained above, your message receiver will respond with your name/section/flight number and then followed by his address. No other words or sentence is required to begin a conversation. Some of the most commonly used terminologies in aviation communication and their meanings are as follows:

Phrase	Meaning
Acknowledge	"Let me know that you have received and understood this message"
Affirm	"Yes"
Approved	"Permission for proposed action granted"
Break	"I hereby indicate the separation between portions of the message" (to be used where there is no clear distinction between the text and other portions of the message).
Break Break	"I hereby indicate the separation between messages transmitted to different aircrafts in a busy environment"
Cancel	"Annul the previously transmitted clearance or message"
Check	"Examine a system or procedure (No answer is normally expected)"
Confirm	"Have I correctly received the following…?" or "Did you correctly receive this message…?"
Cleared	"Authorized to proceed under the conditions specified"
Contact	"Establish radio contact with…"
Correct	"That is correct"
Correction	"An error has been made in this transmission (or message indicated). The correct version is…"

Disregard	"Consider that transmission as not sent"
Go ahead	"Proceed with your message"
How do you read	"What is the readability of my transmission?"
I say again	"I repeat for clarity or emphasis"
Monitor	"Listen out on (frequency)"
Negative	"No" or "Permission not granted" or "That is not correct"
Over	"(Over to you) My transmission is ended and I expect a reply from you." Note: Not normally used in VHF communication.
Out	"This exchange of transmission is ended and no response is expected."
Read back	"Repeat all, or the specified part, of this message back to me exactly as received"
Re-cleared	"A change has been made to your last clearance and this new clearance supersedes your previous clearance or part thereof"
Report	"Pass me the following information…"
Request	"I should like to know" or "I wish to obtain…"
Roger	"I have received all of your last transmission" Note: Under no circumstances to be used in reply to a question requiring "READ BACK" Or a direct answer in the affirmative (AFFIRM) or negative (NEGATIVE)
Say again	"Repeat all, or the following part, of your last transmission"
Speak slower	"Reduce your rate of speech"
Stand by	"Wait and I will call you"
Verify	"Check and confirm with originator"
Wilco	(Abbreviation for Will Comply) "I understand your message and will comply with it."
Words twice	(a) As a request:

Communication

"Communication is difficult. Please send every word or group of words twice."

(b) As information:
"Since communication is difficult, every word or group of words in this message will be sent twice."

There are many more, above are a few.

Note of caution: In the case of important messages, it is always advisable to ask the receiver to read back what he has received and what he understood.

These procedural words and standard phraseologies have been evolved by ICAO. Their use will result in considerable reduction in transmission time, and create standardization and clarity.

Word Spelling in Radiotelephony

1. Communicating/Transmitting Alphabets

Some words or names of people, places etc. are pronounced and spelled differently by different people, whether in person, telephone, or radio. So, when you come across a name or words (not understood) by the person you are addressing, you have to spell it. Again, certain alphabets can sound the same whatever the form of communication e.g. B, D, T, etc. So, each letter of the English alphabet is given an accepted corresponding word. They are,

Letter	Identifying word	Pronounced as
A	Alpha	AL FAH
B	Bravo	BRAH VOH
C	Charlie	CHAR LEE or SHAR LEE
D	Delta	DELL TAH
E	Echo	ECK OH
F	Foxtrot	FOKS TROT
G	Golf	GOLF
H	Hotel	HOH TELL
I	India	IN DEEAH
J	Juliet	JEW LEE ETT
K	Kilo	KEY LOH
L	Lima	LEE MAH
M	Mike	MIKE
N	November	NO VEM BER

Communication

O	Oscar	OSS CAH
P	Papa	PAH PAH
Q	Quebec	KEH BECK
R	Romeo	ROW ME OH
S	Sierra	SEE AIR RAH
T	Tango	TANG GO
U	Uniform	YOO NEE FORM / OO NEE FORM
V	Victor	VIK TAH
W	Whiskey	WISS KEY
X	XRA	YECKS RAY
Y	Yankee	YANG KEE
Z	Zulu	ZOO LOO

For example, if you have to communicate: "The passenger is Mr. John; he is booked on the flight."

You should say it as: "The passenger is Mr. Juliet Oscar Hotel November; he is booked on the flight."

The above alphabetical words should be memorized and should come easily to you.

2. Communicating/Transmitting Numbers

Same as alphabets, numbers can be misunderstood, as they can sound similar. This is very important as numbers and communicating them play a vital and crucial part in ground handling and all aspects of the aviation process. As you will see later, it can have a direct effect on the safety of aircraft, whether on ground, in the air, or on reaching its destination. So, numbers are pronounced as follows:

NUMBERS	PRONOUNCIATION
1	WUN
2	TOO
3	TREE
4	FOW--ER
5	FIFE
6	SIX
7	SEV--EN
8	AIT

Communication

9	NIN--ER
0	ZEE--RO
Thousand	TOU-SAND
Decimal	DAY-SEE-MAL (Do not say the word "point" in between numbers, but say "DAY SEE MAL")

Transmission of Numbers

Numbers 0 to 9 are pronounced as per the table above and transmitted. Ten is transmitted as WUN ZEE--RO. All numbers, except whole hundreds, whole thousands, and combinations of thousands, shall be transmitted by pronouncing each digit separately. E.g.

10	wun zee--ro
75	sev--en fife
583	fife ait tree
38143	tree ait wun fow--er tree

Whole hundreds and whole thousands shall be transmitted by pronouncing each digit in the number of hundreds or thousands, followed by the word hundred or tou-sand, as appropriate. E.g.

600	six hundred
5000	fife tou-sand
11000	wun wun tou-sand

Combinations of thousands and whole hundreds shall be transmitted by pronouncing each digit in the number of thousands, followed by the word tou-sand, followed by the number of hundreds, followed by the word hundred. E.g.

    18900   wun ait tou-sand nin--er hundred

Numbers containing a decimal point shall be transmitted as prescribed with the decimal point in appropriate sequence, being indicated by the word decimal. E.g.

100.3	wun, zee--ro, zee--ro, day--see--mal, tree
38143.9	tree, ait, tou-sand, wun, hundred, fow-er, tree, day-see-mal, nin-er
	or quite simply say:

Communication

tree, ait, wun, fow-er, tree, day-see-mal, nin-er

For identification of VHF frequencies, not more than two significant digits after the decimal point are used; a single zero is to be considered significant. The examples given below will help to illustrate the application of this procedure:

NUMBER	TRANSMITTED AS
118.0	Wun, wun, ait, day-see-mal, zee--ro
118.1	Wun, wun, ait, day-see-mal, wun
118.125	Wun, wun, ait, day-see-mal, wun, too, fife
118.150	Wun, wun, ait, day-see-mal, wun, fife, zee--ro

When transmitting time, only the minutes of the hour should normally be required. Each digit should be pronounced separately. However, should there be any possibility of confusion, the hour should be included, e.g.

1420   Too, zee--ro or wun, fow-er, too, zee--ro

Note of caution: do not assume, always make sure and if possible, write down what is said (especially numbers).

Non-Verbal Form of Communications

There are other forms of communication methods from those mentioned above, which may be comparatively less expensive and be used for matters not requiring urgency.

1) Telex messages e.g SITA (Societe Internationale de Telecommunication Aeronautique), AFTN (Aeronautical fixed telecommunication network)
2) Memo e.g., department circulars, official notifications, instructions etc.
3) Email
4) Notice boards
5) Internet

SITA and AFTN are of prominence. SITA is a company based in France, with a worldwide network. Its subscribers are the airline companies. More and more companies are increasingly using email nowadays, but the formats used are more or less the same when compared to SITA messaging. AFTN is used mostly by civil airports and aviation authorities throughout the world to pass operational messages such as flight plans, weather and airfield information. Lately, email has gained importance, with many airlines switching to it to send messages and information, such as aircraft flight plans, crew information, etc.

Some of the benefits are,

- Easy to maintain
- Hard copy can be kept as a record
- Multiple use
- Clear and less chances of misunderstanding.

Sometimes, the words in a sentence are abbreviated in the some of the above methods of communication, notably in telex messages. This is to reduce time in typing it out, use less space, and cut transmission costs. Use abbreviations which are easily understandable and make sure the meaning is not changed of what you want to convey. For example, "The number of passengers on this flight is 200; all are going to the final destination." This will be written as follows, "The no of pax on this flt is 200 cma all are going to the fnl dest stop"

Some of the common accepted abbreviations on the ramp, other than those used in our daily lives, are as follows:

AA	actual arrival	*COR*	correct message
A/C	aircraft	*CPM*	container pallet message
Act	actual		
AD	actual departure	*CPT*	compartment
ADJ	adjustment	*CRB*	crew baggage
ADNL	additional	*D*	Crew baggage
AHM	airport handling manual	*DCS*	departure control system
AOG	aircraft on ground	*DHC*	crew on pax seat due duty travel
ATA	actual time of arrival	*DIP*	diplomatic mail
ATC	air traffic control	*DIV*	aircraft diversion message
AV6	envelope for airmail documents	*DL*	delay
		DG	downgrade
AV7	delivery bill for airmail	*E*	equipment/ emergency exit
AV8	airmail bag labels	*EA/ETA*	estimated time of arrival
AVI	live animals		
AWB	air waybill (for air cargo)	*EAT*	foodstuff
		ED/ETD	estimated time of departure
ASAP	as soon as possible	*EIC*	equipment in compartment
ATD	actual time of departure	*F*	first class or priority bags
B or Bge	baggage	*FIL*	undeveloped film
Bed	stretcher on board	*FP*	flight plan
BIG	big item	*FWD*	forward
BLKD	blocked	*FOI*	form of indemnity
BKD	booked	*FYI*	for your information
BA	ballast (*see chapter- load control*)	*GD*	general declaration (crew)
C/CGO	cargo	*GMT*	Greenwich mean time
CAB	cabin		
CAO	cargo aircraft only	*GRP*	group
CG	center of gravity	*HEA*	heavy cargo
CIP	commercially important person/passenger	*HEG*	hatching eggs
		HUM	human remains
Com	company mail	*I*	infant

Communication

ICE	solid carbon dioxide (dry ice)	*PAD*	passengers available for disembarkation
IG	imperial gallon	*PAX/PX*	Passenger
J	class of service		
JNG	joining	*PDM*	possible duplicate message
JMP	jump seat		
K/Kg	kilograms	*PEA*	hunting trophies, skin, etc.
L/Lt	liter		
lb	pounds weight	*PEF*	flowers
LD	lower deck	*PEM*	meat
LDM	load message	*PEP*	fruits and vegetables
LHO	living human organs/blood		
		PER	perishable cargo
LPM	load planning message	*PES*	seafood/fish
		PIL	passenger information list message
LT	local time		
M	mail		
MAG	magnetized materials	*PIR*	property irregularity report
MAP	movement after pushback	*PNL*	passenger name list
		POS	position
MAX	maximum	*PWG*	pallet equipped with extension wings
MD	main deck		
MVT	aircraft movement message		
		PTA	prepaid ticket advice
MAAS	meet and assist		
MCO	miscellaneous charges order	*Q/COU*	courier baggage
		R	repeat indicator
N	no	*RCL*	cryogenic liquids
ULD	at position	*RCM)*	corrosive (labeled
NI	time of next information	*RFG*	flammable compressed gas
NIL	no items loaded or manifested	*RFL*	flammable liquid
		RFS	flammable solid
NR	number	*RFW*	dangerous when wet
NOREC/NRC	no record		
		RIS	infectious substance
OBX	Obnoxious load		
OHG	overhang item	*RMD*	miscellaneous dangerous goods
P	class of service		

Communication

RNG	non-flammable compressed gas	*UCM*	ULD control message
ROP	organic peroxide	*ULD*	unit load device
ROX	oxidizer	*US*	US gallon
RPB x	oxidizer	*UWS*	ULD/bulk-load weight signal
RPG	toxic gas		
RR	return to ramp identifier	*U/S*	unserviceable
		UG	upgrade
RRW	radioactive, I-white	*VR*	volume available
		VAL	valuable cargo
RRY	radioactive, III-yellow	*VIP*	very important person
RSB	polystyrene beads	*W*	cargo in security controlled ULD
RSC	spontaneously combustible		
		WET	wet cargo
RXS	explosive 1.4S	*X*	empty ULD
RYT	refer your telex	*XPS*	express parcel service
S	sort on arrival		
SCM	ULD stock check message	*XCR*	operating crew occupying passengers seat(s)
SI	supplementary information		
		Y	class of service Economy class
SEC	item removed from passenger for security reason		
SOM	seats occupied message		
SOC	seats occupied by baggage, cargo and/or mail		
SPCL	special		
STA	scheduled time of arrival		
STD	scheduled time of departure		
SOB	souls on board		
TBA	to be advised		
TBN	to be notified		
TI	transport index		
TTL	total		
TW	total weight		

Communication

You will understand the meaning and use of some of the above abbreviations as we progress through the coming chapters. There are also some more important abbreviations which are best explained and understood in the area of their use. So you will come across them in the chapters ahead.

All forms of messages concerning a flight should start with the message type, flight number, the date, aircraft registration, and your station or airport of departure. For example, when a flight leaves from your station to another, a message called the movement message is send to that station, the airline operations sections, and all relevant sections.

A format is shown below:

QU CDGOOXH DXBOOXH
.DXBKRXH 121450
MVT
XX051/12.A1BCD.DXB
AD1430/1440 EA2100 CDG
DL93/0010
PX200
SI. DCT 1427

Here the QU gives the system, the order of priority for sending the message, and the two groups of seven letters are the addresses, the first three letters giving the airport or city code, the next two letters showing the office code and the last two letters denoting the airline prefixes/code. The next line with seven letters denotes the sender, and then the first two digits denote the date, and then the international time in GMT. The next line denotes the message identifiers. Then come the flight number, date of the flight, the registration, and three-letter city or airport code from where the message is going. The next line gives what time the flight pushed back, took off, what time it is expected at destination. DL stands for delay and that is 10 minutes, for which the code is 93. Some airlines require additional information such as door close time, which is put as supplementary information. It is recommended to start any correspondence regarding a flight with the flight number, date, and registration of aircraft. Any relevant information pertaining to the matter can be added briefly, for example ATA, parking stand etc. Thus there are different types of messages that go about between airport ground handling agents and airlines. Each is to convey a particular information or details of the flight. Three-letter message

Communication

identifiers have been developed by IATA for easy recognition of the type of message. Some of the message identifiers of the airline industry are,

> MVT – Flight movement message. As above.
> DIV – These messages are sent in case of a flight diversion, for example in case of bad weather at destination.
> AOG – Aircraft on ground and will be delayed, where reasons can be, for example, a technical fault.
> LDM – Load message. More on this in load control chapter.
> CPM – Container pallet message. As above.
> LPM – Load plan message.
> PSM – Passenger service message. This message contains special information on the passengers, such as those requiring wheel chairs on arrival, VIP passengers etc.
> PTM – Passenger transfer message. This message contains the list of passengers on board a flight who are transferring to other flight at an arriving station.
> FFM – Freight forward message. This contains information such as consignment, weight, pieces of cargo forwarded on a flight.

Whatever the type of message, each has its own format and gives down line stations and other parties a lot of information regarding the aircraft/passengers/crew/load/meals etc., for necessary preparations or arrangements. Messages should convey to the recipient only the information he needs to know and in a form which he can readily understand. It should be brief, concise, and must be sent promptly and accurately.

Some of the most commonly used terms and phrases in ramp communications are as follows:

1. Back-log – left behind shipments due to lack of space, which continues over a period of time.
2. Down grade – to move a passenger to a lower class compartment.
3. Embargo – the refusal by an airline to accept passengers or cargo on their services for a limited period of time, for various reasons.
4. Go-show – a fare-paying passenger who wants to travel on a fully booked flight and is willing to go to the airport and

accept a seat just before departure if another passenger cancels at the last minute.
5. No-show – a booked passenger who does not present himself for travel at the date and time stated on his ticket and does not board the flight (passengers who do not embark because their connecting flights were delayed are not regarded as No-show).
6. No-record pax – a passenger for whom there is no record of a booking but nevertheless is in possession of a ticket with a booking recorded on it.
7. Off chocks – the actual time the wheel chocks (wedges to prevent the aircraft from moving in the event of brake failure) are removed and the aircraft commences its journey.
8. Off-line city – a city not served by a particular carrier but which maintains a sales office or agency.
9. On-line city – a city served by a particular carrier.
10. Overbooked – a flight with more passengers booked than seats available on the aircraft.
11. Over-fly – the omission of a scheduled stop of a flight at an airport.
12. Pool partner – two airlines whose timetable are jointly scheduled. In some instances the revenue is shared.
13. Portside – It is the left-hand side of the aircraft when looking from the tail section towards the nose; all the passenger access doors are located on this side.
14. Reporting time – the time at which a passenger should present himself for travel at the town terminal or airport.
15. Shipment – one or more pieces of cargo accepted from one shipper to one consignee as a single lot.
16. Standby – commercial or staff passengers who have no confirmed booking, but are prepared to standby at check-in, in case there are seats available.
17. Stopover – a break of journey in a passenger's itinerary.
18. Starboard – It is the right-hand side of the aircraft when facing the nose from the tail section, all the cargo hold access doors are located on this side.
19. Upgrade – to move a passenger to a higher-class compartment.
20. Uplift – to pick-up commercial load and equipment aboard a flight, to remove a flight coupon from a passenger's ticket or excess baggage ticket.

Information for Record or for Action

On the ramp, communicating information will be basically to achieve two main goals. One will be for the receiver to update the records or to create a record. Second will be for taking action or a set of actions immediately or later for the continuation of the handling process, which ultimately leads to its completion. The sender or communicator should decide whether the information is for record or for actioning a task or set of tasks by the receiver. The sender therefore must know the capacity or status of the receiver before passing on the information. The whole aircraft handling process is a multiple of interlinked tasks, which ultimately lead to the same goal. Each task is preceded by a set of instructions or procedure or information. So it is important for all tasks to take place and not stop anywhere due to a break in communication or flow of information. Sometimes information or instructions can be used for both record and also for actioning.

Let us consider examples now. When information is received about the names of team members handling an aircraft loading, it is kept as a record in the flight file. When information is received about a certain baggage or special load coming on a flight and is then supposed to be loaded onto another flight to reach its actual destination, then this information is supposed to reach all the staff responsible to complete all the necessary processes for its transfer, receipt, and finally delivery at destination to the customer. So here the sender is giving information to one or more individuals or sections, who will be prompted to continue a handling process by completing their part in the chain of actions leading to the ultimate goal of safe delivery. They may or may not keep a record of the information and the actions taken. So it is the sender's responsibility to make sure to record to whom an information is communicated for the purpose of continuation of a chain of tasks. The next link in the chain tasks must be informed of the tasks to be done in their capacity, but it is also important to inform the link after the first link also as a back-up. Now the first link will then inform the second link when their part of the handling is complete and so on. This the reason the management of all handling and airline companies insist on the continuation of the communication chain. The staff must take care that this chain is not broken by understanding their responsibilities and those of around them in relation to their area of work. We must be careful to remove all forms of ambiguity and distorted meaning or differences the meaning when duplicated to inform several people. Currently, with increased automation of processes by active induction of cutting-edge technology, computer systems can monitor activities and flight movement electronically. When staff input data or it is captured by the IT systems, this automatically activates other functions or updates other sections. Similarly, all the messaging also can be done automatically between handling agents to airline movement controlling sections or to the next destination airport as necessary.

Always keep in mind that good and clear communication practice in whatever form is the key to successful airport operations. Since English is the accepted or widely used language used in the aviation industry, it is sometimes necessary for personal refinement for staff from other language backgrounds to remove distortion arising from extreme accent differences and other linguistic barriers.

All information should be clear, concise, to the point, and understandable to all. This is the reason for the various standardization and formats which were emphasized here in this chapter. Precision is of the essence in the aviation industry and more so in its basic component, which is communication.

****

Chapter III
Basic Aviation Knowledge

Introduction

As a ramp staff, there is some important basic general knowledge about the civil aviation industry which you must have, this will help you in the understanding processes, rules, regulations, and other chapters ahead. It is highly recommended and very useful for ramp staff to have a fair knowledge of world geography. Not only will it be easier to understand some of the matters mentioned below but also for future professional applications. This chapter's contents are very basic, on a need to know basis for the ramp staff, although it may seem different from each other, each is interconnected in one way or the other.

Chapter Contents

IATA and ICAO
City or airport codes
Airline codes
Categories of flight and five freedoms of air
International time and time calculation
Flight ground times
Airport and aircraft introduction

****

IATA

The international air transport association was formed by the airlines in 1945 to solve the problems created by the rapid expansion of civil air services at the end of the Second World War. Membership is open to any operating company licensed to provide scheduled air service by a government eligible for membership in

ICAO. Although a member airline can have its own operating and safety rules, regulations etc., they must meet some basic requirements set by IATA. Its main purpose is to ensure that all airline traffic moves with the greatest possible safety, speed, convenience, and efficiency, and with the utmost economy. It also aims at structured and ethical commercial growth of the airline industry through cooperation, best practices, and mutual understanding. The creative work of IATA is largely carried out by its standing committees such as financial, traffic, and technical.

Its role in air transport,

a) Operations and commerce – to assist in ensuring that utilized aircraft operates with maximum safety and efficiency. So that people, cargo, mail etc. can move on this vast global network as easily as if they were on a single airline within a single country.
b) Technical activities – such as avionics, telecommunication, engineering, airline requirements at airports, flight operations, medical standards, and security, covering theft, fraud, and terrorism.
c) Air law – supervised by the legal advisory group composed of air law experts.
d) Financial – an outstanding example being the IATA clearing house through which the airlines settle their accounts for interline revenue transactions.
e) Traffic coordination – the negotiation of international fares and rates for submission to governments for approval.
f) Traffic services – covering passenger services, cargo services, and airport handling.
g) Agency operation and accreditation.
h) Assistance to airlines to developing nations.

Its benefits are many, some of them are below,

a) Standardization – through IATA, the airlines define standards and procedures to ensure safe and regular operations while helping keep costs down.
b) Cooperation – through IATA, the airlines deal as one with regularity authorities and world bodies such as ICAO.
c) Exchange – through IATA, the airlines seek joint solutions to problems beyond the resources of any single company to resolve.

d) Training – through IATA, the airlines share knowledge and skills to help each other and assist airlines from developing nations.
e) Publications – through IATA, the airlines operate a publishing and documentation center to integrate and explain industry standards and procedures.

ICAO

The international civil aviation organization is a division of the United Nations organization, and its members are the governments. It is concerned with the standardization of procedures and facilities for international civil air transport. It was founded in the year 1944 at a convention in Chicago, known as the Chicago Convention, and its headquarters are in Montreal, Canada.

ICAO has five standing committees; they are,

1. The air navigation committee, which deals with air routes and air corridors.
2. The air transport committee, which deals the operation of aircraft.
3. The air legal committee, which deals with legal matters.
4. The committee on the joint support of air navigation services, which deals with matters concerning navigational aids.
5. The finance committee, which deals with the accounting/aircraft charges.

Its objectives are:

1. To ensure the safe and orderly growth of international civil aviation throughout the world.
2. To encourage the development of air routes, airports, and air navigation facilities for international civil aviation.
3. To standardize procedures and documentation. These procedures for enforcement by member governments are found in the ICAO Annexes e.g. pilots licensing, aircraft registration, documents required by crew, etc. The most notable among the annexes in recent times is Annex 17, which forms the foundation procedures and requirements to safeguard aviation against acts of unlawful interference through aviation security. The standards and recommended

practices contained in Annex 17 give member countries the necessary set up required for protecting aviation assets and operations.
4. To encourage the art of aircraft design and operations for peaceful purposes.
5. To meet the need for safe, regular, efficient, and economical air transportation throughout the world.
6. To prevent economic waste caused by unreasonable competition.
7. To ensure that the traffic rights of contracting states are fully respected and that they have a fair opportunity to operate.
8. To avoid discrimination between contracting states.
9. To promote safety in flight operation.

City/Airport Codes

IATA has given distinct three-letter codes for cities and airports. Some cities have more than one airport, so each airport will have a different code. These codes are to be used in traffic documents and operational messages, such as movement messages and load messages etc. It would be useful and convenient to memorize as many as possible, especially those in your region/continent if you do not keep a list of codes at hand, because on the ramp you may need to know the code of a particular city quickly. ICAO and civil aviation authorities use four-letter codes instead of the three letters of IATA. IATA has divided the world into three traffic conference areas. This is because fare, rate structure, and regulations can be varied to meet the different economic, social, and business conditions and practices existing in each area. IATA area 1 (TC1) consist of:

- All of north, central, and south America and adjacent islands
- Greenland
- Bermuda, West Indies, Caribbean, and Hawaiian islands

IATA area 2(TC2) consist of:

- Europe and parts of CIS (common wealth of independent states) countries
- Iceland

- The Azores
- African continent,
- Ascension Island
- Parts of west Asia and Iran

IATA area 3 (TC3):-

- Asia
- East Indies
- Australia, New Zealand
- Islands of the Pacific Ocean

Some of the important three letter airport/city codes of IATA are given below,

Country	City	Code	Airport	Code
North Atlantic				
Canada	Ottawa	YOW		
	Edmonton	YEA		
	Gander	YQX		
	Halifax	YHZ		
	Montreal	YMQ	DORVAL	YUL
	Mirabel	YMX		
	Toronto	YYZ		
	Vancouver	YVR		
	Winnipeg	YWG		
U.S.A.	Washington	WAS	DULLES	IAD
	National	DCA		
	Anchorage	ANC		
	Boston	BOS		
	Chicago	CHI	O'HARE	ORD
	Midway	MDW		
	Dallas/ Fort Worth	DFW		
	Denver	DEN		
	Detroit	DTT		
	Honolulu	HNL		
	Houston	HOU	INTERCONTINE-NTAL	IAH
	Hobby	HOU		

Basic Aviation Knowledge

	Los Angeles	LAX		
	Miami	MIA		
	Minneapolis	MSP		
	New York	NYC	JOHN F.KENEDY	JFK
	La Guardia	LGA		
	Newark	EWR		
	New Orleans	MSY		
	San Francisco	SFO		
	Seattle	SEA		

Mid Atlantic

Bahamas	Nassau	NAS
Barbados	Barbados	BGI
Bermuda	Bermuda	BDA
Bolivia	La Paz	LPB
Colombia	Bogota	BOG
Cuba	Havana	HAV
Dominican Republic	Santo Domingo	SDQ
Ecuador	Quito	UIO
Guyana	Georgetown	SEO
Haiti	Port Au Prince	PAP
Jamaica	Kingston	KIN
Mexico	Mexico City	MEX
	Acapulco	ACA
Nicaragua	Managua	MGA
Panama	Panama City	PTY
Peru	Lima	LIM
Trinidad & Tobago	Port of Spain	POS
Venezuela	Caracas	CCS

Basic Aviation Knowledge

South Atlantic

Argentina	Buenos Aires	BUE		
Brazil	Rio De Janeiro	RIO		
	Brasilia	BSB		
	Sao Paulo	SAO		
Chile	Santiago	SCL		
Paraguay	Asuncion	ASU		
Uruguay	Montevideo	MVD		

Europe

Austria	Vienna	VIE		
Belgium	Brussels	BRU		
Bulgaria	Sofia	SOF		
Czechoslovakia	Prague	PRG		
Denmark	Copenhagen	CPH		
France	Paris	PAR	CHARLES DE GAULLE	CDG
			ORLY	ORY
Germany	Berlin	BER		
	Frankfurt	FR		
Greece	Athens	ATH		
Hungary	Budapest	BUD		
Italy	Rome	ROM	FIUMICINO LEONARDO DA VINCI	FCO
Luxembourg	Luxembourg	LUX		
Netherlands	Amsterdam	AMS		
Poland	Warsaw	WAW		
Switzerland	Zurich	ZRH		
	Geneva	GVA		
Cyprus	Larnaca	LCA		
Turkey	Istanbul	IST		
UK	London	LON	PRESTWICK	PIK

Basic Aviation Knowledge

			GATWICK	LGW
			HEATHROW	LHR
Russian Republic	Moscow	MOW	SHEREMETYEVO	SVO
Yugoslavia	Belgrade	BEG		

Africa

Djibouti	Djibouti	JIB
Ethiopia	Addis Ababa	ADD
	Asmara	ASM
Kenya	Nairobi	NBO
	Mombasa	MBA
Libya	Tripoli	TIP
Mauritius	Mauritius	MRU
Reunion Island	Reunion Island	RUN
Somalia	Berbera	BBO
	Mogadishu	MGQ
Tanzania	Dar Es Salaam	DAR
	Kilimanjaro	JRO
Uganda	Entebbe	EBB

Middle East

Bahrain	Bahrain	BAH
Egypt	Alexandria	ALY
	Cairo	CAI
Iran	Tehran	THR
	Bandar Abbas	BND
	Isfahan	IFN
Iraq	Baghdad	BGW
Jordan	Amman	AMM
Kuwait	Kuwait	KWI
Lebanon	Beirut	BEY
Oman	Muscat	MCT

Basic Aviation Knowledge

Qatar	Doha	DOH
Saudi Arabia	Dhahran	DHA
	Jeddah	JED
	Riyadh	RUH
Sudan	Khartoum	KRT
Syria	Damascus	DAM

Asia

Afghanistan	Kabul	KBL
Bangladesh	Dhaka	DAC
Brunei	Bandar Seri Begawan	BWN
Hong Kong	Hong Kong	HKG
India	Mumbai	BOM
	Kolkata	CCU
	Delhi	DEL
	Goa	GOI
	Madras	MAA
	Trivandrum	TRV
Indonesia	Jakarta	CGK
Japan	Fukuoka	FUK
	Tokyo	TYO
	Narita	NRT
Malaysia	Kuala Lumpur	KUL
Maldives	Male	MLE
Nepal	Kathmandu	KTM
Pakistan	Karachi	KHI
	Lahore	LHE
	Islamabad	ISB
Philippines	Manila	MNL
P.R. China	Beijing	BJS
	Shanghai	SHA
Singapore	Singapore	SIN
Sri Lanka	Colombo	CMB
Taiwan	Taipei	TPE
Thailand	Bangkok	BKK
Vietnam	Ho Chi Minh City	SGN
	Hanoi	HAN
Australia	Melbourne	MEL

Basic Aviation Knowledge

| Sydney | SYD |
| Perth | PER |

Airline Codes

All scheduled airlines are given two-letter and numeric codes. The two letters are used in messages, correspondence, schedules, and to identify a flight. The numeric codes are used in all documents such as in the beginning of the serial numbers of airline tickets, cargo air waybill etc. These codes are specific for the airline and act as an identifier. Some examples are as below,

Name of Airlines	**Alphabetic code**	**Numeric code**
Aeroflot	SU	555
Air Canada	AC	014
Air France	AF	057
Air India	AI	098
Air Malta	KM	643
Air Mauritius	MK	239
Air Tanzania	TC	197
Alitalia	AZ	55
American Airlines Inc.	AA	001
Ariana Afhan Airlines	FG	255
Austrian Airlines	OS	257
Balkan/Bulgarian Airlines	LZ	196
Biman–Bangladesh Airlines	BG	997
British Airways	BA	125
Cathay Pacific Airways	CX	160
China Airlines	CI	297
Continental Airlines	CO	005
CSA – Ceske Aerolinie	OK	064
Cyprus Airways	CY	048
Delta Airlines	DL	006
Egyptair	MS	077
Emirates	EK	176
Ethiopian Airlines	ET	071
Finnair	AY	105

Basic Aviation Knowledge

Garuda Indonesia	GA	126
Ghana Airways	GH	237
Gulf Air	GF	072
Iberia – Líneas Aéreas de España	IB	075
Indian Airlines	IC	058
Iran Air	IR	096
Iraqi Airways	IA	073
Jal – Japan Airlines	JL	131
Jat – Jugoslovenski Aero Transport	JU	115
Kenya Airways	KQ	706
KLM – Royal Dutch Airlines	KL	074
Korean Air	KE	180
Kuwait Airways	KU	229
Libyan Arab Airlines	LN	148
LOT – Polish Airlines	LO	080
Lufthansa German Airlines	LH	220
Malaysian Airlines System	MH	232
Malev – Hungarian Airlines	MA	182
Mea – Middle East Airlines	ME	076
North West Airlines	NW	012
Olympic Airways	OA	050
Oman Aviation Services	WY	910
Pakistan International Airlines	PK	214
Philippine Airlines	PR	079
Qantas Airways	QF	081
Royal Air Maroc	AT	147
Royal Brunei Airlines	BI	672
Royal Jordanian	RJ	512
Royal Nepal Airlines	RA	285
SAS – Scandinavian Airlines	SK	117
Saudia	SV	65
Singapore Airlines	SQ	618
South African Airways	SA	083
Sudan Airways	SD	200
Swiss	LX	085
Syrian Arab Airlines	RB	070
SriLankan Airways	UL	603

Basic Aviation Knowledge

Thai Airways International	TG	217
Thy – Turkish Airlines	TK	235
Tunis Air	TU	199
Uganda Airlines	QU	673
United Airlines	UA	016
Varig – Brazilian Airlines	RG	42
Yemenia – Yemen Airways	IY	635

Categories of Flight

An aircraft can be termed as a flight when it is scheduled to fly to another station, and this flight is given a flight number, which is alpha-numerical. In airline codes we mentioned that the airline codes are used to identify a flight. So the first two characters are the two-letter airline code, and the next three or four characters are numbers given by the airline operations department. Normally, the number series may be for a certain country, continent etc., so the flights operating to the different airports of a country/continent may have flight numbers starting with the same number e.g. XX123/XX145 etc. Flight numbers with the two-letter airline code and four numbers are for off-schedule flights such an extra flight, a delayed flight, VIP flights, etc. For example, XX1234. The civil aviation authorities, on the other hand, use three-letter ICAO code, instead of the two-letter IATA codes, but the numbers remain as above. The IATA flight numbers are used to identify the flight, used it in all communications, schedules, and for all ground handling activities.

Sometimes we notice that although a flight comes to the airport but goes back to its origin airport with a new flight number. E.g. XX500 DXB/BOM, XX501 BOM/DXB.

Let us examine the different categories of flight to understand this.

- Departure flight – This is for a flight which is originating or starting its journey from an airport and for all the staff involved in all activities connected with its departure process.
- Arrival flight – This is for an incoming flight for the staff at the arriving airport.
- Transit flight – This is a flight arriving from an airport, making a stop at your airport, and continuing onwards to

Basic Aviation Knowledge

another airport. The reason for the stop may be for taking additional fuel, for discharging passengers or other load, uplift of passengers or other load, for a crew change etc. depending on the airline requirement and traffic rights available to it. E.g. XX500 from Dubai, stop over at Mumbai, and going onwards to Cochin. Here XX500 is said to be a transit flight at Mumbai.
- Turnaround flight – This is for a flight which comes to your airport, after load change (discharge and uplift), goes back to its origin station, via the same route it had taken initially or directly. So the flight will be known as a turnaround flight at Cochin airport. In the above example, XX500 after arriving in Cochin from Dubai and Mumbai, will go back to Dubai, either via Mumbai or directly to Dubai. At Cochin, for the return flight, there will be a change in flight number, so in the example above the flight number will change to say XX501. This is an IATA requirement and avoids confusion.
- Stopover flight – These are flights which come to an airport and stay for a longer period. Normally, the stay-over may be for 6 hours, a day, or more. During this time there may be a change of load. The reason for stay-over or stop-over may be for schedule requirements or for crew rest etc.

Five Freedoms of Air Traffic (Commercial)

Airlines cannot start operating to anywhere, when they please. Many airlines were part of government-owned enterprises in the beginning. When competition grew, there was intense protectionism among the various countries in regards to its airline or aviation industry. The convention on international civil aviation (Chicago, 1944) introduced the freedoms of air. Countries will negotiate and sign bilateral agreements with each other. These agreements will be based on trade, commerce, infrastructural development, aviation, etc. needs of the two countries. The bilateral air transport agreement relating to aviation will list the conditions under which flights can be operated between the two countries. For example, it may specify the number flights allowed between the two countries, to be operated by the airlines registered in those two countries, if commercial load can be transported, which types of loads can be transported, etc. Each agreement will have specific basis of consideration for formulation and agreement. The conditions of carriage or air transport can be grouped into five basic scenarios (related to commercial aviation) and are called the five freedoms of air between the two signing countries. And the bilateral agreement will say which of the five or all of the conditions are applicable or not. It can be further elaborated to say how many passengers can be carried or seats are to be sold per week, etc. The copy of the agreement which stipulates the applicability of the five freedoms or rights, agreed between the country where is registered and another country it intends to operate, can be obtained by the airline from its civil aviation authority or the foreign affairs ministry or the applicable authority. This must be clarified before planning an operation to any country. Five freedoms as per IATA are as follows:

First freedom: It is the permission to over-fly a country. E.g. an aircraft on international routes normally have to fly over several countries to reach its destination. For this the airline needs to take prior permission of all the countries it flies over. The airline is even charged for it.

Second freedom: It is the permission to make a technical stop at an airport in a country. A technical stop means there will not be any commercial load coming off the flight and no uplift of commercial load (passengers/cargo/mail etc.).

Normally, this is for the uplift of additional fuel in case of long routes, or for a crew change in case of crew operating time limitation. Legally, the crew (cabin or deck) are supposed to operate an aircraft for a certain number of hours only. After that they must have a rest period. This is called crew time limitation.

Third freedom: This is the permission to carry commercial load from the home country of the airline to another country.

Fourth freedom: This is the permission to carry commercial load from another country to the home country of the carrier airline.

Fifth freedom: This is the permission to uplift commercial load between two intermediate countries, other than its home country, by an airline. E.g., the commercial airline belonging to the U.A.E is Emirates. The fifth freedom takes effect when Emirates takes commercial load from Mumbai to Singapore.

Based on the above five freedoms, airlines and governments mediate and grant traffic rights between the commercial airlines based in their countries. Taking from the above example, Emirates may be granted the fifth freedom between Mumbai and Singapore, if similar permission is given to the carriers based in India and Singapore, when they operate between an airport in the U.A.E and any other airport in some other country. Again, this depends on whether their airlines find such an agreement beneficial to their commercial interests. There are again many other factors that determine granting of permission to an airline. These five freedoms are to avoid conflicts and unhealthy competitions. Sometimes the airlines of two countries can uplift only cargo between the countries. So there can be different types of traffic rights.

Other than this there can be agreements between airlines to carry each other's passengers on their aircrafts (code sharing). Some airlines get permission from the government to operate in their country only if a certain number of seats are blocked for the passengers of the airline based in its country. This may be because its airline may not find it commercially viable to operate an aircraft to the country the other airline is coming from.

Some airports have the open skies policy. Sometimes governments of countries liberalize rules and regulations for operating to its airports. They negotiate and enter into bilateral air traffic agreements that include these liberal conditions which will be applicable for operating flights between these two countries. The main aim is to create a free market environment, stimulate growth, etc. There are also multilateral agreements, which include more than two countries as well. Other than the above, airlines have come up with loyalty clubs. The airlines group together to give better service, cover more routes, and cut costs. Most airlines have passengers from countries where they do not operate directly, but have another member airline operating there. So its passengers can use the special passenger waiting lounge or other services/facilities at the airport belonging to that airline and then travel on that airline or any other member airline belonging to its club.

International Time

The earth completes a full rotation around its axis in 24 hours, turning from west to east. This means that the sun shines on 360 degrees of the earth's surface once every 24 hours. Hence, it passes through 15 degrees every hour (360 degrees divide by 24 hours).

The earth's surface has therefore been divided into 24 imaginary time zones of 15 degrees each. The difference between each is one hour. These imaginary lines on the earth surface, running between the north and the south poles are called Lines of Longitude or Meridians or Means.

There are two important lines of longitude:

1. Greenwich Meridian or Degree Line of Longitude.

   The longitudes running through a country are used to determine the standard clock time for that country. When a flight goes from one country to another, it may fly over many countries too. The time in the country of departure, time in the countries along the way, and the time in the country of arrival are all different. Also, when calculating the estimated arrival time at the destination, which time would you use? If you use the time of the country you are in, it will be confusing for the others. Hence, to have uniformity and to remove ambiguities, the time along Greenwich Meridian is used the world over by airlines. All times are calculated from this longitude and all schedules, messages etc. will be based on this reference time, whatever the flight or destination. This meridian passes through the Greenwich Village in England. The time along this longitude is known as Greenwich Mean Time or GMT. Some term it as UTC or ZULU, here UTC means Universal Time Coordinate.

   Each country is given a variation factor that is the time difference in relation to the Greenwich Time. This could be plus or minus depending whether the place is situated to the right or left of the GMT (east or west of GMT). Places to the right of GMT i.e. east of GMT always have a plus (+) variance, and places to the left of GMT i.e. west of GMT always have a minus variance factor (−). UTC or GMT are used by all stations in the aeronautical telecommunication services. Midnight is designated as 2400 for the end of the day and 0000 for the beginning of the day.

   A date time group consists of six figures, the first two representing the date of the month and the last four figures the hours and minutes in UTC.

2. The International Date Line.

   If you see a political map of the world, the Greenwich Meridian will show as 0 degrees and on both sides of it the longitudes are in increasing order till both sides end at the last longitude of 180 degrees. That is half of 360 degrees. It is called the International Date Line or the 180 degrees longitude. It passes through the center of the Pacific Ocean, with the continents of Australia and Asia to its west and Americas to its east. It is diverged in places to include a whole country or a whole group of islands. When a journey involves crossing of this longitude, it affects the date. On the map you will see the clock at the Greenwich Meridian will show 12 noon, and on the 180 degree longitude it will show 12 midnight.

Time Calculations

1) The 24-hour clock

In our daily life, the time after 12 noon is 1pm, 2pm etc. and the time after 12 midnight is 1am, 2am etc. In the airline industry, the use of AM and PM are avoided, whether GMT or local time, with the use of the 24-hour clock. In the 24-hour clock system, the hours after 12:00 noon are continued as 13:00, 14:00, 15:00 etc. for 1pm, 2pm, 3pm etc. till 24:00, which is 12:00 midnight. After this it goes to the normal 01:00, 02:00, etc. for 1am, 2am etc. till 12:00 noon. The time is always in four digits. For example, 2:25am as 0225.

Conversion from AM/PM to 24-hour clock time

- a- AM time between 1am and 12noon
  List the time as it is, in 4 digits,
  e.g., 4:30 am = 0430
- b- PM time between 1pm and 12 midnight
  Add 12 hours.
  E.g., 8:40 pm = 2040
- c- AM time between 12:01am and 12:59am
  Deduct 12 hours.
  E.g., 12:17 am = 0017
- d- PM time between 12:01pm and 12:59pm
  List as it is.
  E.g., 12:50 pm = 1250

Conversion from 24-hour clock time to AM/PM time

- a) Between 0100 and 1200
  List the time as it is. The result will be AM.
  E.g. 0135 = 1:35am
- b) Between 1300 and 2400
  Deduct 12 hours. The result will be PM.
  E.g. 1930 –1200 = 7:30pm
- c) Between 0001 and 0059

Basic Aviation Knowledge

Add 12 hours. The result will be AM.
E.g. 0010 + 1200 = 12:10am
d) Between 1201 and 1259
List the time as it is. The result will be PM
E.g. 1250 = 12:50pm

2) GMT

As mentioned earlier, in the airline industry we use only GMT. It is then up to the airport staff or airline staff to convert it to the local standard time of the country they are in, for the general public. Find out the variance factor or in other words the time difference between the standard time/local time of the country you are working in and the GMT; it will be a plus or a minus figure based on where you are located in relation to the Greenwich Meridian, as mentioned before.

Conversion of GMT to Local time (LT)

To the GMT add if the variance factor of a given place is + or subtract if it is −
E.g., THU 1455 GMT, the variance factor for DXB is (+4), so local time in DXB is 1855.
FRI 0930 GMT, the variance factor for NYC is (−5), so local time in NYC is 0430.

Conversion of local time (LT) to GMT

To the local time of a given place, add if the variance factor of the place is − and subtract if it is +
E.g., THU 1855 DXB LT, the variance factor for DXB is +4, hence GMT is 1855 − 0400 = THU 1455 GMT
FRI 0430 NYC LT, the variance factor for NYC is −5, hence GMT is 0430 + 0500 = FRI 0930 GMT

Formula I

When time cannot be deducted because of the greater figure of the variance factor,
E.g., SUN 0255 − 4 hours
then,
Step 1: add 24 hours
Step 2: deduct 1 day

Basic Aviation Knowledge

Thus:
0255 + 24 hours = 2655
SUN – 1 Day = SAT
SAT 2655 – 4 hours = SAT 2255

Formula II
When the result is greater than 24 hours,
e.g., SAT 2255 + 4 hours = SAT 2655
then,
Step 1: deduct 24 hours
Step 2: add 1 day
Thus:
2655 – 24 hours = 0255
SAT + 1 day = SUN
SUN 0255

Formula III

In case of addition of hours and minutes, another method can be used,
e.g., to add 03 hours and 40 minutes to 2355 SAT.
We all know 60 minutes make 1 hour. And any hour over 2400 will be the next day,
so first add the minutes 40 + 55 = 95 minutes, there cannot be 95 minutes on the clock, since the maximum is only 60,
so 95 – 60 = 35 minutes and the 60 minutes, which we deducted/took out is actually 1 hour, so it is added to the hours in the next step.
Now add the hours, since we mentioned earlier after 2400 we take the next hour as 0001 of the next day.
So 2300 + 0300 = 0200
Then add the 1 hour accumulated after adding the minutes above = 0200 + 0100 = 0300.
Finally, put the hours and the minutes together, 0335 SUN.

This form of calculation is required when a flight is airborne and the next airport is to be advised when it will arrive. First convert your local time to GMT and then as per the example shown in formula III, if the aircraft takes off the ground at 2355 GMT on a SAT night and the estimated flying hours it needs to reach its destination (to be obtained from the captain) is 03 hours and 40 minutes, then its estimated time of arrival at its destination will be at 0335 on SUN early morning the next day.

Flight on Ground Times

Scheduled Time of Arrival (STA) and Scheduled Time of Departure (STD)

When we look at the time table of a flight for a particular station, we see the arrival time at the station and then a departure time from that station. This is called the scheduled time of arrival (STA) and the scheduled time of departure (STD). The scheduled time at which an aircraft will come to a stop after completing its flight at its designated parking stand and the safety chocks will be applied to its tires to stop it from moving is the STA. The scheduled time at which all the required activities are to be completed and the safety chocks removed from the tires of the aircraft so that it can move off from its parking stand to begin its flight is called the STD.

Similar to the importance of a schedule for any mode of transport, the need for a strict schedule for arrival and departure of flight is of particular importance and cannot be over emphasized. The maintenance of the flight schedule and where possible or required the safe reduction of time an aircraft is on ground at an airport is the responsibility of all handling staff, involved either directly or indirectly whether belonging to the airline or to the handling company. Some of the reasons for this are as follows:

- An aircraft is a very valuable mode of transport requiring specialized care, so it is important to have a detailed plan and schedule for its use, thus ensuring maximum operating profit, safely.
- Every activity in handling of a flight is dependent on the schedule. For example, the check-in of passengers by some airlines stops 40 minutes to its scheduled time of departure. This will give it the time required for the passengers to report to the aircraft from the check-in and also for the bags to be processed by the baggage handling section to be forwarded on the aircraft and to be loaded.
- Quite simply, for obvious reasons, it is important for the passengers and other customers to know the schedule of the flight they are going to use.
- Commercially, the thumb rule in civil aviation is that keeping an aircraft in the air for transporting revenue load is the most ideal and preferred practice to ensure profitability. So the least amount of time it is on the ground

Basic Aviation Knowledge

will mean completing its schedule/routing quicker and thus making the aircraft available for another operation.
- Less use of ground support staff and equipment to service or handle the aircraft and its load will be required. This means reduced handling fees and thus complementing the airline profits.
- The less amount of time an aircraft stays on ground means less pollution from support equipment and reduced human activity required for the aircraft handling, thus, protecting the environment.
- The less amount of time an aircraft is on ground, when it arrives off-schedule, would mean the handling capacity of the handling company is not stretched or strained as it will be handling other customers.
- The performance and quality of service of the station is measured by monitoring adherence to schedules.

The above reasons are a minute glimpse of the importance of a flight schedule and were only meant to make you understand its importance.

Transit Time and Turnaround Time of a Flight at a Station

The length of time or duration between STA to STD is known as transit time or turnaround time and depends on the flight routing. Let us understand these terms using examples. If the flight is coming from one origin, say LHR, to your station and then going onwards to another station, say CMB, then the duration of time between the STA and STD will be known as transit time. This is because the flight is in transit at your station. Whereas if the flight is terminating at your station and is going back to its origin or previous routing, e.g. in the example above, if it goes back to LHR, then the duration of time between STA and STD is called turnaround time. Here it is turning around and going back. Another example is if your station is DXB, then for a flight XX123 with a routing of CDG/IST/DXB/IST/CDG, the duration of time between the scheduled arrival and departure while coming to DXB, or on the return leg of the journey at IST, will be known as transit time and at DXB it will be known as turnaround time.

The transit or turnaround time at a station can be different for different airlines, and for the same airline the times for the different aircrafts can also be different. The STA, on-ground time, and STD at a station are planned by the airlines at its headquarters. The determination of STA, the on-ground time, and thus the STD for flight at all stations depends on various factors. Some of them are,

- Government approvals
- Bilateral agreements
- Air traffic control or handling slots availability at destination
- Commercial considerations
- Protection of its network schedules
- Handling time required for the type of aircraft
- Capacity constraints and facilities available at a station, etc.

Each of the above factors is stated in very general terms and thus can have its own several number of factors for consideration.

How do we know the transit or turnaround time for a flight at a station from its STA and STD, unless advised by the airline? Let us do this with an example.

Example I. For a flight XX123 the STA at DXB is 0120 and the STD is 0220 for the next destination, then the duration of time in between STA and STD or the allocated ground time is 01 hour at DXB, during which time all passengers must disembark, cleaning and catering needs to be done, load is to be unloaded and joining load is to be loaded, passengers are to board the aircraft for the next flight, and all other related activities are to be completed within this 01 hour duration. Hence, this 01 hour allocated ground time will be known as transit time or turnaround time.

Example II. If the STA is 2200 and the STD 0115, then the allocated ground time is 03 hours and 15 minutes.

What Is Actual Time of Arrival (ATA) and Actual Time of Departure (ATD)?

The STA and STD are planned times and it is not necessary that an aircraft arrives and departs at these planned STA or STD at your station. So it may not be the exact time an aircraft comes to a stop at a destination after a flight or departs for the next destination. The aircraft may arrive early or late at your station, depending on various factors, a few can be,

- It may have left early or late from its previous station.
- It must have experienced strong tail winds or head winds.

- It must have been held up by air traffic control for landing, etc.

So the exact time a flight comes to a stop at its allocated parking stand after a journey at a station is called the actual time of arrival or ATA. It is also referred to as on chocks time by the airport staff, because of the placing of safety wheel chocks in the front and back of the aircraft tires as soon as it comes to stop. This is to prevent the aircraft from moving due to any surface incline of the parking stand when the captain releases the brakes. The captain will release the brakes of the aircraft as soon as the chocks are put in. This is because the aircraft touches down on the runway at very high speed and the brakes are engaged to slow it down, may be right till it comes to a stop at its parking stand. This results in the brakes getting heated and hence they are disengaged to avoid damage and prevent malfunction.

The ATA can be earlier than STA, same as STA, or later than STA, depending on the factors mentioned above and more.

Similarly, an aircraft may depart earlier than the STD, at STD, or later than STD from your station. Normally, if it departs early, it is well and good, this is much appreciated by the airline. If it departs at exactly the STD, again there are no complications arising out of exceeding the allocated ground time. The flight may depart later than the STD due to various reasons; some of them can be as follows,

- It must have arrived late from the previous station.
- It may be delayed due to servicing or handling processes not being completed on time.
- It may be deliberately held back due to adverse conditions en-route or at the next station, etc.

Hence, the exact time an aircraft starts moving out of its parking stand at a station for the next leg of its journey is called the actual time of departure (ATD), and airport staff may refer to it as off chocks time also. This is because the wheel chocks are removed to enable the aircraft to move. Thus, the ATD can also be earlier than, same as, or later than the STD. The duration of time between the ATA and ATD is the used ground time.

What Is Estimated Time of Arrival (ETA) and Estimated Time of Departure (ETD)

Estimated time of arrival or ETA is the time an aircraft is planned or calculated to arrive at a destination airport. It is planned when the operations department of the airline estimates a flight will depart from an airport at a specific time plus the estimated flying time required to reach its next station. The ETA is calculated with the take-off time (the time the tires of the aircraft leave the ground at the end of its take-off run) at its previous airport plus the time required for the flight, i.e. flying time to its destination or next airport of arrival. Take-off time + flying time = ETA. A flying time is calculated by the airline flight dispatcher or the captain of the flight. It is calculated after considering various factors; a few are,

- The distance between two airports,
- Obstructions in the flight path,
- The amount of load and fuel on board,
- The wind blowing from the front (nose wind) or back (tail wind) of the aircraft,
- The flight route,
- The weather conditions along the flight route, etc.

Example I, Flight XX234, routing CAI/AMM/MOW/CAI. If the flight was delayed to depart at CAI, then the operations department of the airline will then calculate and ascertain the planned ETA at all down line stations, i.e., AMM, MOW, and back to its origin CAI station. It will also send a planned ETA or delay message to these down line stations. These are normally in the case of long delays and when the flight timings have gone off its original schedule.

Example II, Flight XX345, routing CAI/AMM/MOW/CAI. The moment the flight takes off from CAI, the airport communications staff will add the flying time between CAI and AMM to the take-off time and advise AMM and MOW the ETA of the flight at AMM from CAI. Let say the take-off time is 2340 in the night from CAI and the flying time is 03 hours between CAI and AMM, then the ETA of the flight at AMM airport will be 2340 + 0300 = 0240 the next day early morning.

Calculated ETA is more accurate than planned ETA, since calculated ETA is derived from actual time the flight took off. Planned ETA messages are always sent by the airline operations or flight scheduling department in the form of a schedule change or delays advisory message, whereas the calculated ETA is send by the communications staff at each departing airports in the form of a flight status message or flight departure message. Calculated ETA may be send by flight crew from on board the flight also.

The ETA tells down line stations if a flight is expected to arrive early or late or when to expect the flight to enable them to make necessary preparations accordingly to handle the flight load and aircraft. It also allows them to inform waiting relatives, friends, etc. of arriving passengers when to expect the flight. It allows for decisions to be taken if departing flights are to wait or not to wait for connecting passengers from an arriving flight at a down line airport. It allows the airline's scheduling sections at its headquarters to ascertain when the flight will arrive at its down line stations or at its base and when the aircraft or crew can be utilized for the next operation on its network.

Estimated time of departure or ETD is the planned or calculated time a flight is to depart from an airport. It is planned when the flight is running off schedule, or due to other reasons or restrictions the operations department of the airline decides as to what time a flight must depart from a station. The off schedule or delay advisory message sent by the operations or scheduling department of the airline will contain the planned ETA and planned ETD at each station or at a particular station along the route. It is calculated when the flight arrives late from its previous station and is based on the allowed ground time. In other words, ATA + allowed ground time = ETD. Calculated ETD is send by the airport communications staff to down line stations in the flight status message, when the flight is delayed at their station. They also briefly mention the reason for the delay in departure.

Calculated ETA and ETD can be sent by the operations or scheduling department of the airline also.

Thus, ETD is required under three conditions,

First, when the flight suffers a long delay at the departure station and the lost time cannot be made up during flight or by reduced ground time in any of the stations along the route, thus resulting in the flight arriving late at down line stations and back to the base. So, a flight delay advisory or rescheduled time message with ETA and ETD at each down line station and back at base station is sent to all concerned.

Second, when the flight arrives late from its previous station, the allowed ground time is added to the ATA to determine at what time (ETD) the flight must depart without suffering a station delay.

They will only incur a late arrival delay, which will be non-accountable delay and not affect the performance of that station.

Third is when the flight may be delayed beyond its STD or will need more time than the allowed ground time, due to some unfinished flight handling or servicing requirement. For example, delay in completion of aircraft loading, technical repairs, etc. Here the airport communication staff will get an estimate time for the completion of the process that is delaying the flight departure from the party concerned and transmit this estimate time as the ETD to the operations or scheduling department of the airline and the down line stations. If a long delay is expected, then the flight operations or scheduling department will send a delay advisory to all down line stations and concerned departments with the rescheduled timings (ETA and ETD), as explained in the first condition.

The planned ETA and ETD message for a flight at a particular station sent by the flight operations or scheduling department of an airline will then replace the original STA and STD for that particular flight. The new ETA and ETD will then be known as rescheduled times.

Using STA, STD, ATA, ATD, ETD and Allocated Ground Time for Delay Calculation

An aircraft arriving early or late (ATA) in relation to the STA has a profound effect on the time available to handle passengers and other load and for servicing the aircraft. Also, the allocated ground time from the ATA of flight will determine at what time the flight must depart without incurring a station-accountable delay. Let us understand the relationships between the different times and allocated ground time.

Scenario I – When the flight ATA is same as the STA, it is said to have arrived on time. E.g. flight XX123 STA is 1130 and it actually arrived on its parking stand at that time, i.e. ATA is 1130. Thus, the flight has arrived on time. Similarly, when the flight departs at the same time (ATD) as its STD, then it is said the flight departed on time. Here there is no arrival delay or late arrival. Also, there is no station delay, as the flight used its planned or allocated ground time, thus departing on time. In other words, ATA + allocated ground time = ATD, which should be less than or same as STD, then there is no delay.

Scenario II – Flights that come in early are extremely desirable, as the ground time increases. When the ATA is earlier than the STA, then there is extra ground time to handle the flight load and service the aircraft. The extra time will be the time duration between ATA and STA. It then needs to depart on or before the STD, without incurring any station delay.

Example I, Flight XX123 from BAH to DXB, STA at DXB was 0120 and the STD was 0220.

So allocated ground time as per schedule is 01 hour or time duration between STA 0120 and STD 0220 is 01 hour.

The flight actual time of arrival (ATA) was 0100 and actual time of departure (ATD) was 0220. Then,

- The flight has come in early, ATA 0100 instead of 0120 STA.
- That is 20 minutes early.
- It is only scheduled to go at 0220 STD.
- The allocated ground time was 01 hour.
- This does not mean you have to send the flight in 01 hour, i.e., ATA 0100 + 01 hour = 0200,
  but you can take 01 hour and 20 minutes of ground time to handle the flight load and service the aircraft.
- Here the STA does not have relevance.
- Thus, ensure to send the flight on or before STD 0220, thereby no station delay will be incurred.

You basically get more time to do the same amount of handling and servicing as it were to have come on schedule, which is largely preferred by operational units at an airport and the staff. Unless it comes at peak or busy time of operation at an airport, leading to strained facilities and manpower availability, since other normal scheduled on ground flights handling is going on. When a flight comes in earlier than its STA and departs earlier than its STD, with the consent of the airline and airport authorities, it is well and good.

<u>Scenario III</u> – If the flight ATA is later than STA, i.e. it has come late at a station, then how much ground time can be utilized to complete all activities and then at what time should it depart, without incurring a station delay? Here the allowed ground time to complete all activities and the allocated ground time will be the same. Thus, adding the allocated ground time to the ATA will give the exact time within which the flight must depart without incurring a station delay.

By taking Example I,

Basic Aviation Knowledge

- If the flight comes at 0130 ATA, instead of the STA of 0120.
- Here it has come 10 minutes late.
- This does not mean you have only 50 minutes of ground time that is the duration between ATA 0130 and STD 0220.
- And it is not necessary that the flight must go on or before STD, in order not to have a station delay.
- The allocated ground time at your station is 01 hour between STA and STD and so the allocated ground time will be 01 hour from ATA,
  0130 ATA + 01 hour = 0230, all activities must be completed before this time. OR another method can be employed,
- The time difference between the ATA and the STA can be added to the STD to get the maximum time within which the flight must depart,
- Here, ATA 0130 − STA 0120 = 10 minutes + STD 0220 = 0230, Thus the ATD of the flight should be on or before 0230, and then no station delay will be incurred.

Theoretically, also it makes sense, a flight arrived late and hence departed late, thus no delay is accountable to that station.

If the flight has departed at say ATD 0225, that is 05 minutes later than the STD of 0220. Although there is no accountable station delay, as per the allowed ground time calculation we employed above; in fact, there is a 05 minutes delay in relation to the scheduled time of departure (STD). Basically, any delay to the schedule must be accounted for and recorded. This is because every activity throughout the airline operation is dependent on the flight schedule. Therefore, in the example above, the 05 minutes delay will be attributed to late arrival of flight, or in other words, late inbound aircraft, which is a non-accountable delay as far as the station is concerned. Another point to be noted is that the flight could have departed at 0230, thereby utilizing the entire 01 hour of allowed ground time. But by going at 0225, the remaining 05 minutes between 0225 and 0230 was saved. Thus, as far as the station is concerned, it has saved the flight ground time by 05 minutes by completing all activities earlier than allowed. This is a positive point for the station concerned. When a flight departs later than its STD, i.e. ATD is later than its STD, for whatever reasons, whether due to late arrival or due to some station delay, then the flight is said to have departed late or departure delay.

Basic Aviation Knowledge

Scenario IV – When the flight comes in later than its STA, i.e. its ATA is later than STA, then the flight is said to have come in late or as per airport handling terms, late inbound or late arrival. E.g. flight XX123 STA is 1250 and its ATA is 1305, so the flight has arrived late. If the flight ATA is later than the STA and all activities are completed within the available ground time or duration of time in between the ATA and the STD, thus enabling the flight to depart on or before the STD, it is well and good. This is because the flight has cleared a delayed arrival by departing at STD or before, after completing all the handling and servicing, thus maintaining the flight schedule. Here again, the flight ground time is saved in respect to the allowed ground time for that station.

Example, Flight XY456, routing BAH/DOH/BAH, STA at DOH from BAH 2000, STD from BAH back to DOH 2055, ATA2010/ATD2050.

- Here the flight had arrived late by 10minutes,
- The allocated ground time for handling and servicing at DOH is 55minutes (time between STA and STD),
- So, departure should be on or before, ATA 2010 + 55 minutes = 2105 or by another method STD 2055 + 10 minutes = 2105.
- With the flight departing at 2050 ATD, the DOH station used only 40 minutes to complete all activities to turnaround the flight. That is the duration between ATA 2010 and ATD 2050. Thereby, saving 05 minutes from its allocated ground time, as it was scheduled to depart only at 2055(STD 2055 – ATD 2050 = 05 minutes), i.e. it was 05 minutes early.
- They have also saved 10 minutes from the allowed ground time, as they were allowed time till 2105, what we calculated above ATA + 55 minutes of allocated ground time for that station.
- So the total ground time saved will be 05minutes + 10minutes = 15 minutes to the credit of DOH station.

Scenario V – The flight is said to have suffered a delay when the allocated ground time i.e. transit time or turnaround time is exceeded. More clearly, when the used ground time is more than the allocated ground time, then the flight has incurred a station delay. In the example above, the flight although came late, departed earlier

Basic Aviation Knowledge

than its STD. Now if the flight was delayed beyond STD, then we have to consider two cases:

i) The flight had arrived late and departed after the STD, but within allocated ground time of 55 minutes, i.e. on or before 2105 ETD.
In this case it will be similar to scenario III, the delay will be the amount of time between STD and the ATD, but on or before 2105 (known as the estimated time of departure or ETA). Formulae, ATD – STD = amount of late arrival delay. This is only if the
ATD is <= ETD. The reason will be late inbound aircraft.

ii) If the flight had arrived late and departed after the allocated ground time had elapsed, obviously after the STD and the ETA. Let us examine this case with an example.
Flight XX789, THR/BND/THR, at BND the STA is 0700 from THR, STD 0800 from BND and back to THR, ATA was 0715 and ATD 0835.

Step 1, Was the flight was delayed at BND, to find out:
The ATD must be less than or equal to STD.
ATD < = STD
Here STD was 0800, but the flight departed at 0835 (ATD), i.e. after STD.
Thus answering the question, yes the flight was delayed at BND.

Step 2, Calculate the total delay at BND.
The amount of time between STD and ATD will give the total flight delay from STD or after how much time the flight actually departed from its schedule or STD.
ATD – STD = amount of delay.
0835 – 0800 = 35 minutes.

Step 3, Calculate the ETD or the allowed ground time within which time the flight should have departed BND, without a station delay.
What is the allocated ground time for the flight at BND?
STD – STA = allocated ground time.
0800 – 0700 = 01 hour. Hence, the allocated ground time will be 01 hour.
What is the ETD or the time within which time the flight must depart without a station delay but only a late inbound/arrival delay?

ATA + allocated ground time = ETD.
0715 + 1 hour = 0815 ETD.

Thus the flight must depart on or before 0815, within which time if it departs, there will be only a late arrival delay because it arrived late and no station delay. In other words, it came 15 minutes late (STA 0700, but ATA was 0715); hence, it can go 15 late from STD of 0800, that is at ETD of 0815 instead.

Step 4, Calculate the amount of late inbound or arrival delay.

The duration of time between STD and ETD is the late arrival delay and you find that this will always be obviously same as the duration of time between the STA and the ATA.

Here, since the ATD is after ETD the, ETD − STD = amount of late arrival delay.

0815 − 0800 = 15 minutes of late arrival from THR.

This form of late inbound calculation with the departure times of STD and ETD is better for the next step where we have to calculate the station delay. Otherwise it can be easily found that the flight was delay inbound by ATA − STA = amount of late arrival, when ATA is after STA. Here 0715 − 0700 = 15 minutes. But either way, you must get the same duration of time, in this example 15 minutes.

Step 5, Is there a station delay?

Check the example above meets which of the conditions below,

- If the ATD is less than or equal to STD, then no late arrival delay and no station delay. Not applicable to this example.
- If the ATD is less than or equal to ETD but obviously after STD, then a late arrival has occurred, but no station delay.
- If the ATD is after the ETD (obviously after STD), then there is a late arrival delay and a station delay.

So, from the above, we can see that the example meets the third condition. That is the ATD 0835 is after the ETD of 0815.

Hence, answering the question, yes, there is a station delay.

Step 6, Calculate the station delay.

Basic Aviation Knowledge

Now you must have noticed that there is a total delay of 35 minutes.

Of this 15 minutes is already established as late arrival delay, which was derived using the allocated ground time, thereby establishing the ETD.

Hence the total station delay will be ATD − ETD. 0835 − 0815 = 20 minutes of station delay.

OR another method is total delay − late arrival delay = station delay.

Thus, the flight suffered a delay of 35 minutes in total, which is divided into

- 15 minutes of late arrival of flight from previous station, here THR, and,
- 20 minutes of station delay at BND, due to whatever reason.

To confirm your calculations are correct, the following method can be applied,

STD + late arrival delay + station delay = ATD.
Here, 0800 + 15 minutes + 20 minutes = 0835 ATD.

A flight may be delayed at a station for one or more reasons. The root cause of the delay is ascertained and the whole station delay is automatically put down to that. But if there are more than one unrelated root causes for the delay of flight for departure at a station, then the total station delay is divided further into the amount of time consumed for each contributing delay reason. In the example above, the 20 minutes may have been caused by one or more different root cause reasons and thus may be divided further. For example, a passenger after boarding the flight may have to get off due sickness, which took about 15 minutes in total. And the rest 05 minutes out of the 20 minutes were used for waiting for clearance from the control tower for departure. Then the delay breakdown will be as follows:

- 15 minutes late arrival of flight from previous station,
- 15 minutes offloading sick passenger and baggage,
- 05 minutes awaiting local air traffic clearance.

Thus, 15 + 15 + 05 = 35 minutes of flight delay from the STD of 0800 from BND to THR.

Some airlines reduce the allocated ground time when the flight has arrived late at a station from its previous station. This is to minimize the effect of the delay on the entire schedule. This reduced ground time or RGT is normally by 05 to 15 minutes, depending on the aircraft type and station on the airlines network. This RGT is decided by the airline operations center at its headquarters and will notified in advance or will be mentioned in its aircraft handling manual. Once advised, the RGT or the allowed ground time will then replace the allocated ground time. Thus, from step 3 in the above example, the RGT is to be used instead of the allocated ground time for the calculation of delays. Although the total station delay will remain the same that is from the STD, obviously it will effect allocation of the amount of delay on late arrival and station accountable delay. With RGT, the late arrival delay will be reduced or may be eliminated and then this reduced or eliminated delay time will get added to the total station delay. This is not beneficial to the station, as it gets taxed because the flight came in late, which is not their fault in the first place. Here the sentence "it came late, hence it went late" cannot be used. The RGT is not desirable to the station handling agent because the allocated ground time was given to a station based on several reasons and one was the amount of facilities and the amount of load to handle at that station. Now to handle the same amount of load, the ground time is reduced, thereby putting pressure on its manpower and facilities, when the flight comes in late at that station. It may be beneficial to the airline on a short-time basis, but in the long run, it is not. This is because obviously pressure is applied to handle the flight in lesser amount of time and the facilities also may be strained. This can give rise to errors and adversely affect the quality of service provided. Also, it can affect the service being provided to other customer airlines. The use of RGT has to be agreed by the handling company at the station also.

Flight Station Delays

As mentioned earlier, the airline will want to maintain its schedule. The transit or turnaround time at a station should be sufficient to handle the aircraft and load, at the necessary required minimum level of standards. But when the flight suffers a delay, either by arriving late or at departure, then there is the need for service recovery. For example, when the flight comes in late, passengers may miss other connecting flights or other appointments, which will have a negative impact on the airline's reputation. Similarly, a delayed departure can again cause difficulties in down line stations, other scheduling problems, extra handling charges, the aircraft getting held-up on the route and thus cannot be used for other route deployment, etc. Part of the service recovery or schedule recovery is to ascertain the actual cause of a delay and to take corrective steps to make sure it does not occur in future. Delays can be due to two causes, which are non-controllable and controllable. A good example of non-controllable delay is the weather element, flight getting delayed due to adverse weather conditions. Here, although nothing can be done, airlines sometimes take precautions to avoid or minimize some non-controllable delays, e.g. possibly depart early to avoid foggy weather at departure station or at destination, etc. Controllable delays may be due to a service delivery failure e.g. late receipt of baggage for loading on the aircraft, aircraft repairs, etc. The list of most common delay reasons, whether controllable or non-controllable, can be found in the aircraft handling manual of an airline, otherwise categorized into the most suitable category based on appropriate area of applicability.

Delay reasons are used to measure the level of service delivery punctuality of a station. These can be used to negotiate renewal of handling agreements. For example, airlines can ask for reductions or discounts in charges after a certain amount or length of delays caused by the handling agent at a station. Another need for determining delay reasons is to pinpoint the actual area, analyze the reason or causes to take corrective steps and thus avoid recurrence. It helps to improve service levels also and increase accountability.

Each delay reason is also given a code, which can be numeric or two/three-letter words. This helps in the statistical analysis. There are IATA recommended delay codes used by airlines, while others have amended versions as well.

Delay Codes starting with 0 are used for internal airline purposes. Airlines are free to define these codes and to determine particular application fields according to their operational requirements.

A few of the standard codes are as follows:

00–05:	These codes are left blank so that each airline may develop codes specifically to meet their own individual requirements, e.g. 03: "Three-class system" moving curtain.
06 (OA):	No gate/stand availability due to own airline activity
07:	Aircraft connection by maintenance

08:	Aircraft connection by miscellaneous, traffic, marketing flight operations, ground handling, cabin services, etc.
09 (SG):	Scheduled ground time less than declared minimum ground time.

Delay Codes starting with 1 are related to passenger/baggage handling.

11 (PD):	Late check-in, acceptance of passengers after deadline
12 (PL):	Late check-in, congestion in check-in area
13 (PE):	Check-in error
14 (PO):	Over sales, booking errors
15 (PH):	Boarding, discrepancies and paging, missing checked-in passenger at gate
16 (PS):	Commercial publicity, passenger convenience, VIP, press, ground meals, and missing personal items
17 (PC):	Catering order – late or incorrect order given to supplier
18 (PB):	Baggage processing, sorting, etc.
19 (PW):	Reduced mobility – boarding/de-boarding of passengers with reduced mobility

Delay Codes starting with 2 are related to cargo/mail handling.

21 (CD):	Documentation, errors, etc.
22 (CP):	Late positioning
23 (CC):	Late acceptance
24 (CI):	Inadequate packing
25 (CO):	Over sales, booking errors
26 (CU):	Late preparation in warehouse
27 (CE):	Mail over sales, packing, etc.
28 (CL):	Mail late positioning
29 (CA):	Mail late acceptance

Delay Codes starting with 3 are related to other ground handling.

31 (GD):	Aircraft documentation late or inaccurate, weight and balance (load sheet), general declaration, passenger manifest, etc.

Basic Aviation Knowledge

32 (GL):	Loading, unloading bulky/special load, cabin load, lack of loading staff
33 (GE):	Loading equipment – lack of or breakdown, e.g. container pallet loader, lack of staff
34 (GS):	Servicing equipment – lack of or breakdown, lack of staff, e.g. steps
35 (GC):	Aircraft cleaning
36 (GF):	Fueling, de-fueling, fuel supplier
37 (GB):	Catering – late delivery or loading
38 (GU):	ULD, containers, pallets, lack of or breakdown
39 (GT):	Technical equipment – lack of or breakdown, lack of staff, e.g. pushback

These are just a few examples. The lists above are showing two letter or numerical codes; as stated, some airlines also use three letters.

Some airlines use the term accountable delays and non-accountable delays, instead of controllable and non-controllable delays. Accountable and non-accountable delay terms are more specific because delays are analyzed station-wise, on the basis of each station's performance. For example, if a flight departure delay occurred because it arrived late, but used only the allowed transit or turnaround time, he delay should not be accounted to that station. Whereas if a flight departure was late due to a service failure, then that station is accountable for that delay. Sometimes a delay will be combination of accountable and non-accountable delay reasons. For example, a flight may arrive late and take more than its allocated ground time. So you have a late arrival delay as well as a station delay.

Now let find out how to calculate the delay at a station. The important fact that all station staff must understand is that a station-accountable delay is not meant as an accusation but for adaptation of new procedures or improvement of existing processes to avoid recurrence. In any case, a station-accountable delay needs to be thoroughly investigated with the concerned parties involved. A detailed report is to be compiled by the senior operations controller, who is directly in charge. The investigations must be done with or through the concerned direct supervisor if a junior staff is involved and must be done as follows,

a) Must be formal, factual and fair,
b) Always maintain a high level of integrity,

- c) Avoid preconceived opinions or past conclusions,
- d) Avoid personal or cultural or religious remarks and opinions,
- e) Avoid personal like or dislikes.
- f) Avoid conspiracies and institutional grapevine,
- g) Where confidentiality is required, adhere to it strictly,
- h) Where applicable, use the necessary level of support and empathy,
- i) Avoid arguments and never get irritated or angry,
- j) Approach should be calm and focused.
- k) All questions must be leading and probing questions rather than questions where the answer will be just a yes or no.

The report can be for higher management, for records, for procedural changes, etc. It must be precise and most importantly, avoid any form of generalizing and personal remarks. It must comprise of the following,

- a) Relevant details of the flight, e.g. flight number, date, routing, load, aircraft type, etc.
- b) Staff involved.
- c) The precise nature or contributing factors leading to the service delivery failure, which resulted in the flight delay.
- d) Conclusion as to whether the cause was due to any lack of or existing faulty procedures.
- e) Practical and workable suggestions and actions taken or to be taken to avoid future recurrence.

All delays or service failures must be looked on as a learning and correction process only. Learning from mistakes ultimately leads to success and perfection.

Airport and Aircraft introduction
Airport

The size of airports differ from country to country and city to city, depending on where it is located. It all depends on the economic activity in the area/region nowadays. Also, it has become multi-functional i.e. as mentioned earlier, it is not just a place associated with travel, but is nowadays used for shopping, resting, socializing, etc. Whatever the size, layout, and functions, it can be divided into two main areas, namely, airside/operational area and landside/general area. Airside area is that sterile operational area of the airport, access to which is controlled. Which means only security-cleared operational staff or immigration and security-cleared traveling public has access. The movement of all those authorized to enter this area is again restricted to their area of concern. For example, after security clearance, passengers have access to the duty free, waiting or pre-boarding lounge, and embarking or disembarking areas (under guidance), but are not supposed to go to any other aircraft handling areas. Similarly, a catering staff working in the aircraft may not be given access to the terminal due to security reasons. Some of the other areas are:

- Baggage claim area,
- Passport control,
- Customs control,
- Security control,
- Baggage build-up/storage area,
- Cargo build-up/storage area,
- Maintenance areas,
- Catering,
- Ramp areas, etc.

Here ramp area includes aircraft parking stands and other flight handling areas, which are off limits to the general public.

Landside, on the other hand, is where the general public and the traveling public mingle and as such there are no security controls for access to these areas. These areas consisting of car parks, food courts, shopping areas, pre check-in areas, meet and greet areas, etc. This form of segregation is to stop any form of unlawful interference to civil aviation. Our main area of concentration will be the ramp, which can be a beehive of activities done by professionals, using highly sophisticated and expensive equipment and systems to ensure smooth movement of passengers, crew, aircraft, and other load through the airport.

An airline appoints a general sales agent (GSA) in a country or city when it decides to operate to that country/city. This GSA holds the ticket stock, which is then given to travel agents, for selling it to the passengers on the basis of a commission from the fare for each along the line. In the case of cargo, there are also GSA who are given air waybill stocks – IATA approved cargo agents who accept, document, mark, label, and ensure proper packing of export cargo on behalf of the airline and earn a percentage of the air freight charges. There are air freight forwarders who cover all aspects of cargo processing such as consolidation, pick-up, forwarding, customs clearance, delivery, safe keeping, etc. A consolidated shipment is a bulk shipment with one or more individual consignments from different shippers. All this cargo is handled at the airport by the cargo handling agent on behalf of the airline. The functions of the cargo handling agent are:

- Receive export cargo from IATA cargo agents and interline cargo from other airlines or their agents and arrange the load for outgoing flights.
- Accept import cargo from incoming flights and check it with customs and arrange storage. Prepare transfer manifests and transfer interline cargo.
- Notify consignee about the arrival of incoming cargo and assist them in taking delivery from customs.
- Take and in some cases track mishandled and undelivered cargo.
- Get all export cargo build-up into the correct ULD and complete the proper documentation as per the airline requirements.
- Get import cargo accordingly removed from ULD and stored till consignee takes delivery.
- Hand over all build-up and processed cargo to the aircraft handling section for loading onto aircrafts. Similarly, import cargo brought from the aircraft once it is offloaded.

Basic Aviation Knowledge

Aircraft

Let us first see what each part of the aircraft is called (*see figures*). On the outside, the aircraft comprises mainly of:

Fig. III.1: The aircraft nose cone.

Fig.III.2.a.

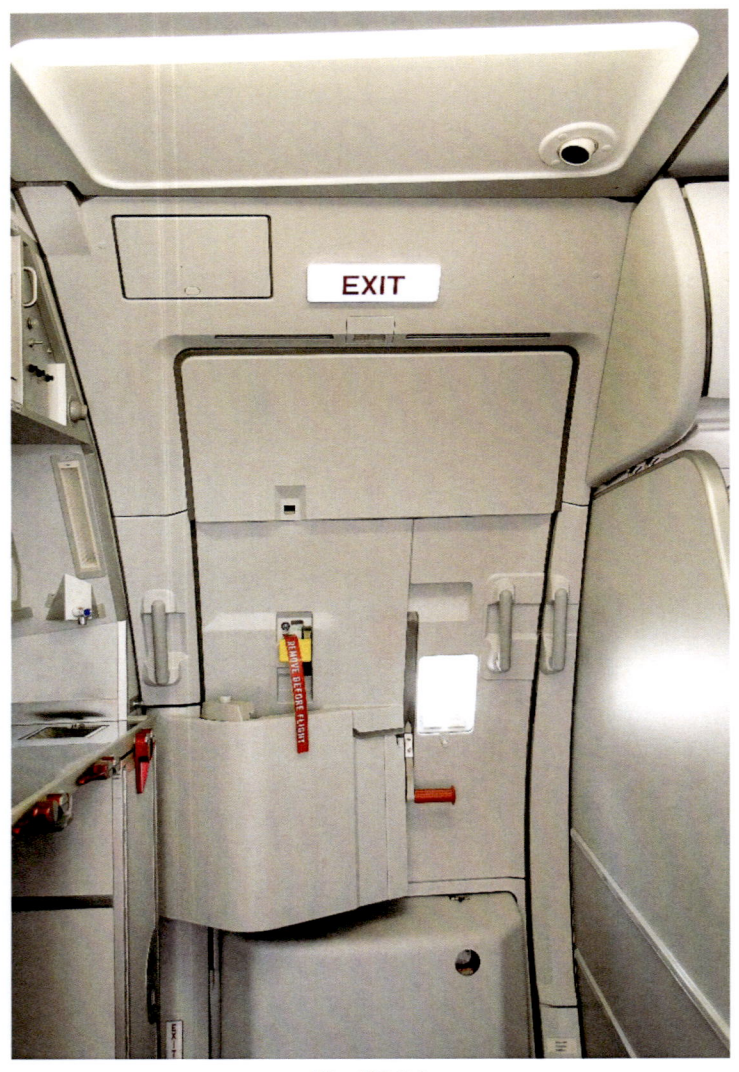

Fig. III.2.b.
Fig. III.2: Aircraft door.

Fig. III.3: Forward landing gear, which is the nose wheel and wheel assembly.

Fig. III.4: Wheel assembly.

Basic Aviation Knowledge

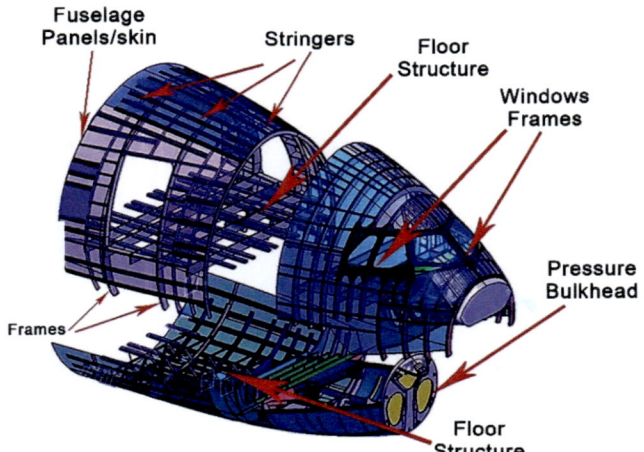

Fig. III.5.a.

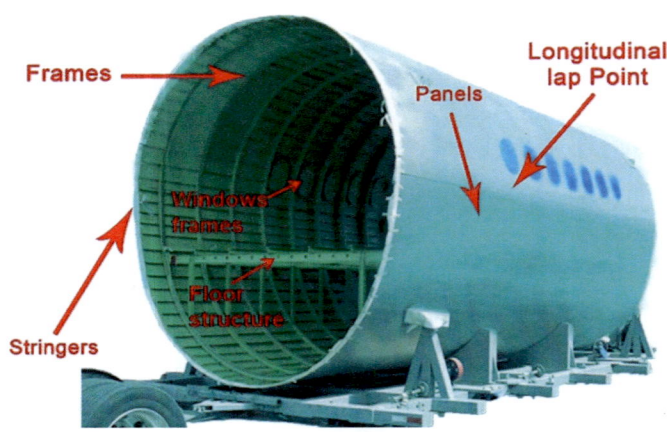

Fig. III.5.b.

Fig. III.5.c.
Fig. III.5: Main body called fuselage.

Fig. III.6: Rear / Main landing gear.

Basic Aviation Knowledge

Fig.III.7.a: Engines on the wings – provides the thrust required to create forward motion and generate lift.

Fig. III.7.b: Aileron on the aircraft wing – forms part of the <u>trailing edge</u> of each <u>wing</u> of a <u>fixed-wing aircraft</u>. Ailerons are used in pairs to control the aircraft in <u>roll</u> (or movement around the aircraft's <u>longitudinal axis</u>), which normally results in a change in flight path due to the tilting of the <u>lift vector</u>. Movement around this axis is called 'rolling' or 'banking'.

Basic Aviation Knowledge

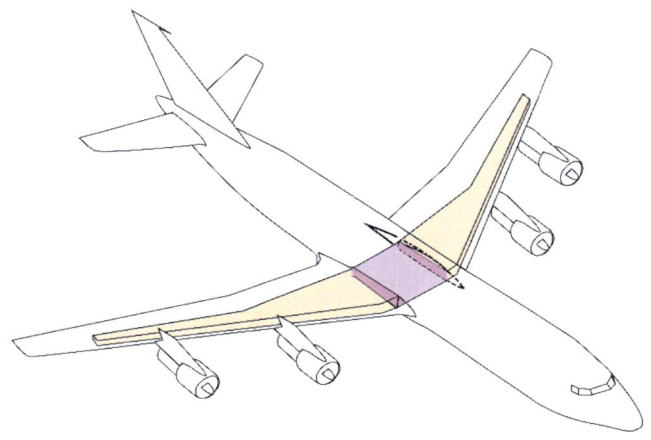

Fig. III.7.c: Fuel tanks – situated inside the wings.

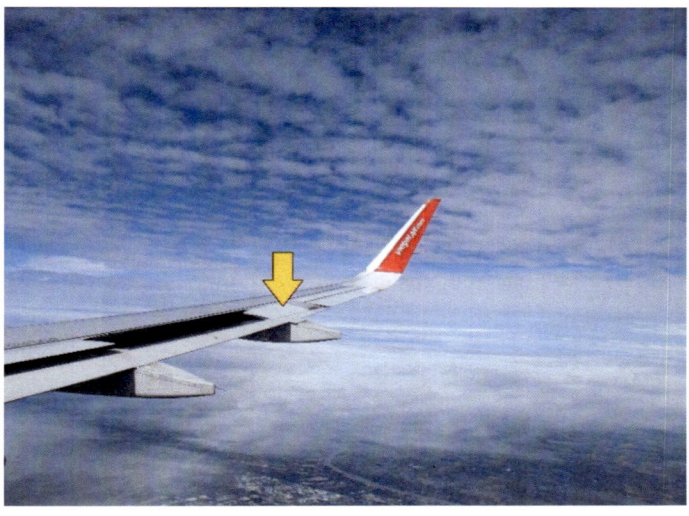

Fig. III.7.d: Spoilers – Spoilers are plates on the top surface of a wing that can be extended upward into the airflow to spoil it. By doing so, the spoiler creates a controlled <u>stall</u> over the portion of the wing behind it, greatly reducing the lift of that wing section.

Basic Aviation Knowledge

Fig. III.7.e: Flaps – devices used to alter the lift characteristics of a wing and are mounted on the trailing edges of the <u>wings</u> of a <u>fixed-wing aircraft</u> to reduce the speed at which the aircraft can be safely flown and to increase the angle of descent for landing.

Basic Aviation Knowledge

Fig. III.7.f: Slats – Slats are <u>aerodynamic</u> surfaces on the leading edge of the <u>wings</u> of <u>fixed-wing aircraft</u> which, when deployed, allow the wing to operate at a higher <u>angle of attack</u>.

Fig. III.7: Aircraft wings comprising of engines, ailerons, fuel tanks, spoilers, flaps, and slats.

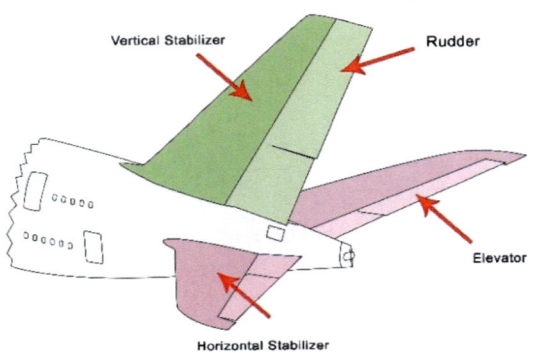

Fig. III.8.a.

Fig. III.8.b

Fig. III.8: Tail section with the rudders, the stabilizers, and elevators.

Now let us briefly see the functions of the wings, rudders, stabilizers etc. in flying (*see figures*).

Basic Aviation Knowledge

1) Wings:
    Have you ever thought how does the aircraft lift off the ground and fly? This is due to the action of air pressure on the wings. Take an A4 size paper, hold it horizontally just below your lips, with the other end drooping downward and blow straight, over the paper (*See figure. III.9.a*). You will notice the drooping end of the paper rising up to the level of the air blow. This happens because the pressure all around the paper is same, but when you blow air in the area above the paper, low pressure is created there and the area below the paper experiences high pressure build-up comparatively.

    Consider a typical cross section of the wing, which is designed to have a camber (that is the top needs to be slightly curved, like a hump, and the bottom is left flat or straight). An object with this shape is called an aerofoil (*See figure. III.9.b*). An air stream hitting the leading edge of the aerofoil will split and flow over and below the wings. Camber causes the air that flows over the top of the airfoil to move faster than the air that flows beneath it. In the 1700s, Daniel Bernoulli showed that a fluid that flows faster over a surface will create less pressure on the surface than fluid that flows more slowly. This concept later became known as Bernoulli's Principle. Further, since air is a fluid, air follows Bernoulli's Principle. Thus, we have a situation where there is less air pressure on the top of an airfoil than underneath. This difference in pressure will cause the wing to move. That is, the difference in pressure will generate a force. The force that is generated is called "lift". Bernoulli's Principle applies only to subsonic flight. By virtue of its shape alone, an airfoil will generate lift as air flows over it. However, even more lift can be generated by the airfoil if it is tilted with respect to the airflow. This tilt is called an airfoil's angle of attack. As the wing is tilted, the air flowing over the top of the wing flows even faster than the air flowing underneath. As the difference in the speed of the two airflows increases, the difference in pressure increases also. Remember that it is this difference in pressure that generates the lift force. So, as its angle of attack increases, the wing generates more lift. Imagine an airplane taking off heading into the wind. As the airplane speeds along the runway, it is already feeling the effect of the lift generated by the shape of the aerofoil. Farther along the runway, the pilot pulls the nose up. This increases the angle of attack of the wings, which causes more lift to be generated.

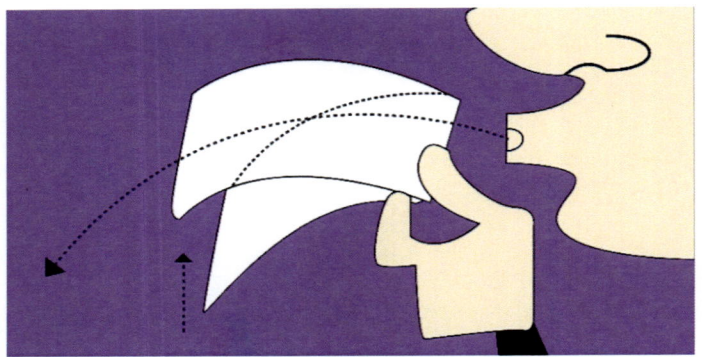

Fig.III.9.a.

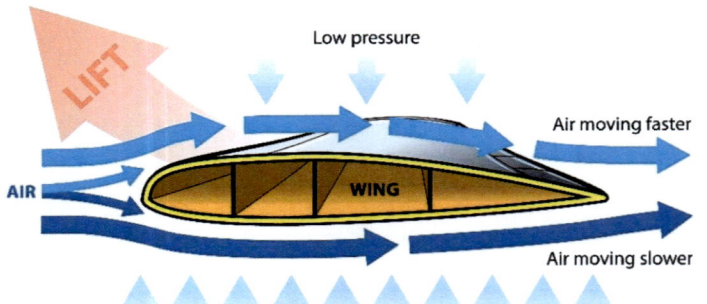

Fig.III.9.b.
Fig. III.9: Effect of airflow on the wings.

The force to move forward is called thrust and is provided by the engines. To move forward, the thrust must be more than the resistance caused by friction of the atmospheric air on the fuselage of the aircraft. This force of friction is called drag and acts backwards. Manufacturers try to reduce the drag by streamlining the fuselage. Thus, when the engine provides sufficient thrust, the aircraft moves forward, creating the air flow over the wing, which ultimately gives the lift. This is how an aircraft flies. There are four forces acting on an aircraft:

Basic Aviation Knowledge

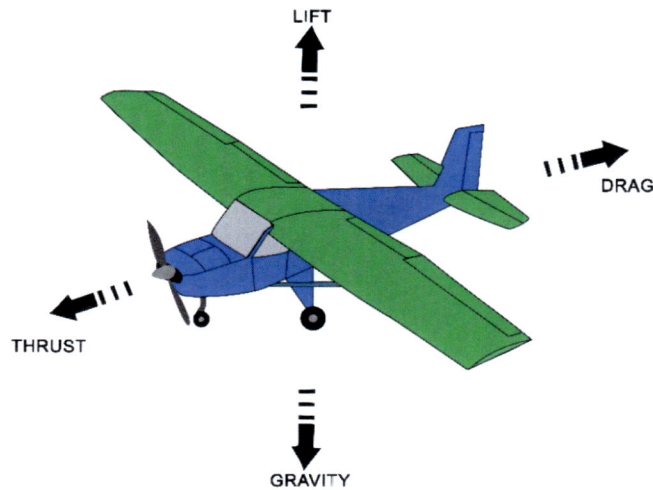

Fig. III.10: Forces acting on an aircraft.

- Weight of the aircraft – downward due to weight/gravitational pull.
  To counter this force
- Lift of the aircraft – upward force provided at the wings.
- Drag of the aircraft – backward force due to the friction.
  To counter this force
- Thrust from the aircraft – forward force from the engines. *(See figure.III.10).*

All forces are interactive. The thrust created by the engines must exceed the drag for the aircraft to move forward. Only when it moves forward is the lift created. The lift must exceed the weight in order to get airborne.

The fuel inlets are located on both the wings of the aircraft. The fuel tanks are inside the wings and in some aircrafts there are fuels tanks in between the wings and even at the tail section of the wings. Having fuel tanks in the wings gives additional strength and stability to the aircraft.

2) Engines:
   We saw how an aircraft is lifted off the ground due to the effect of fast moving air over and below the wings. The fast movement of air can be achieved only when the aircraft is

Basic Aviation Knowledge

moving forward equally fast. Here the jet engines come into use. The fan blades of the engines are designed to suck in the air in front of it when it is rotating and this air is then pushed out the rear with high intensity, propelling the aircraft forward. A basic example is like your kitchen exhaust fan. Note of caution: it is extremely dangerous to be near a running engine. In front of it there is possibility of getting sucked in, and at the rear, there is the risk of very hot jet blasts, or in other words, jets of very hot air. So never approach or go near an aircraft engine when it is running. Tests have shown that jet blast can send vehicles hurtling several meters away. Coming back, when this propulsion is increased, the aircraft moves forward faster, thereby when a certain desired speed is achieved, the desired lifting effect is created.

3) Stabilizer:
This looks like small wings, situated near the tail section of the aircraft. For smaller aircrafts, this is normally on the tail, and for bigger aircrafts, it is attached to the rear end of the fuselage, below the tail. This is turned/adjusted and set up or down by the captain, before departure from an airport. When the aircraft is flying, if the front side of the stabilizer is adjusted at a downward angle, the rushing air currents hit against its surface side, causing the level of the nose or front part of the aircraft to stay above the level of the rear of the aircraft (*see figures.III.11*).

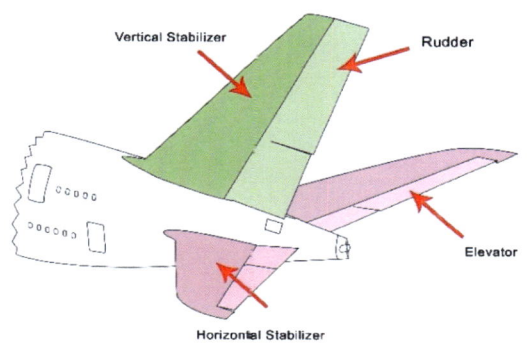

Fig. III.11.a.

Fig. III.11.b.

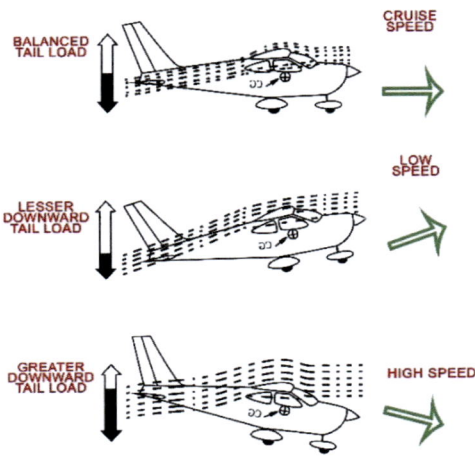

Fig. III.11.c.
Fig. III.11: Aircraft stabilizer.

The level depends on to what degree the stabilizer is adjusted, and this degree is arrived at by the load controller, who plans and makes sure the aircraft is well balanced, with the passengers seating and other load loaded in the cargo hold below. This is most desired by airline companies, as it saves on fuel. When the front part of the aircraft is slightly elevated than the rear, the underside of the aircraft has a skimming effect over the air currents passing underneath it, thereby reducing the need for more engine power and thus less fuel. Similarly, the effect is reciprocated if the stabilizer is adjusted upwards, causing the front of the aircraft to dip down while in the air. This increases the fuel consumption.

4) Elevator:
   These are extensions attached to the stabilizer and are for longitudinal control. The captain uses them to raise or lower the front of the aircraft during flying (*see figures III.11.a and III.12*).

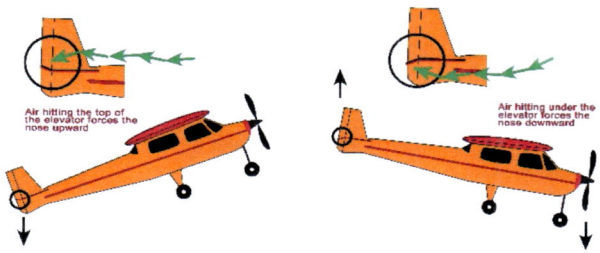

Fig.III.12: Elevator.

This is done by the effect of air currents on it and is similar to the action of the stabilizer.

5) Rudder:
   These are longitudinal extensions on the tail and are for directional control. These are used to turn the aircraft left or right. If the rudder is turned left, the air currents coming from the front on the left side of the aircraft hit against the rudder, whereas on the right side there is no resistance, causing the aircraft to turn left. Similarly, in the case to turn right. (*See figures. III.11.a and III.13*)

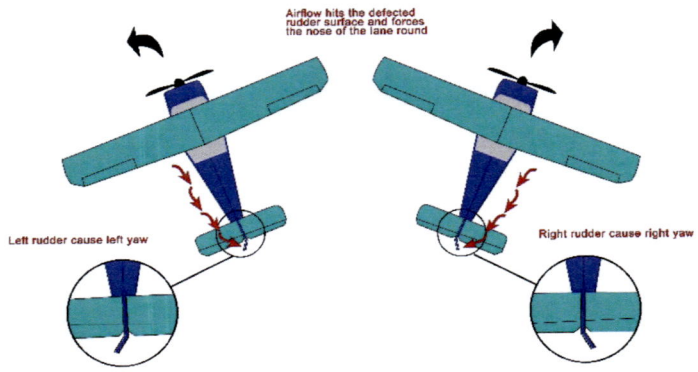

Fig. III.13: Rudder.

6) Aileron:
   These are found on the wings and are for lateral control. During a turn to any side, that side of the aircraft has to dip down and the other side is to be elevated. This is achieved due to the effects of the air currents on both sides of the aircraft on the ailerons found on both the wings (*see figures: III.7.b and III.14*).

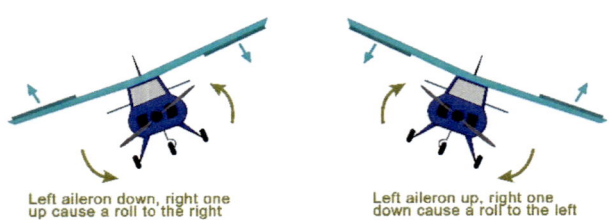

Fig. III.14.a.

Basic Aviation Knowledge

Fig. III.14.b.
Fig. III.14: Aileron.

7) Spoilers and trailing edge flaps:
   (*See figures III.7.d and III.7.e*): These are found on the wings and are used to slow the aircraft during landing. The spoilers come up and the trailing edge flaps extend downwards causing the air currents to hit against it. This resistance gives an additional braking effect to the aircraft than that offered by the brakes on the wheels.

The inside of an aircraft is like a hollow tube, imagine seeing it from one end of the tube, it will look like a circle, with a divider in between. The top is the passenger cabin and the bottom half is the cargo holds (*see figure.III.15*).

Basic Aviation Knowledge

Fig. III.15: Cross-section of an aircraft fuselage.

The upper cabin or the main deck inside the aircraft consists of the cockpit/flight deck in the front, where the captain and first officer fly the aircraft,

Fig. III.16: Flight deck or aircraft cockpit.

there are the galleys where the food, drinks, cutlery etc. are stored, heated, and prepared for serving by the crew, crew lockers for storing blankets/trays/newspapers/passengers coats etc.,

Fig. III.17: Aircraft galley and catering trolley.

then there is the cabin with seats divided into different classes such as first /business/economy class etc., these seats have overhead

Basic Aviation Knowledge

stowage lockers for handbags, announcement/entertainment systems/visual display units (VDU), and of course, the toilets.

Fig. III.18: Aircraft passenger cabin.

There are many other important components and features in an aircraft; for example, the emergency exits, the chutes for emergency evacuation etc.

In the lower section of the aircraft or the lower deck, there are two holds; one is the forward hold, which is forward of the wing, and the aft hold, which is at the rear of the aircraft or aft of wing (*see figures: III.19*).

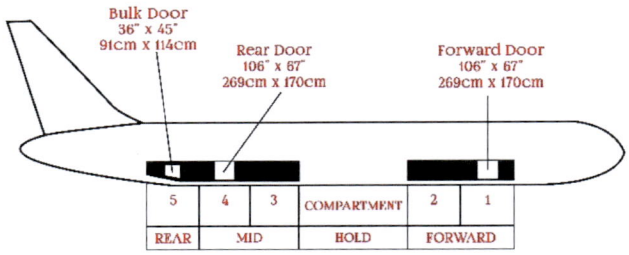

Fig. III.19: Aircraft hold division.

Basic Aviation Knowledge

Now if you are in the aircraft facing the front and your back towards the rear of the aircraft, then your left will be the left of the aircraft and your right will be the right side of the aircraft. The left of the aircraft is called portside, and the right side of the aircraft is called starboard side (*see figure.III.20*).

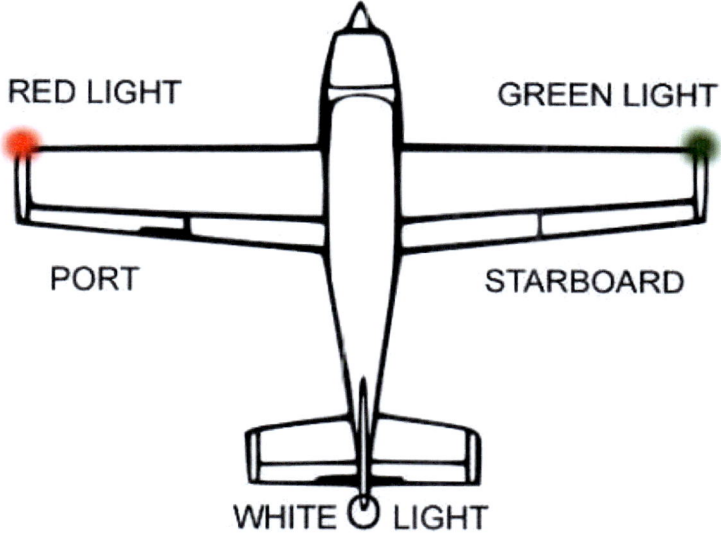

Fig. III.20: Port and starboard side of an aircraft.

There are beacon lights on each wing and the tail section of the aircraft. These can also be used for identifying the aircraft port and starboard sides.

Basic Aviation Knowledge

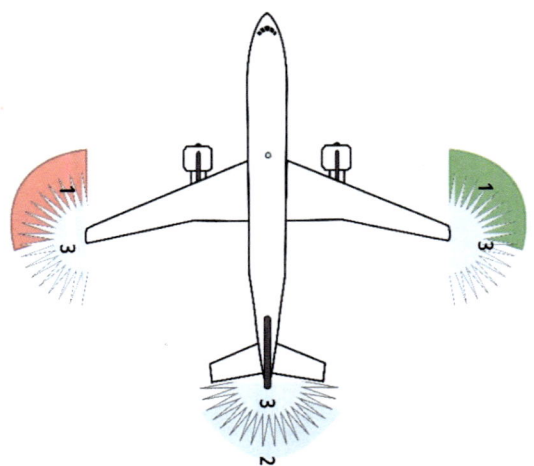

Fig.III.21.a.

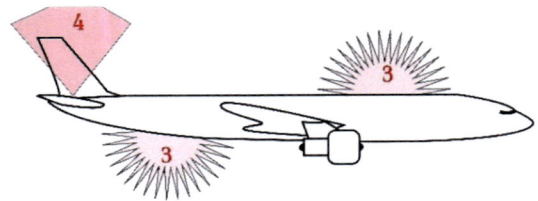

Fig.III.21.b.
Fig. III.21: Beacon lights.

The captain normally sits on the portside side, and the first officer sits on the starboard side. The captain will have a four stripes on the epaulets, and the first officer will have lesser stripes (depends on the airline). Some older aircrafts have a flight mechanic/engineer sitting behind the first officer. Doors in the upper passenger cabin can be found on both starboard and portside. The doors at the portside are used for passenger/crew embarkation/disembarkation, whereas the starboard doors are used for loading or unloading of catering items or for servicing the aircraft. The number of doors on the starboard and portside depend on the type of aircraft. For example, if there are two on the portside, one located forward of the wing and one at rear of the aircraft (aft of the wing), then the first forward left side or portside side door is called L1 and the rear left side door is called L2. Similarly, the doors on the starboard side or right side are called R1, R2, R3, etc., from the front to the rear of the aircraft, depending on the number of doors. You may find other door or doors (normally smaller) in between, marked as emergency exits. These are not to be taken as L2 or R2 etc. but are used in cases of extreme emergency situations, which are activated by and used with the assistance of the crew or authorized personnel. Opening of any aircraft cabin door from the inside at any time must be done by the crew only and no one must touch any components of the door. When the aircraft has completed its operation and all passengers, crew, etc. have disembarked, the aircraft is then handed over to the aircraft engineers; at this time aircraft doors and everything else can be operated by the authorized airline engineers on the ground.

The lower hold doors are located at the starboard side of the aircraft. There are normally two doors, one for the forward hold and the other for the aft hold, located aft of the wing. There can be more than two hold doors, it depends on the type of aircraft (*See figure.III.22*).

Fig. III.22.a.

Fig. III.22.b.
Fig. III.22: Location of aircraft holds.

For some long-range flights additional fuel tanks or sometimes crew rest area or bunks may be fitted in one of the holds also, which can be accessed from the cabin. These bunks will enable the crew to take rest and do rotational duties on long haul flights. Access to this area is restricted for passengers. In the case of additional fuel tanks,

Basic Aviation Knowledge

they will help the aircraft fly for a longer distance without having to stop for refueling on long haul flights, which would be expensive.

Although there are many types of aircrafts made by different manufacturers, for the ramp staff there are basically two types, narrow-body and wide-body aircrafts (*see figures:III.23*).

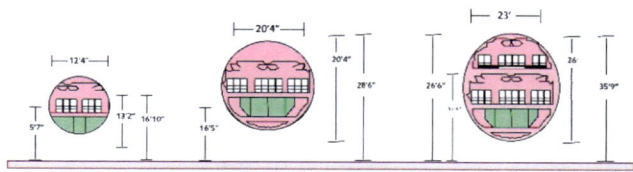

Fig. III.23: Basic types of aircraft.

Normally, narrow-body passenger aircrafts are smaller, have a single aisle in the upper passenger cabin, all load (baggage/cargo/mail/etc.) is stalked/stored/bulk loaded as it is in the lower cargo holds, and they have lesser capacity.

Wide body aircrafts have twin aisles in the passenger cabin, ULD loading (units in which the joining load is loaded, which in turn is loaded into the aircraft hold), and has a higher capacity. Some of the common types of aircrafts and their manufacturers are as follows:

Manufacturers	**Wide body aircrafts**	**Narrow body aircraft**
Airbus	A310/A300/A330/A340/A380	A319/A320/A321 (lately some airlines have converted them to ULD versions)
Boeing	B767/B747/B747combi/B777	B707/B727/B737/B757
Ilyushin		IL96 /IL62
McDonnell Douglas	DC10/MD11/MD11combi	DC8/DC9/MD90
Tupolev		TU154
Fokker		F50/F100

Above you may notice two aircrafts (B747 and MD11) having the word combi attached to them. These aircraft models have, like other aircrafts, a passenger cabin on top and a cargo hold below, but

Basic Aviation Knowledge

additionally, in the main deck the passenger cabin length is shortened to add an extra cargo hold after it *(see figure.III.24)*.

Fig. III.24.a.

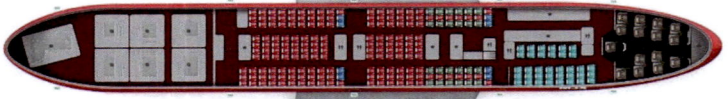

Passenger cabin Main deck Cargo hold
Fig. III.24.b.
Fig. III.24: Combi aircrafts.

You may think that just like cars, where each manufacturer has different models, it is similar in the case of aircrafts. But these aircrafts have different versions for each model shown above. For example, the Boeing Company makes different versions of its B747 aircraft, such as B747-200, B747-300, B747-400 etc. Although all the versions of a particular model may look the same, they have varying capacities and limitations. The airline selects the model, version, and engines it wants based on its requirements. Please note the aircraft manufacturer does not make the engines. Two major engine manufacturers are:

- Rolls Royce
- Prat & Whitney.

Basic Aviation Knowledge

Here too there are different versions of engines, with varying capacities such as range, fuel consumption, etc.

All aircrafts, whatever the make or type, must be registered with the government aviation authority of a country and is in turn given a distinctive alpha-numeric or only alphabetic registration. The first two characters will denote the international civil aviation code of the country. This is like the registration plate of your car. On an aircraft this registration is found painted, always visibly, at the rear of the aircraft fuselage on both sides (nearer to the tail section), under the wings, and in some aircrafts on the nose wheel well cover.

The technical regulation process of ICAO is for international legislation to be made effective at the national level. This takes place through the enactment of the civil aviation act in each member country. This addresses a broader legal framework, so the next level is the civil aviation regulation (CAR), which focuses specifically on the management and operation of air transport. This means all matters pertaining to registration of aircraft, airworthiness requirements, maintenance, and air crew qualifications come under its preview.

****

Chapter IV
Aircraft Documentation (Ramp Operations)

Introduction

There are a lot of necessary traffic documents a flight must have on board before it can depart from a station. These documents contain names of crew operating the flight, passengers, the load details it's carrying, etc., and is required on board for the crew, for the airline, handling agent, and authorities at the departure and destination airports. There is a lot of information in these documents and is used to provide good service, meet safety/security requirements, for operational requirements, for accounting, and as a record. Each document has a specific purpose and format. With the advent of automation, these documents can easily be printed quickly, provided the necessary data is input. The main activities of this section are collecting incoming documents, preparing the outgoing documents as per the requirements of the airline, and then putting it on board the particular aircraft for departure. There are two files per flight, one with copies of all inbound documents and one with all outgoing documents. The information from these files are used to feed data regarding the flight into the computer systems for statistical purposes, billing, accounting, and future quick reference and then these files are stored for a minimum period of six months. In some airports, these functions are done by a separate section, usually attached to the load control section, called the documents section, and in some airports this is done by the load control staff, depending on the extent of operations. Again, with the advent of automation, the need and recording process requirements have been negated or greatly reduced. Thus, these can easily be assimilated into the load controller's functions. Here we will study it as a separate section.

Chapter Contents

Classification of documents and types
Pre-flight preparation
Incoming documents
Finalizing outgoing documents
Data input and filling

****

Classification of Documents and Types

All documents must be placed in an envelope, as per IATA recommendations; the envelopes' minimum size to be such that it can accommodate A4 size papers, with holes of approximately 7–9 mm diameter at intervals of 7cm, separate columns or boxes for writing the flight number, date, and destination where the documents are to be off-loaded. These envelopes must have the words "Passenger Manifest" or "Cargo Manifest" etc. printed in bold letters and broken lines along their edges. The color of the letters and broken lines for the different documents' envelopes should be as follows: red for passenger manifest envelopes, green for cargo documents, blue for mail, and dark yellow for load sheet and clearance documents. Normally, these are provided by the airline, with its logo and name on it. Basically, the documents to be on board the aircraft can be classified into two groups and are put into their respective envelopes before placing them on board the aircraft,

1) Passenger documents
2) Cargo and other load documents

Passenger Documents

These comprise of the passenger manifest, passenger information list, passenger seat list, passenger security list, etc. Each give certain information about the passengers on board the flight. It depends on the airline and the destination airport requirements if all of the mentioned list or any other list is required to be forwarded on board. These documents are always placed in the cabin of the aircraft, normally in a documents bag in the care of the cabin crew. A brief of the passenger documents mentioned above are as follows,

Aircraft Documentation (Ramp Operations)

- Passenger manifest – This is the list of passenger names who are traveling on the flight. This list is prepared or printed once check-in is completed or boarding is over.
- The passenger security list contains the traveling passenger's name, his reference number, the number and weight of bags for that passenger, his seat number and if he is traveling with a group, etc. for each passenger on the flight.
- The passenger seat list contains the seat plan of the aircraft, with the seats occupied by passengers marked accordingly.
- The passenger information list contain special information about the passenger, e.g. wheel chair passenger, VIP, special meals requests etc. For example, this will help the crew serve the meal requested by the passenger, which he had booked while purchasing the ticket.
- A baggage reconciliation list contains the list of all the passengers' bags loaded on the aircraft, with the baggage tag numbers against the passengers' reference numbers. If it is a wide-body aircraft, this list will show in which container the bags are loaded.

In places where there is no automation or in the case of a system outage, there will always be provisions for getting the lists manually.

For example, passenger manifest will be then made manually by the check-in section based on the passengers actually checked in by them and is then forwarded to the documents section for hand-over to the cabin crew. Currently, these documents in some airports are printed by the boarding staff at the boarding gate and handed over to the crew on board directly as soon as the boarding is completed or as early as possible when the flight has been finalized by check-in.

Cargo and Other Load Documents

These comprise of the air waybill (inclusive of any declaration/certificates in case of special cargo), cargo manifest of the cargo being carried, and the courier documents, and is forwarded in a cargo documents envelope. The mail manifest and the AV7 are put in its (blue broken lines on its edges) envelope. Both these envelopes are placed in the documents bag with the passenger documents envelopes on board in the cabin. Some airlines have a separate documents bag only for the cargo documents envelope in the cargo hold of the aircraft. One of the reasons for this is that the cargo documents are handled by staff from a different section in some airports, who do not have access to the cabin, and the passenger documents are handled by the passenger services section. Briefs about some of the cargo documents are as follows,

- Air waybill – An air waybill has the same relation to cargo as an airline ticket (with coupons) to a passenger. It is a documentary evidence of the contract of carriage between shipper and the carrier. The air waybill is made, or in airline terminology "cut", when a shipper delivers a cargo consignment after all airline and government formalities are completed, with all necessary details such as cost of carriage, weight, volume, contents, etc. to the forwarding agent of the airline. It acts as a guide to the carrier's staff in handling, dispatching, and delivering the consignment. It consists of two parts; the first part identifies the airline, and the second part identifies the individual consignment. The air waybill is made in duplicate, with each copy for different parties involved in the process of transportation. E.g. one copy is taken by the airline for accounting, one copy goes to the shipper, one copy for the consignee on receipt of consignment, etc. An air waybill may be used for the transportation of individual shipments or consolidated shipments. In case of special consignments such as live animals or pets, the veterinary certificate, permission for carriage from destination country (if required) etc. is also attached to the air waybill.
- Cargo manifest – There can be many consignments going on a particular flight, with each having its own air waybill; hence, like a passenger manifest, we have the cargo manifest. The cargo manifest contains all the air waybill numbers, against which the designated name of the cargo, number of pieces, weights, the total pieces, and weight are detailed.
- AV7 is a revenue document and is prepared by the postal authorities. This has similar role like the air waybill as it is used for the transportation of airmail. The airline recovers money from the postal authorities for the transportation of airmail on the basis of AV7. This document contains the dispatch number of the post office mail bag (tagged with

the number), number of pieces, weights, and final destination in case of re-routing.
- Mail manifest – This is the list of all the mailbags going on a particular flight. It shows the number of mailbags, dispatch numbers, weights of each bag, destination, and total weight.

Other than the above two sets of documents, there are two more sets of documents required, one for the crew and the other for the load planner or controller.

The cabin crew needs the following documents to operate the flight: the general declaration, passenger information list, passenger seat list, and any others as per airline requirement. A brief about general declaration (GD) is as follows,

In some countries the arrival crew will need to make a declaration that the crew and passengers on board are free of any contagious or communicable diseases to the best of their knowledge to the health authorities at the arriving airport. This is based on ICAO – Annex 9, appendix 1, where it is agreed to formulate a general declaration form. It is the list containing the names of all the crew on board the aircraft. It also has the flight number, origin station, destination, aircraft registration, number of passengers, governing rules, regulations, etc. It also states that the crew, whose names are on it, does not have any contagious or communicable diseases. Nowadays, the crew GD list in the correct format (multiple copies) is used widely by immigration authorities in many departure airport and the arrival airport to allow travel, short stay, and departure, instead of visas or a crew card for operating on a flight or for short duty travel. This will be clarified by the airline to its crew, but the need for the GD to be on board with the operating crew list details is mandatory. So the GD must be prepared from the list of crew operating a flight and handed over to the crew after it has been approved and verified by the origin immigration authorities. (*Refer to figure.IV.1 for a copy*)

GENERAL DECLARATION

OUTWARD/INWARD ICAO ANNEX 9, APPENDIX I

O W N E R OR O P E R A T O R : **EMIR**
MARKS OF NATIONALITY AND REGISTRATION : **A6-ABC**
FLIGHT NUMBER AB**9889** DATE: **15 AUG 15**
DEPARTURE FROM MUMBAI INDIA
ARRIVAL AT . . . DWC DUBAI
FLIGHT ROUTING: BOM-DWC

Crew
CA SALEM JESSANI CA XX997733 M 01JUL1955
FO NIKOLAS TEPPELIS CX KX0036532 M 26JAN1974
CA OLOF STEFAN ORESTEN SA LX093835 M 31AUG1977
FO RAWLE ALVIN BASANTA HENRY UK JJ0668066 M 17JUN1989

NUMBER OF PASSENGERS ON THIS STAGE: C A R G O

--DEPARTURE PLACE: MUMBAI INDIA
THROUGH ON SAME FLIGHT: …
ARRIVAL PLACE : DWC DUBAI
DISEMBARKING: ………. …
THROUGH ON SAME FLIGHT: …

FOR OFFICIAL USE ONLY

DECLARATION OF HEALTH

PERSONS ON BOARD KNOWN TO BE SUFFERING FROM ILLNESS OTHER THAN AIRSICKNESS OR THE EFFECTS OF ACCIDENTS, AS WELL AS THOSE CASES OF ILLNESS DISEMBARKED DURING THE FLIGHT. ………………..
ANY OTHER CONDITIONS ON BOARD WHICH MAY LEAD TO THE SPREAD OF DISEASE. ………………………..
DETAILS OF EACH DISINSECTING OR SANITARY TREATMENT --PLACE.DATE. TIME, METHOD-- DURING

Aircraft Documentation (Ramp Operations)

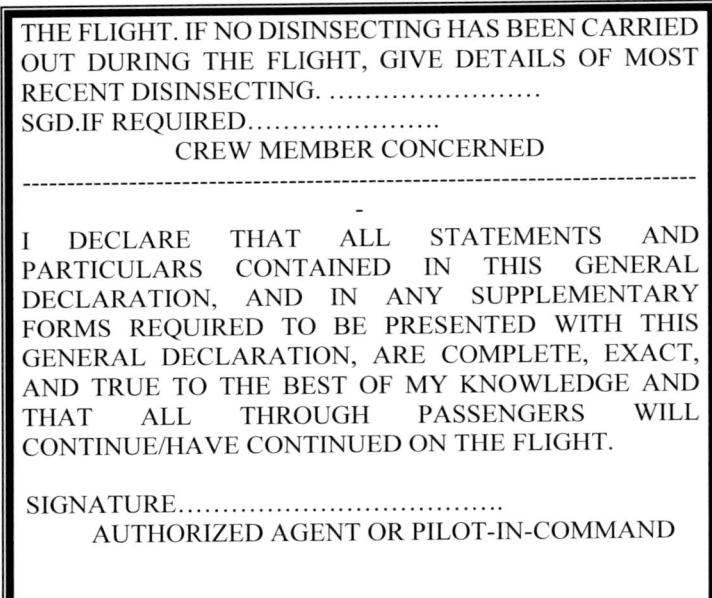

> THE FLIGHT. IF NO DISINSECTING HAS BEEN CARRIED OUT DURING THE FLIGHT, GIVE DETAILS OF MOST RECENT DISINSECTING. ....
> SGD.IF REQUIRED......................
> CREW MEMBER CONCERNED
> --
> -
> I DECLARE THAT ALL STATEMENTS AND PARTICULARS CONTAINED IN THIS GENERAL DECLARATION, AND IN ANY SUPPLEMENTARY FORMS REQUIRED TO BE PRESENTED WITH THIS GENERAL DECLARATION, ARE COMPLETE, EXACT, AND TRUE TO THE BEST OF MY KNOWLEDGE AND THAT ALL THROUGH PASSENGERS WILL CONTINUE/HAVE CONTINUED ON THE FLIGHT.
>
> SIGNATURE....................................
> AUTHORIZED AGENT OR PILOT-IN-COMMAND

Fig. IV.1: General Declaration.

The documents required by the load planners, which must be handed over to him timely by the documents staff, are as follows,

Cargo manifest, mail manifests, courier manifest, the GD, NOTOC, and the unit weight statement. These documents must be handed over to him well in advance so that he can plan the flight.

NOTOC means notification to captain. This document contains information regarding any special cargo such as potentially dangerous cargo, animals, etc. going on the flight, which has to be brought to the attention of the captain. It has a lot of information, which we will go into detail in the load control chapter.

Unit weight statement (UWS) – The loose cargo for loading on aircraft is transported on trolleys to the aircraft in case of narrow-body aircraft for loading in it. In a wide-body aircraft, the cargo is loaded in unit load devices (ULD); this is weighed and taken to the aircraft for loading in it. There can be many ULDs and trolleys for a flight. The UWS gives a list of all the ULDs, with airline ULD serial numbers, net cargo weight, gross weight (i.e. weight of actual cargo in the ULD and the weight of the ULD), remarks in case of any special cargo in the ULD, and trolley numbers in case of bulk

Aircraft Documentation (Ramp Operations)

or loose cargo. The load controller uses this UWS for the actual planning of the aircraft, as the weights shown are more accurate than the manifests. You will know more about ULD in the next chapter.

Pre-Flight Preparation

Some of the documents must be kept ready well in advance, before arrival of the aircraft, in case of a turnaround or for a departure flight. The passenger, cargo, and mail envelopes are kept ready with the following documents,

a) GD – The airline will give names of the crew operating a flight well in advance to the documents section. This is to enable the documents staff to prepare the GD forms with the names and forward the required number of completed copies to the crew counter. When the crew report at the crew counter in the airport, they check in their crew bags, pick up the GD copies, and then proceed to the immigration counter. A few more copies are printed or prepared at the documents section as per the standing instructions of the airline. From these, one copy is given to the load planner, for him to calculate the weight of the crew, and one copy to the airline station. In some countries the crew may need more copies of GD at the destination airport; hence, the rest of the copies are attached to the outside of the passenger manifest envelope. In case of a transit flight, the airline will inform you if the same incoming crew are operating, then the outgoing GD is to be prepared from the in-coming GD, which will be on board, that is if the airline staff already does not know the names.

b) Manifests – The planned cargo for the flight is always ready much ahead of its arrival, that means it has been weighed and the air waybills, AV7s, manifests are send ahead to the documents section. Here the air waybills are checked against the flight cargo manifests, sorted, and put into the cargo manifest envelope, along with any NOTOC and courier documents. Even if there is no cargo for a destination, then a nil cargo manifest must be placed in the cargo envelope. Similarly, with the mail documents. A copy of the manifests and NOTOC is given to the load planner. In some airports, the cargo section accepts

Aircraft Documentation (Ramp Operations)

cargo/mail/courier, etc. till 40 minutes to departure time, so there is chance of some last minute urgent load going on the flight. In this case, the documents staff is informed by the cargo section and then he must make sure the documents are received, one copy given to the load planner and the rest put into the respective envelopes. The envelopes' address boxes are then filled (preferably with bold marker pens) with the flight number, date, destination of the cargo documents. In case the flight is going to two or more destinations, then the cargo documents for each destination must be in separate envelopes and addressed accordingly.

c) UWS – This document is only required by the load planner for planning purpose and in some cases the airline for records. This has to be handed over to the load planner as soon as it is received because it is crucial for planning. Always keep one copy of all the cargo manifests and one copy of the UWS to handover to the loading staff who will be actually loading the aircraft. It will help him in cross-checking what he is loading against the loading instruction given to him by the load planner.

Incoming Documents

Make a list of the airlines operating through your airport, with the passenger documents' bag location and the location of the cargo documents bag or if both are kept together on board their aircrafts. Take the out-going cargo documents envelope and the loading staffs manifest and UWS copies with you when you go to the aircraft to collect the incoming documents an arrival of the flight. Once the aircraft comes, the doors are opened, and before the passengers begin disembarking, the crew will normally hand over the documents bag to the documents staff. You must

a) Collect the incoming load sheet, trim sheet (if available), and any copies of NOTOC (Notification to Captain) if it is pertinent for his station.

b) Check the destination box on the passenger manifest envelope and take it only if it mentions your station, as the aircraft may be in transit and will have documents for the next destination/s, which must not be taken. Open the envelopes and check if the passenger manifests and any

Aircraft Documentation (Ramp Operations)

other documents specified by the airline or authorities required at your station are present in it.
c) Take the GD copies, after checking with the crew if they have enough copies for immigration formalities, if they are disembarking. Remember, if the crew are staying on board and continuing on the flight, a fresh GD is always required from the airport of departure. So check with them if there will be any changes to the GD list, as there may be one or more crew getting off at your station, in which case the outgoing GD must be prepared accordingly.
d) If there is only one bag for all documents, then the cargo envelope must also be offloaded if it is for your station, similar to the passenger envelope. If the cargo documents are in the bag placed in the cargo hold of the aircraft, go and collect that. Wherever it is found, open the envelope to ascertain that the cargo documents are for your station. Take one copy of the cargo manifest and hand it over to the offloading staff that is offloading the incoming load in the cargo hold of the aircraft. Place the outgoing cargo and mail envelope in the bag and give the loading staff the copies of outgoing cargo manifest and UWS copy.

If any document as per the requirement of the airline, your organization, or the airport authorities is missing or if any additional documents addressed to your station is found in the bag or the envelope, immediately inform the crew, airline representative, your supervisor, and the aircraft dispatcher, or your organization's senior most staff at the aircraft.

Once back in the office,

a) Immediately handover the incoming copy of the load sheet and trim sheet to the load planner.
b) After taking your filling copy and the copy for the airline representative of the incoming cargo and mail manifests, send the rest of the cargo documents to the cargo import section.
c) Similarly, take keep copies of the passenger names list for your office records, for airline records and send rest to the airport authorities or information desk (if required).
d) In case the same incoming crew is operating, prepare a new GD from the incoming GD, after making the necessary changes in case of any deletions or additions to the names.

Aircraft Documentation (Ramp Operations)

Get the necessary immigration authority's approval, give one copy to the load planner, one copy to the airline, and keep the rest ready.

Finalizing Outgoing Documents

The check-in counters in airports close normally 30 to 40 minutes before departure. This varies from airline to airline and airport to airport. The next step in the documents handling activity takes place after the check-in counters are closed, because only then we will know the actual passengers traveling on the flight. The airlines use different computer check-in and departure control systems, so different airlines will use different systems at an airport. With the development of certain interface systems, you will be able to log into any of the airline systems of the airlines your company is handling, provided the necessary authorizations and programs are in place. You must first know what is the passenger information required by the crew and the lists to be forwarded on the flight of the airlines your company handles. Next, you must know the different commands to be given in the system to get the necessary print-outs. After gaining all of the above knowledge, let us go through the next set of activities step by step.

a) All the airlines require a passenger name list, so print it and any other list, such as the security list, passenger information list etc., and then place it in previously prepared passenger documents envelope. Depending on the number of destinations the flight intends to go, prepare the appropriate number of envelopes. If there is no passenger for a particular destination, then place a nil passenger manifest in the envelope.
b) Take a print-out of whatever information the crew will need for service, security, etc. e.g. special information list, seating list, etc. and keep it separately. There will be prior standing instructions from the airline on this requirement.
c) A security list will be needed by the aircraft dispatcher, in case a passenger is missing after check-in. He will be able to know if there is any bag for this passenger, number of pieces, name, reference number, and if he is with a group.
d) Unless provided by the baggage services section, a baggage list containing the list of tags for all the baggage on the flight, including the units they are loaded in etc.

must also be printed out. Copies of this are required to be kept in the documents bag on board, for the aircraft dispatcher (to find out where the bag of a missing passenger is loaded against the security list), for the airline, and for filling purposes.

Once all of the above documents have been printed and are ready, take all of them to the flight with the GD copies. At the aircraft

- Place the passenger documents envelope in the documents bag after informing the cabin crew, and make sure the GD is correct by asking the crew to check it.
- Hand over the necessary list required by the crew to them.
- Hand over the security list and baggage reconciliation list to the aircraft dispatcher.
- In case of any additional cargo, documents of any last minute urgent shipment accepted and loaded on the aircraft must be placed in the cargo documents bag.
- Finally, check with the loading staff whether all the cargo has been loaded. If any cargo is offloaded, due to no space or if the aircraft cannot carry that much weight, then remove the air waybill for the shipment that is offloaded. In case only part of the shipment is offloaded, then remove only one copy of the air waybill and then amend the cargo manifest accordingly. Amending the cargo manifest will enable the destination station staff to know that the cargo was offloaded at the origin station. Inform the aircraft dispatcher that all documents are on board and the necessary amendment has been made, if applicable.

Data Input and Filling

Once the aircraft has departed, the load planner then hands over his flight file, containing the inbound load sheet, the outgoing load sheet (signed copies), all the copies such as the manifests, GD etc. which you had initially given for planning the flight. Normally, the incoming load sheet is for the airline representative or the airline traffic department; if not, then with all the documents, two files are always made for a transit or a turnaround flight. The inbound file will have the copies of all the documents received on arrival from the origin station. The outbound file will have the copies of all the outbound documents, which you had put on board, including the load sheet, and in case if the load sheet is not system-generated, then the trim sheet. If the flight is only an arrival or if the flight was only a departure, then there will be only one file, an inbound or an outbound file. There will be a checklist according to which each document has to be arranged in the files, and then the checklist is to be ticked off accordingly and signed off. After the files have been made, the airline representative is given copies of all the inbound and outgoing documents. Next, your company may require you to feed data in the computer system with details of the flight, such as the number passengers, cargo, mail, etc. on the inbound flight and similarly for the outbound flight. This will be used, as mentioned before, for billing, accounting, statistical purposes, etc. Finally, at the end of every shift, the files of all the flights are sent for storage and safe keeping.

The staff in this section should be thorough, orderly, and keep the office in immaculate condition. This is because since a lot of papers and documents are handled, there are chances of misplacing important documents, and the office becoming untidy with papers thrown all over the place. Each airline should have its documents stowage positions labeled and marked, from which the airline representative can take what is pertinent to him. The documents staff must promptly advise his supervisor if he is missing any documents or if any of the documents are delayed or not received on time. It is in this section that the staff get ample opportunity to observe and learn more about the aviation industry.

This section functions as a support arm to the bigger load control section. In some airports this section does not exists independently or not at all. The functions described above can also be merged with functions of other major sections or some functions are performed using minimum staff utilization. For example, the collection of incoming and outgoing cargo documentation may be performed by the cargo handling staff; similarly, the traffic documents such as passenger manifests etc. may be handled by the passenger handling staff. Sometimes the entire function is done by the load control staff or the aircraft dispatcher of the flight. It all depends on the organizational layout of the handling agent, cost factors, and the kind of service agreed to be provided or required by the customer airline.

****

Chapter V
Unit Load Devices

Introduction

During apple picking time, there are thousands of apples to be transported from the orchard. These apples are first sorted and crated, before the arrival of the wagons or trucks for transportation, so when the trucks arrive at the orchard, the categorized crates can be quickly loaded. This saves a lot of time and protects the apples from damage during handling. Similarly, you may have 200 passengers traveling on your aircraft, with maybe 400 pieces of baggage and say 10000 kilograms of cargo. Passengers start coming in for check-in approximately three hours, nowadays even 24 hours before actual departure time. By the time the aircraft comes, say 375 pieces of bags have been checked-in. So if you wait till the flight arrives, all the incoming load is offloaded, and then start loading each cargo and each bag into its hold, it is going to take a lot of time and manpower. This is because checking in a passenger can take anywhere between 2 to 5 minutes or more, then the bags have to reach the baggage build-up area and then be taken to the aircraft and loaded into it. The aircraft may not leave on time.

The solution for this are the Unit Load Devices, commonly known as ULDs. They are units used for the carriage of pre-loaded dead load, or in other words these, ULDs are units into which the joining bags, cargo, mail, etc. are loaded as per each category of load and kept ready before the arrival of the flight. So once the aircraft arrives, the incoming ULDs with inbound baggage, cargo, etc. are offloaded and the joining ULDs, which were kept ready are loaded straightaway. The wide-body aircrafts and a few narrow-body aircrafts holds are built in such a way that you can load only these ULDs and no loose loading is possible. These ULDs interface directly with the aircraft loading and restrain systems, and meet all the restrain requirements, without the use of any supplementary equipment. On an aircraft there may be more than 30 ULDs coming and more than 30 going. At a major airport with many airlines operating, thousands of ULDs of different airlines are handled in each shift. Since these are expensive equipment, the airlines need continuous information on all its ULD movements at the airport. The answer to this is the unit load devices section/department of the handling agent handling their aircraft. Let us learn more about the different unit load devices and the section that is responsible for it. The airline's own local representative as well as its headquarters coordinate with this department.

Chapter Contents

Unit load devices
Identification of unit load devices
Accessories
ULD handling
ULD section activities

****

Unit Load Devices

Some aircrafts have very huge cargo holds with very high capacities. The floor of an aircraft hold that can carry ULDs has powered unidirectional rollers. They are fixed at intervals, with free rollers in between. You need to only bring the ULD to the doorsill of the aircraft hold, from there on the powered rollers can be used to move it in or out of the aircraft, using its control switches (*see figure. V.1*).

Fig. V.1: Cargo hold of ULD-version aircraft with PDUs.

Some aircrafts do not have these Power Drive Units (PDU) and hence must be pushed into position or pulled out accordingly. It must be understood that the latest PDUs are light sensitive, i.e. they do not function when the control stick is moved but start only if they sense additionally an ULD over it. This is to reduce the wear and tear of these systems when there are no ULD over it to move and also reduce power waste that is generated from the aircrafts power unit (APU), which is even more expensive.

Use of ULDs helps in utilizing the maximum available space in an aircraft hold. This is of high commercial value for the airline and has an impact on its profits. Some of the benefits of the ULD are as follows,

1. Saves time.
2. Improves handling of baggage, cargo etc. as it is grouped into a larger unit with a ULD.
3. Gives additional strength to the aircraft structure.
4. Provides safety to the items loaded in it.
5. Easier and quicker to find any item, in case of large numbers of load in several ULDs.
6. Better utilization of its aircraft hold space.
7. Flexibility in distribution of load in the aircraft hold.

There are different types of ULDs and these are not manufactured by the aircraft makers but by other companies specialized to design, test, and make them. These ULDs are designed as per the hold layout of most aircrafts, so that maximum space is utilized safely. Then they are put through several rigorous tests such as the effect of fire, fall from heights, etc. After these tests, the limitations and capacities of the ULD are established such as the maximum weight that can be loaded in it, its rate of burn, etc. Once they are of the established international standards, they are registered with IATA and then produced. All ULDs cannot be loaded into any aircraft as different aircrafts have different hold sizes and inner contours/shapes. Some ULDs are also custom-made to carry special loads such as perishable items which have to be kept frozen always or for the carriage of garments that cannot be folded etc.

The three major and common types are,
- Pallets
- Containers
- Igloos

Of these, pallets are big metal plates of different sizes, the most commonly used size is 88inches by 125inches, as it can be loaded on all wide-body aircrafts. This is a PAJ pallet. The load is loaded or stacked on it, the pallet has a net which is then thrown over the load and then lashed down into grooves found on the edge of the pallet. These nets have special pins that can be locked into the pallet grooves. The important point to note is that the maximum height allowed for ULDs in the lower hold of any wide-body aircraft is 64inches. The pallet will be built up to 64inches in height. As per IATA rules, there should always be a gap of 50mm between the surface of any sides of a ULD and the wall of the aircraft.

The containers are smaller fully covered (metal/fiberglass, etc.) units with one side may be shaped in such a way to fit the contour side of the aircraft. That means some containers have a protruding contour on one side and the other side is straight, while others will be square shaped on all sides. (*See figures.V.2.*)

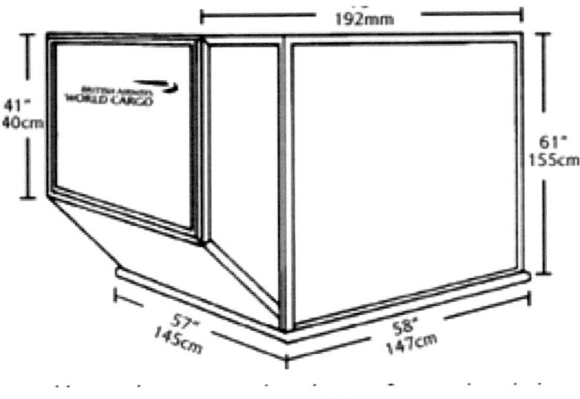

Fig. V.2.a.

Unit Load Devices

Fig. V.2.b.
Fig. V.2: Containers.

The Igloos are larger containers and can be considered a covered pallet, as its base dimensions are similar to a pallet, but covered (hard cover – metal, fiber glass, etc.) on the sides and top, instead of nets. (*See figure: V.3.*)

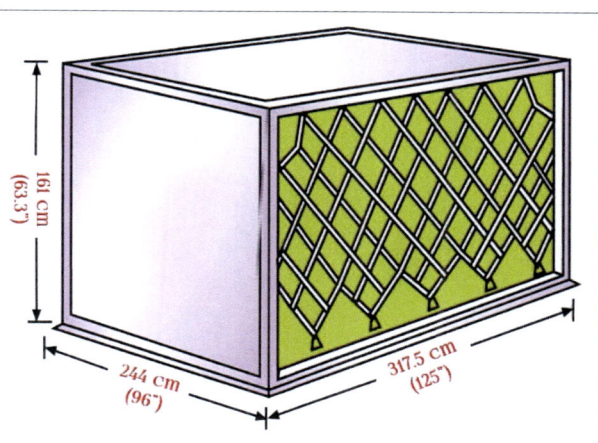

Fig. V.3: Example of Igloo.

Unit Load Devices

As mentioned before, the height of any ULD for the lower aircraft hold is constant i.e. 64inches, but the factors that make each type to differ from the other are as follows,

1) For purpose intended for or use.
2) Its base dimensions.
3) Its contour or shape.

1) **Category:** The ULDs are given codes by IATA, which specifies its category. They are as follows,
- A- Normal certified aircraft container
- P- Normal certified aircraft pallet
- N- Certified aircraft pallet net
- R- Thermal certified aircraft container
- U- Non-structural igloo
- H- Horse stall
- K- Cattle stall
- V- Automobile transport equipment

Fig. V.4: Example of ULD.

Here, normal loads such as baggage, cargo, etc. can be loaded in the A and P category ULDs. N is for the pallet nets, mentioned earlier. (*See table. V.5.*)

| ULD | Code | Dimension | Volume | Approx | Approx | *Remarks* |

	(LxWxH, cm)	(cm)	Max Gross Weight (kg)	Tare Weight (kg)	
PQP	244x153x163	5	2,440	70	For B767
AKC	233x153x163	3.5	1,580	80	
DPE	157x153x163	2.5	1,220	90	
AKE	201x153x163	3	1,500	80	
RKN	201x153x163	3	1,580	210	Cool container
AKH	156x153x114	3	1,130	75	For A320
DQP	244x153x163	5.5	2,440	120	
ALF	406x153x163	6.5	3,170	230	
P1P PAG	317x224x153	10	6,030	105	

Unit Load Devices

 PMC   317x244x163 10.9   6,804   110

Table. V.5: Common ULD types and specifications.

Thermal containers are used for those items which need to kept cool or if the temperature needs to be kept constant. The others are self-explanatory.

2) **Base:** Aircraft hold floors have differing lengths, heights, and widths based on the various types of aircrafts. The height and width of almost all wide-body aircrafts are more or less standard. There are also locks in the aircraft hold floor to lock the ULDs from unintentional movement. These are at certain locations or intervals along the length of aircraft floor based on the base dimensions of the type of ULDs that can be loaded in the aircraft hold. ULDs, depending on the aircraft type, aircraft hold, and hold door clearance, may be loaded lengthwise or sideways. So the intervals or distance between the locks will depend on the base dimensions (length and width) of the ULDs compatible for loading in the aircraft hold. As there are various base dimensions, these have been converted to codes. The loadable width (base of sidewall to the opposite side wall base) of the lower deck aircraft hold floor is 125inches, except in the case of B767 aircraft types. The codes are as follows.

New code	Dimension	Old code
M -	88 x 125 inches	A or 1
M -	96 x 125 inches	Q or 6
K -	60.4 x 61.5 inches	V or 5
L -	60.4 x 125 inches	W or 9
G -	96 x 238.5 inches	S or 7
P -	47 x 60.4 inches	--------

The "G" base category ULDs can be used in the main deck of cargo aircrafts only. These are big pallets used to load heavy and oversized cargo, e.g. a car, big power plants, aircraft engines, etc.

3) **Contour:** The aircraft, as mentioned earlier, is like a cylindrical tube, so the inside walls of the holds are not a perfect

square like a room. The two side walls of the aircraft hold don't meet the floor directly but have a contour due to the outward convex shape of the aircraft fuselage (*see figure. V.6*)

Fig. V.6: ULD contoured as per aircraft cargo hold contour.

The container ULDs also have a contour to make use of this additional space and fit into it. Since different types of aircrafts have different contour sizes due to the different fuselage sizes, there are containers also with different contour sizes. The length at the top will be different to that at the bottom of the ULDs (*See table. V.5*). The different codes are E/C/J/K/D etc. These codes are shown as the third letter of the prefix in a ULD serial number.

A K E 1234 XH

Here the "E" contour can be loaded on all types of wide-body aircrafts and "C/J/K" contour may be loaded only in B747 aircrafts. The "D" category is for the main deck of cargo aircrafts only. Therefore, all closed-type ULDs have codes that specify the contour, with which it is possible to identify the aircraft cargo holds they are loadable in.

4) **Height:** The floor to ceiling measurement of the cargo hold is considered as the height. In a bulk-loading aircraft hold, the entire length will be available. However, a certain gap is required at the top due to light fittings and smoke detectors on the ceiling panel of the cargo hold. In the case of the ULD-only compatible cargo holds of the aircrafts, there are roller bed trays on the floor of the aircraft

hold in addition to the smoke detectors and light fittings on the ceiling on the top. However, the cargo hold of the ULD-version type aircraft are much larger than the bulk-loading aircraft holds. Now the ULDs that are designed for the ULD-version cargo holds are such that the distance between the floor (including the roller tray) and ceiling of the aircraft cargo hold is considered. The distance between the top of the roller trays on the floor to the ceiling of the aircraft lower cargo hold in most aircrafts are more less standard (64inches). Therefore, the height of ULD in the lower hold of wide-body aircrafts should not exceed 64inches, but the main deck of freighters, or in other words, cargo aircrafts and combi aircrafts can accommodate higher ULDs as these holds are much larger and higher.

The ULD compatibility for a particular aircraft hold is determined by the height and contour of the ULD. Each ULD type has been designed based on the specific height and contours of specific types of aircrafts. Some ULDs may fit most cargo holds, whereas other can be very specific to only a few types of aircraft cargo holds. It is important to check the ULD compatibility to the aircraft type being operated, before planning the ULDs for build-up of load for that flight. As otherwise, after build-up of load or after bringing the ULD to the aircraft, it is found the ULD cannot be loaded as it is too high or does not have sufficient clearance between the walls or contours of the aircraft cargo hold, then it could be too late to make changes, or it could cause damage to the cargo hold if the loading team tries to load the ULD, without checking the compatibility. It would be like trying to fit a square box into a smaller circular tube. Therefore, it is important that both the height and contour of the ULD fits or is compatible with the inner height and contour of the aircraft cargo hold. There is a certain level of standardization of the height and contours in regards to the various aircraft cargo holds, which has been translated to the related ULDs' specifications as well. As there are still numerous types, it is not easy to remember every ULD type based on its height and contours. In the above paragraph on contours, specific codes are given for closed-type ULDs that specify the contour compatibility. Other than closed-type ULDs, there are ULDs like the airline pallets, which are basically a certified purpose-built metal base with nets that can be used to hold the load onto the metal base. Here it is possible to build-up load on the airline pallet to the specific height and contour desired. One must make sure the height and contours are not exceeded. It must have sufficient clearance between the aircraft hold door edges/dimensions, the aircraft ceiling and the side walls as well. If not the cargo on the pallet may not be loadable, touch or scrap the inner roof panels or wall panels, causing damage. These pallets can be built up for upper deck loading on cargo flights and for lower deck hold loading as well. But the height and contours differ from aircraft holds to aircraft types. There are other benefits as well. Therefore, there are IATA approved height codes for airline pallets to maintain a level of standardization, which is a designation that is a combination of the specific height and contour given to a ULD. Some airlines use their own height codes or terminology. A few examples of height codes are as follows:

- LD = Lower deck
- MD= Main deck followed by the following (applicable for cargo and combi aircrafts):
  Here base dimensions (length and width) will depend on the airline pallet used. Whereas the height on the length-wise sides will differ, to be compatible with the aircraft contour:
- Q4= one lower side will be 132cm/52inches and the other higher side 294cm/116inches.
- Q5= one lower side will be 193cm/76inches and the other higher side 300cm/118inches
- Q6= both sides will be 244cm/96inches.
- Q7= one lower side will be 244cm/96inches and the other higher side 300cm/118inches
  Here just MD will not be sufficient, as different freighter aircrafts will have varying heights clearance in its main deck due to the shape of its fuselage. (*Refer to figure. V.7 for understanding.*)

Unit Load Devices

Fig. V.7: Aircraft interior contour.

It is therefore very important to understand the compatibility of a ULD is a combination of its base dimension, contour, height, and gross weight allowed in relation to the intended cargo hold of the aircraft.

5) **Weight:** The weight of an empty ULD i.e. a ULD with nothing loaded in it is called the tare weight. The tare weight of a ULD can wary, depending on the make, type, maintenance done on it, etc. The same type or category of ULDs can have different weights, but the difference will be minimal. Some carriers use the

actual weight of the each ULD and some use a predetermined average weight for a particular category. The weights are provided by the manufacturer or the maintenance company after each maintenance. The gross weight is the weight of a loaded ULD i.e. the tare weight plus the weight of the load in it. Here we mentioned weight of ULDs, but you will know its relevance in the load control chapter. In brief, anything you put on an aircraft will have weight and that weight has a direct effect on the balance and capacity of the aircraft. To give you an idea, here are some of the approximate ULD weights, but please note this is only for training purpose.

- Containers (AKE/AVE/AVA)– 80kg
- Pallets (PMC/PAJ)– 110kg
- Igloos (AMF)– 220kg
- Igloos (ALF)– 160kg

ULDs have floor loading limitations, gross weight limitations, linear load limitations, etc., and details can be found in the airline ground handling manual. For example, the floor loading limitation is the maximum permissible weight that can be loaded per square area of the ULD floor. Gross weight limitation is the maximum allowed weight of a ULD, which is inclusive of the tare weight and the total weight of the items in it.

Identification Code of Unit Load Devices

There are several types of ULDs an airline may have that can be loaded on the different types of aircrafts it operates. The ramp staff has to know which ULD can be loaded on which type of aircraft. This will allow him to arrange the ULDs that are loadable in that particular type of aircraft of the arriving flight in advance and do the build-up. Also when he receives the ULDs at the aircraft for loading, he must know if it is loadable on that aircraft type and in which hold it will go. There are some aircrafts where one ULD type can be loaded in the forward hold but cannot be loaded in the aft hold. IATA has given identification codes for the different types of ULDs. The ULD identification codes are simple to understand, are intended to fully describe the ULDs, and are derived using the category, base, and contour codes mentioned above. They consist of the following characters, *see example:*

A K E 1234 XH

Example of a typical ULD serial number sequence.

The first character will signify the ULD category.

The second character will signify the base dimension.

The third character will signify the contour or compatibility.

Next comes the serial number of the ULD given by the airline, normally four or five digit numbers.

And finally, the last two letters will be the owner airline code.

So, for all ULDs, there are identification codes.

This identification code have many benefits, a few are:

- To identify the ULD type,
- For communication purpose,
- To help keep stock records,
- In storage,
- In locating it,
- In flight documentation, etc.

Accessories of Unit Load Devices

There are certain accessories which can be used with ULDs. Sometimes the ULDs as such will not be sufficient to load certain loads and may need additional support or the requirements may warrant additional accessories. Some of them are as follows,

1) Studs/pins – These can be clipped/locked to the attachment points found on pallets/containers/igloos etc. These pins can be found permanently attached to the four sides of the pallet net. When thrown over the load on a pallet, the studs are used to lash down on the four sides of the pallet. They have rings to which the nets are attached in the case of pallet nets. Sometimes you may have to tie down heavy and bulky items in the ULDs or in the aircraft holds of narrow-body aircrafts. So these studs can be first attached to the tie down points found in ULDs or aircraft holds and then using ropes/lashing belts, the load can be secured. There are two types of studs,

Single stud and double studs. (*See figures. V.8.*) These studs have certain capacities and limitations set by the manufacturer e.g. the maximum weight they can hold down.

Unit Load Devices

Fig. V.8.a.

Fig. V.8.b.

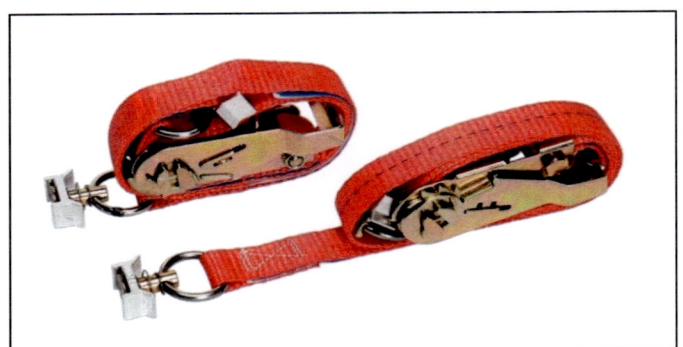

Fig. V.8.c.

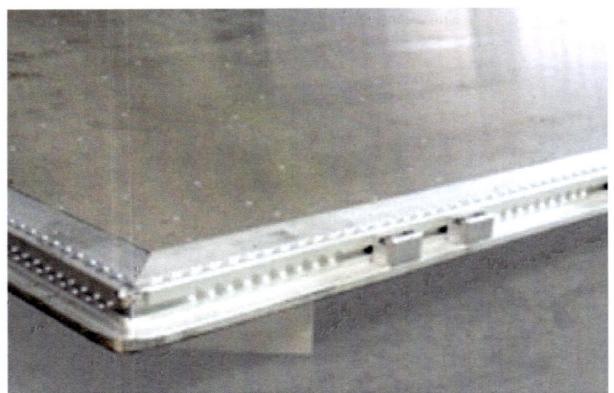

Fig. V.8.d.

Unit Load Devices

Fig. V.8.e.
Fig. V.8: Type of studs/pins and grooves / tie down points on pallets.

2) Nets – There are two types of nets, strap net with square mesh and rope net with diamond mesh. The ropes and straps are made of strong capacity materials, such as nylon, to be able to hold down very heavy weights. The manufacturer gives its capacities and limitations. Since the pallets can be made to different heights and the base dimension of pallets are different, the nets are also of different sizes. So like the ULDs, nets are also given different codes, as per the pallets it can be used on, such as,

- PAG   NAD, NAE, NAF, NAJ, NME, NMF
- PAJ   NAE, NAJ, NMF
- PLA   NLA
- PMC   NMA, NMB, NME, NMF
- PGE   NGE

As you can see, some nets can be used on mostly all pallets. It is because these nets have hooks on them and the tie down points on the pallets are continuous, so once it is over the load on the pallet, the nets can be tied down and tightened, whatever the shape/height.

3) Adjustment buckles – These are found on the straps of nets or single straps. These nets are usually used outside of the covering flaps in the front of igloos or on pallets using such straps (*see*

Unit Load Devices

figures. V.9). Since it is difficult to tighten a thick strap by tying it, these buckles have the straps running through them, so it is easy to tighten or loosen the strap using the adjustment clip on it and pulling the end of the strap.

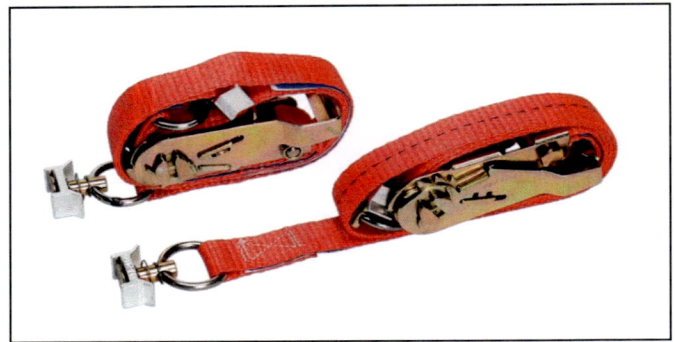

Fig. V.9: Adjustment buckles on straps for tightening.

4) Lashing belts – These are again very strong, single, thick and wide strap or belt. Both ends have studs, some also include hooks, which are attached to the tie down points in the aircraft floor or on the ULDs (*See figure. V.9*). In between there is a buckle, when the loose end of the belt – which goes through the buckle – is pulled, the belt gets tightened and it can be locked. Some belts have buckles which can be used to tighten them, instead of pulling the loose end, more like a wrench. The straps or belts will have its capacity and owner airline name written on it. They are used to tie down exceptionally heavy or volumetric loads. Sometimes the pallet nets may not be sufficient. Also, in the aircraft hold this is the only safe method of securing such loads.

5) Dollies – The ULDs don't have wheels to move them from one place to another, e.g. say a container (AKE) is loaded with the joining baggage for a flight at the baggage build-up area and the aircraft is parked far away. Its gross weight can be anywhere between 800 to a 1000kg; how will you transport this container? For this we have dollies or a kind of trolley. It consists of,

    - A platform of bi-directional rollers, for the ULD to be rolled onto it or off it,

    - Controllable locks on both sides to keep the ULD locked in position while it is on it while being transported and so it doesn't fall off,

- Tires,
- Handles in front for towing it. These handles, when raised, engage the brakes on the tires, so that the dolly doesn't roll off during high winds or jet blasts. This must be always engaged when not being towed as a safety precaution.
- Connectors at the back are used to connect a train of dollies to each other, but not more than six at a time should be connected for towing, again a safety measure.

There are different types of dollies to accommodate the different base sizes of ULDs. There are commonly three kinds and are called LD3 or container dollies, 10-foot dollies, and 20-foot dollies. *(See figures. V.10 for LD3 and 10-foot dollies.)* The container dollies are small dollies on which only ULDs with base dimensions 60.4 x 61.5inch and 47 x 60.4inch (ULD base code "K" and "P") can be loaded. On some container dollies the smaller "P" base code ULDs cannot be loaded due to non-availability of locks. The 10-foot dollies are normally for "A", "M", "L" base dimension ULDs. These dollies can also accommodate maximum two "K" base dimension ULDs on them, provided the necessary locks are available. They can also accommodate a maximum four "P" base dimension ULDs. The 20-foot dollies are for "G" base dimension ULDs and a maximum of two "A" or "M" base dimension pallets can be loaded on them.

Unit Load Devices

Fig. V.10.a.

Fig. V.10.b.
Fig. V.10: Types of dollies compatible with various ULD types.

As mentioned earlier, the ULDs are moved in or out of the aircraft hold using rollers. Now for this, the underside of the ULDs have to be smooth. So the underside must be protected always from getting damaged. This is another important use of a dolly. Since these dollies are costly and to make minimum use of them, some companies use stationery dollies to store ULDs. Stationery dollies are similar but don't have tires and they are basically stands with beds of rollers. They are used for staging of built or for storing ULDs. The ULDs are transferred onto normal dollies when required for transporting from one place to another. This does not keep the moveable dollies occupied and thus they can be used elsewhere, since they are more expensive and maybe in short supply in the airport.

Trollies are used for loose cargo transportation. These are normally large platforms on tires, with rails on all four sides (sides can be lowered/raised) and handles to push or pull them (*Refer to figure. V.11*). The loose cargo is loaded on to it for transporting to the aircraft only using tractors, then the cargo is removed and loaded straight into the hold.

Fig. V.11: Trolleys.

6) ULD tags – A ULD is loaded with only one category of load e.g. only baggage or only cargo, etc. All loaded ULDs must have tags to show what they are holding (cargo/baggage/etc.) and some additional information such as the destination, flight number of the

flight on which they are to be loaded, the date of flight, weights (tare and gross), in some cases the position on the aircraft where they are loaded, etc. There are four main types of ULD tags. They identify the different categories of load. E.g.

- Baggage tag
- Cargo tag
- Empty ULD tag
- Serviceability tag

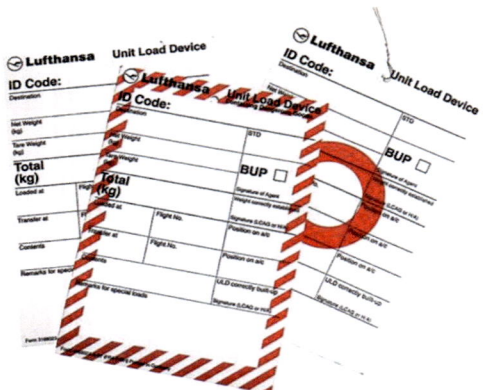

Fig. V.12: Samples of various ULD tags.

Baggage ULD Tags:

There are different categories of bags and these bags are mostly not loadable together. If the first class bags are loaded with economy passengers' bags together in one ULD, then the offloading and delivery of first class bags at the destination to first class passengers may be delayed or hindered. Again, if bags for the destination of the flight are mix loaded with transfer bags belonging to passengers going onwards i.e. transfer passengers, it can cause delays and maybe misconnections or mishandling of those bags. In such situations, the passengers are caused unnecessary inconveniences, as the airline is unable to provide the basic or quality service which the airline is supposed to provide to its customers. Some carriers use separate tags for the different categories of bags, e.g.

- Priority baggage ULD tag – for ULDs containing priority bags (first class/business class, etc.) for a destination.

Unit Load Devices

- Economy baggage ULD tag – for ULDs containing economy bags.
- Transfer baggage ULD tag – for ULDs containing bags of passengers with confirmed travel onwards after arrival at a destination airport.
- Quick transfer baggage ULD tag – for ULDs containing bags of passengers with confirmed travel onwards from the destination of the flight with a short connection time on another flight.

Hence, there can be different types of tags, depending on the airline requirements and its services/operations. So the staff, after checking the tag at the destination, segregates the ULD and sends it to its particular handling sections. For example, the bags for the arriving passengers will be sent to the baggage arrival area for offloading on the conveyor belt, and the transfer bags may be sent to the baggage transfer section for onward connection. In some airports, different types of bags may be handled in different terminals altogether. So it is important the ULDs are loaded correctly and the tags marked accordingly. This is done by the staff at the baggage build-up area as only they will know what bag is loaded in each unit.

Cargo ULD Tags:

Like the baggage ULD tags, there are different tags to show the different categories of cargo. There are basically three types of cargo ULD tags.

- For general cargo.
- For special cargo such as dangerous cargo, courier, etc.
- For transfer cargo.

Unit Load Devices

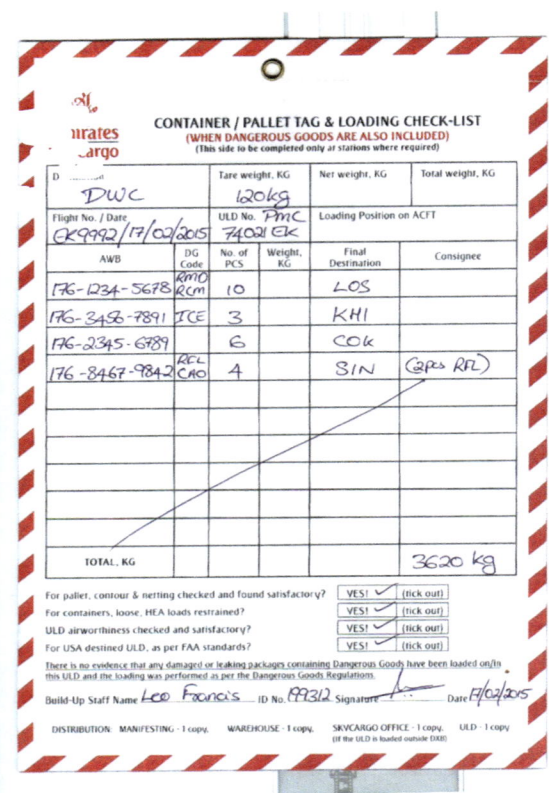

Fig. V.13: ULD Tag with dangerous goods loaded in it (Hashed boundary lines).

Here if the special cargo e.g. a consignment of potentially dangerous chemicals (meeting all packing and carriage rules) going on a flight are only a few pieces and you have more of general cargo, both for the same destination, then both these cargo consignments can be loaded together, but the ULD tag will have a special cargo tag on it. The tag will have broken lined edges, and will show the total gross weight, destination, flight number, date, the dangerous cargo category code etc. This tag is used only to show the ramp staff handling the unit that there is a dangerous consignment loaded in it, whatever the number or amount. He can do his handling checks and take the necessary precautions. Like transfer bags, there are also

Unit Load Devices

cargo coming on a flight and then sent on flights to its final destination, for this we use the transfer cargo ULD tag.

Empty ULD Tag:

When a container or igloo is closed, it may not be possible to know if it is empty. Normally, airlines have the rear side of baggage or cargo ULD tag printed with an X or the words "empty". So the baggage or cargo build-up staff can reverse the tag if the unit is empty. At the aircraft the ramp staff on seeing the empty ULD tag can know that it is empty and then load or not load it in the aircraft as per whatever is in his loading instruction. This tag makes it convenient for the ramp staff at the arriving airport and also for anybody seeing a unit.

Serviceability Tag:

A ULD if damaged must not be used and must be sent for repairs. So once a damage is noticed, an un-serviceability tag must be put on it. So that no one else uses it, unknowingly.

Fig. V.14: Unserviceable ULD tag.

Unit Load Devices

ULD Handling

Unit load devices and their accessories are costly items and their maintenance are also a costly affair. Additional to repairing costs, there are the costs of transporting to the maintenance facility, and the time and revenue wasted to the airline. As ramp staff, if you had not given the necessary care while handling a ULD, you may have difficulty offloading or loading it in an aircraft hold. A damaged ULD can cause handling problems. They may cause damage to the ground handling loading equipment, the aircraft loading, and restrain systems. Remember, serviceable ULD is important for the safety of the load in it, the aircraft, and the people traveling on it. If you think a ULD is damaged, immediately remove it from service, put an unserviceable tag on it, make a report, and send it for repairs. Certified units must be maintained in fully airworthy condition throughout their service life.

A few dos and don'ts:

- Always store and transport the ULDs on dollies, even if empty.
- Before towing the ULD on a dolly or dollies, check all the locks, securing that the units are engaged.
- Load evenly in a ULD.
- Never cut the nets or straps of a net.
- Always protect the base of the ULD and never drag it on the ground.
- A lot of damage can take place if you use a forklift carelessly.
- Never use a forklift to lift a loaded ULD, unless it is designed accordingly.
- Empty ULDs must be protected and secured from adverse weather, like rain and wind.
- ULDs must be protected from unauthorized persons and handling.

ULD Section Activities

Let us briefly examine the main activities of the ULD control section. As mentioned earlier, the handling agent at an airport may handle many airlines. Each airline will have lots of ULDs coming in and going out on each of its flights. Furthermore, there will be lots more in stock. The owning airlines will have its own ULD control section at its base and may have sections or its staff at other airports monitoring the movement and stock of its ULDs. The handling agent may also have a ULD section, as they are the ones who actually handle the ULDs. The primary functions of the ULD section are as follows:

For inbound ULDs
a) After the incoming units are offloaded from an aircraft, the staff gives the list with the ULD identification code or numbers of all the ULDs that came in on the flight to the ULD control section. They in turn feed these number codes into the computer system which can then be used to automatically generate a message called the UCM or ULD control message.

UCM
XH0566/25JAN.DXB
IN
.N
OUT
.AKE11385EK/BLR/C.AKE11686EK/BLR/Q.AKE13714EK/BLR/X
.AKE13757EK/BLR/B.AKE14424EK/BLR/B.AKE15516EK/BLR/B
.AKE16410EK/BLR/B.AKE17099EK/BLR/B.AKE18588EK/BLR/Q
.AKE19350EK/BLR/X.AKE41174EK/BLR/C.AKE42709EK/BLR/B
.AKE46154EK/BLR/B.AKE45184EK/BLR/X.AKE47964EK/BLR/B
.AKE48299EK/BLR/B.ALF80660EK/BLR/C.ALF80969EK/BLR/C
.AMF50531EK/BLR/C.PLA6637EK/BLR/C.PMC30549EK/BLR/C
.PMC30855EK/BLR/C
SI

a) This message is sent to the base station of that particular airline, copied to the local airline office and to the down line stations. This way the handling agent and the airline has a record of what type of units came in on a flight on a particular date, the total number of a particular type of units in stock, etc. This information or record is used to maintain stock for future departure flight operations also. There are several computer packages available for ULD control.

b) Once the incoming ULD is dismantled i.e. the load (bags, cargo, mail, etc.) is removed from these units at the different sections, these are then collected or handed over to the ULD control section for storage.

Unit Load Devices

c) In case of any visible damage, the airline is advised accordingly, who in turn liaise closely the ULD section for sending it for repairs.
d) There can be leased units of some other airline arriving on a flight. In this case, as per the particular airline's requirement, the unit is either included in the stock of the actual owner airline or maintained in the stock of the leaser.
e) The staff ensures the ramp is cleared of any empty units that was not loaded on an aircraft.

For outbound ULDs

a) Much before the arrival of the flight, even before checking starts, the load planner or the airline will release the space for cargo to the cargo section on a flight, after reserving space for baggage. In other words, they will determine the number and type of units that will be required to load the joining baggage, cargo, mail, etc. Then the ULD control section and the concerned sections responsible for their build-up are advised. Accordingly, the serviceable units from the airlines station stock are given to cargo and baggage sections for build-up of these loads, so that the joining load is kept ready before the arrival of the flight. A stock debit record is also maintained.
b) At the aircraft, once all the loading is completed, another list is made by the loading staff with the number codes of all the units they have loaded on that flight. This list is used by the ULD section to send the UCM and for updating the airline stock record. Depending on the load factor and frequency, the airline is able to know when they are low in stock, from these records. They will take the necessary steps to replenish the station stock. Sometimes it is the ULD section that informs the airline of the low or high number of ULDs. For all arriving and departing flights, it is necessary to send a UCM; for transit flights this can be combined into one message.
c) Sometimes airlines need to lease units from other airlines due non-availability; in this case, the ULD section either leases out its own units or acts as intermediary.
d) In some cases, the ULD section also has a maintenance or a repair facility.

e) They maintain stock as per the airline requirement. Excess units are sent to the airline base as empty (if space permits). If there are five pallet positions on an aircraft after loading the other load and you have to send at least six or more pallets from your excess stock, then a stack of the pallets are made i.e. five pallets are loaded on top of each other and are lashed together with lashing belts. This will avoid having to occupy all the five positions and thus only one position is needed. Wooden spreaders are used in between the base pallet and the pallets on top, to avoid the pallets on top touching and getting stuck on the side locks in the aircraft hold floor. Similarly, containers are sometimes sent lashed on top of pallets. This is commonly called piggy back. It is the ULD section that makes these stacks.

f) They are also responsible for the storage and stock maintenance of ULD accessories, except ULD tags.

g) They are responsible for providing, maintaining, and repairing of ULD dollies and carts for loose loads. In some airports they only acquire dollies.

Although most work done is using custom-made computer packages to suit the various setups at different airports, the ULD control of a handling agent also has manual back-up procedures. The number codes lists provided by the loading staff, requirement list for baggage, cargo loading and the units release list to the various build-up sections form the manual back-up procedure. There is more to learn in this section if you want to go deeper, but for ramp staff, I have given only must-know information in this chapter.

****

Unit Load Devices

Chapter VI
Passenger Baggage Handling

Introduction

In an airport there will be passengers flying in and flying out. They obviously will have bags and handling these bags is an essential element of the overall airport operating system. All bags cannot be loaded in the passenger cabin with the passengers, as there are space and capacity constraints, safety issues, and above all it is not practical. So these bags need to be loaded in the lower cargo hold. This is not as simple as it sounds, as there are some very important requirements such as of security and rules of the airline to be met before any bag can be loaded in an aircraft for flight. Further, there are the processes of segregation, sorting, loading, and dispatch of bags in the case of a departure flight. In the case of arrival, there is segregating/sorting and offloading of bags. This is because of the different types of bags and the different sections to handle each type. In busy airports the number of bags handled can be very high. A passenger checks-in his bag at departure, expects to retrieve it on arrival at the destination in the same condition. But sometimes the bag may be delayed, damaged, lost, or pilfered. As per IATA figures in 1995, on an average 5.2 million bags per day were carried by the airline industry. The baggage handling processes are a long chain of activities, which has a direct effect on the ramp handling of a flight. There are interrelated and parallel activities that support these activities such as a baggage reconciliation system etc.

Chapter Contents

General information
Baggage tags
Passenger and baggage reconciliation system
Baggage handling stages
Handling tips

****

General Information

1) Aircraft type and baggage

As mentioned earlier, there are two types of aircrafts, the narrow-body and the wide-body aircrafts. In most narrow-body aircrafts the load, whether baggage, cargo, etc., are bulk load, and in the wide-body aircraft the load is always in the ULDs. Please note even in wide-body aircrafts there is one compartment in the cargo hold at the extreme rear of the aircraft where bulk loading can be done. It is a small compartment compared to the forward and aft cargo compartments *(See figure. VI.1)*.

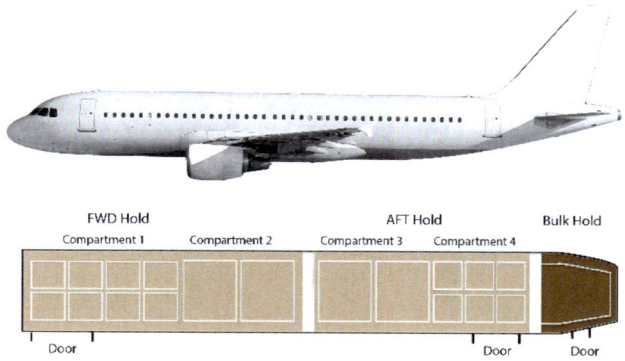

Fig. VI.1: Aircraft bulk hold / hold 5 (compartment located at the extreme rear of the aircraft lower holds).

This compartment is normally called hold 5 or bulk hold, compartment 5. Some airlines term it as hold 4. So even in wide-body aircrafts, there is a bulk hold for loading any item (but with certain restrictions put in place by the airline, aviation authority, etc.), and thus you must not be under the impression that bags from or for a wide-body aircraft will be only in ULDs.

2) Baggage security

There are mainly two areas of concern: baggage theft and terrorism.

a- Baggage theft or pilferage can be theft of a bag or theft of some contents of a bag. This is normally done by airport staff and the thief can be a member of the handling agent, airline staff, or non-airline personnel. The places where a

Passenger Baggage Handling

theft or pilferage may be carried out are while the bag is moving in the conveyor belt tunnel, in containers or carts, or in the aircraft holds. The stolen bag or pilfered items may be then stored in places like storerooms, closets, rubbish bins, etc., till the item or contents of the bag can be removed from the airport. To avoid this, the steps to be taken are close supervision, brightly lighting areas, and using surveillance cameras. In cases of severe problems, undercover policemen are recommended.

b- Terrorism – The airline industry has been target of terrorists or potential acts of terrorism, causing loss of lives and increase in security requirements and screening. Terrorists have in the past managed to get explosives on board aircrafts and have committed other acts of sabotage. To prevent this, airlines must be aware of the different ways used by terrorists and take necessary precautions to prevent loop holes. Terrorists have used baggage, both hold loaded and hand carry bags to conceal explosives or weapons, to carry out sabotage. So it has become necessary to screen bags more strictly and carefully. Terrorists are always trying new ways to cause damage, so just as the authorities have to stay in the forefront to outwit them with new technology, the ramp staff should also be alert, trained, and knowledgeable. An increased security screening requirement may cause inconvenience both to the passengers and to a ramp employee. This is a small price to pay when compared to the repercussions if these security screening are not there. Furthermore, stepped up security screening gives additional peace of mind and relaxation to the passengers of the airline. As ramp staff, you have an important role to play in the security screening process. Some of the duties are as follows:

- You must be patient, understanding, and within your limits and capacities help in the security procedures of the authorities/airline.
- You must be aware of the security requirements of the authorities and of the airlines, especially for the part of the airline handling chain that you are responsible for.
- You must be extra vigilant and if security staff is unaware or unavailable to carry out a required security procedure, report the matter immediately to the concerned authorities through your superiors.

Passenger Baggage Handling

- It may not be part of your job, but it is your responsibility as airport ramp staff to report any irregularity or breach of security.
- If you feel suspicious or are not satisfied with a security process or a safety incident outcome during a flight handling process, immediately bring it to the attention of your superiors and seek clarification. Do not leave it to later.
- Never assume anything in an airport work environment. This is a golden rule for all airport employees as you are directly or indirectly responsible for many lives in the air and on the ground. Do this for the comfort/convenience of passengers, profitability of the customer airline and safety of yourself and of your colleagues.

The above steps are not confined to this chapter, any particular job, individual, or handling process, but are the duty and responsibility of all airport staff. To prevent acts of terrorism, ICAO has adopted some conventions, protocols, and annexes which are intended to protect international civil aviation against acts of unlawful interference. Most countries are using the standards and recommended practices formulated by ICAO in their own legislation and have introduced their own security controls. The security standards and recommended practices are enforced and monitored by the civil aviation authority of that country. For example:

- Airport authorities in most countries security screen all bags, bags intended for hold loading in the aircraft (i.e. checked-in bags or transfer bags) and hand carry bags (i.e. hand baggage).
- In some airports the checked-in bags are x-rayed before passengers check-in and the hand carry bags are hand searched by security staff before the passengers board the aircraft. They use x-ray machines and explosives trace detectors or sniffers for the baggage screening process.

The number of security screening steps taken at an airport depend on the requirements as stated by the country's civil aviation authority. The airline or airport authorities can do additional screening if required, depending on the level of threat or if the situation warrants it.

3) Baggage classification – Baggage can be divided into four categories:

- Originating (local check-in).
- On-line transfer (different aircraft, same airline)
- Interline transfer (different aircraft, different airline)
- Direct transit (continue journey on the same aircraft)

To understand the above four categories, let us take an example, a flight EK500 going from Dubai/Muscat/Bahrain. There may be passengers for different destinations on the flight e.g. for those going from Dubai to Muscat, their bags come under the originating bags category, and bags of those going from Dubai to Bahrain will be called transit bags at Muscat. There can also be passengers disembarking in Muscat but going on another aircraft of the same airline because the routing of this aircraft is to Bahrain next, say EK600 to Doha, their bags will be checked in accordingly and come under the on-line transfer category. Finally, interline transfer bags are of passengers coming on one airline and transferring onto another aircraft belonging to another airline. From the above example, for a passenger arriving on EK 500 to Muscat and then going to Bombay on another airline, his bag will have a interline tag.

As ramp staff you must know into what category a bag will fall into when you read the tag on it. The loading sequence and position of each category on a flight will be different. For example, if you load local check-in bags with interline bags, at the destination the bags have to be segregated for the arriving passengers and of the interline passengers. This will require extra time and manpower, resulting in delay in delivery of bags to the arrivals area and possibly bags of the interline passengers not connecting onto the next flight. The handling process and section for each category of bag at an arriving airport may also be different.

Baggage Tags

Passengers can check-in several pieces of baggage and with many passengers traveling, the number of bags can be a lot. Also, passengers can check-in similar looking bags, and it will be difficult for them to know which belong to them. Passengers may be traveling to other airports from the arrival airport. Finally, the ramp staff and everyone who handles the bag must know if it needs any special care, on which flight the passenger is traveling so that it could be loaded, and what is the destination, etc. To meet these requirements, in addition to security needs, all bags are tagged with the necessary information. Baggage tags enable proper handling, routing, identification, etc. Baggage tag design can be done in different ways and can cause confusion to others who read them. So IATA has specified a design or tag layout in its resolution 740, which is followed worldwide by airlines. So now all baggage tags can be read and understood worldwide. The identical design of tags has greatly helped in the baggage handling process standardization in the airline industry. The purpose of baggage tags can be divided into two general categories. They are,

- Routing tags – it shows the routing of the bag, its destination airport, flight number, date, passenger reference or sequence number, and importantly a tag number, etc. (*see figure. VI.2.*)

Fig. VI.2: Baggage tag samples

- Handling tags – it is used in addition to the routing tags, to give special information to the handling staff, as the bag may require special care or priority handling. For example, fragile tags, heavy bag tag, travel class of passenger like first or business class, quick transfer tag, etc. (*See figure. VI.3*).

Fig. VI.3: Baggage handling tags samples.

IATA members have developed specifications for some types of tags that give the routing as well as give special handling information about the bag. They are,

- On-demand tag – e.g. there are hold loaded bags which cannot be loaded in the cabin such as baby prams that the passenger will need at the aircraft door instead of at the arrival terminal.
- Limited release tag – these are bags taken from the passenger for hold loading as it may not be loadable in the aircraft cabin due to being oversize, heavy, etc.
- Expedite or rush tag – this is for sending a found bag claimed by the passenger at his destination airport, which was lost/misrouted.
- On-line – no change of airline
- Interline – change of airline
- Bar coded tag

Now let us examine a normal routing baggage tag. If you can read a baggage tag, then if you have the necessary information, you can also fill up a manual baggage tag.

1. All baggage tags have a tag number, which comprises a two or three letter airline prefix followed by a six digit random number *(See figure.VI.4)*.

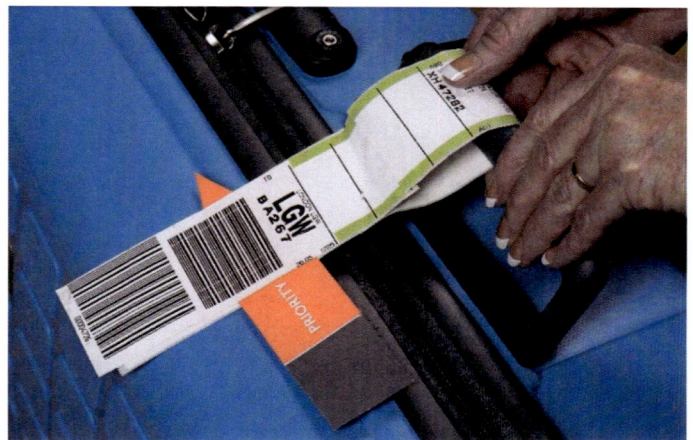

Fig. VI.4: Examples of baggage tag serial numbers.

e.g. XX123456. This number is encrypted into the bar code and the bar code is also printed on the tag at check-in, so that the tags are machine readable also. So in airports with automated baggage sorting and reconciliation systems, the tags are read by the laser scanners and the baggage is automatically diverted to the correct conveyor belt for that flight where the baggage build-up is taking place. This is because it will access the data base with the number it has read to know for which flight this bag belongs. Some systems can even know the class of travel of the owning passenger. When the bar code is scanned with laser gun at the baggage makeup area, the baggage reconciliation system (BRS) will know if the passenger has boarded the flight, and if he has boarded, it will give the go ahead signal for the handling staff to load the bag in a ULD.

Previously, airlines had their own interline baggage tagging system, which made it impossible for other airlines to read those tags. So Air Transport of America (ATA) and IATA members developed the bar codes and standardized its format. The alphanumeric tag, which we can read, is transformed into a 10 digit number by the computer system to facilitate the bar coding of the baggage tag number. As you may know, the bar codes can only signify numbers. This 10 digit number is printed instead of the normal alpha-numeric tag number, along with the bar code on the tags by some airline system. The 10 digits give additional information, which when transmitted in the BTMs or BSMs, help down line transferring stations to know how many transfer or interline bags are coming, even before the flight arrives. Let us now examine the 10 digit baggage tag number.

a) The first digit can be:
   0 – means interline
   1 – fall back for sortation system
   2 – interline expedite
   3 till 9 – interline or on-line use, the value will be decided by the airline.
b) The second to fourth digit (that are the next 3 digits) signify: The three letter IATA airline accounting code.
c) The fifth to tenth position (that are the next 6 digits) signify: The six digit random number which is specific to that bag.

E.g. The alpha-numeric number is EK123456

the 10 digit number for it will be 0176123456

So, the first digit '0' signify that it is an interline bag, the next three digits '176' is the three letter airline code for EK and the last six digits '123456' is the specific number for that bag.

2) With the exception of expedite baggage, all routing tags have two parts, one part is attached to the bag and the other part called the claim tag is given to the passenger. In case the passenger needs to identify his bag or if the bag is lost or misrouted, this claim tag is proof of hand over for the passenger. The claim tag must have the tag number and the destination at the least.

3) Let us now learn to read or write a routing tag. All routing tags are written from the lower end to the top of the tag. E.g. for a passenger going on UA912 from Dublin (DUB) to John F Kennedy airport (JFK), the tag will be local check-in tag, showing the flight number and date and above that the three-letter code for destination (JFK). (*See figure. VI.5.*)

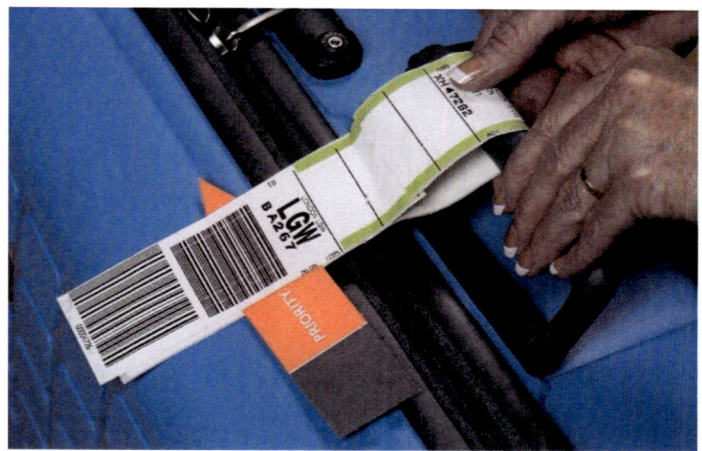

Fig. VI.5: Single sector baggage tag sample.

In case of transit bags, for a flight EK500 operating Dubai/Muscat/Bahrain, the tag will show flight number/date and BAH. As it is not expected to be offloaded and reloaded in Muscat, since the aircraft is continuing onwards to Bahrain. As far as the passenger is concerned, he is travelling till BAH and the transit stop at MCT is not his concern nor is he concerned about his bag, which is checked in till final destination BAH.

In case on-line transfer or interline bags, e.g. passenger wants to travel from SYD to final destination MCO. There is no direct flight. So his itinerary will comprise of several connecting sectors. He will travel from SYD to AKL on NZ airline, AKL to SFO again on NZ airline and from there to final destination MCO (as NZ airline may not fly there or for other reasons) on UA Airline from SFO to MCO. His bag tag will have all the three sectors with the flight numbers and dates, starting with the first sector at the bottom, the second sector above it, and finally, the last and final sector above the previous two. (*See figure. VI 6).* Here the first and second sectors are on the same airline and so it will be an internal transfer wth the airline. The aircraft actually flying may be the same or different, but the bags needs to be processed for connecting onto the next flight. The last sector is on another airline and hence will be an interline sector.

Fig. VI.6: A transfer and interline baggage tag sample.

Passenger Baggage Handling

Passenger and Baggage Reconciliation System

ICAO has stated in its annex 17, developed in 1987, that a carrier must not transport the baggage of passengers who are not on board the aircraft, unless the baggage has been subjected to other security screening. It is the responsibility of the handling staff (check-in and boarding staff) to make sure that passengers of all bags loaded on an aircraft are also on board the flight before it leaves their station. Also, it is the responsibility of the baggage loading and aircraft loading staff to ensure that all the baggage loaded on the flight they are handling has the passengers of those bags also on board. The case of expedite baggage is an exception. The expedite or rush baggage are baggage belonging to passengers who had already traveled before but the bags were either lost, left behind, or misrouted. These bags can be loaded only if certain security requirements have been completed e.g. 24 hours cooling period (means bags have been stored for 24 hours or more before being forwarded on a flight), or additional to that bags have been x-rayed or security searched, etc. The requirements depend on the airport authorities and airlines. Let us now take the normal checked-in bags. When a bag is checked in, the tag number is transmitted from the check-in system to the sorting and reconciliation systems. This bag is then sorted and diverted by the automated sorting system to the particular baggage build-up area for the flight. Here there can be several ULDs lined up for the different bag types for that particular flight. Each of these ULDs, in addition to the normal ULD tags, will have a baggage reconciliation system tag on it, with the encrypted bar codes. These tags are printed when certain information such as flight number, ULD number, date, class of service, etc. are fed into the system by the baggage reconciliation staff. Now the baggage build-up staff will scan the bag tag with laser gun and against the ULD BRS tag bar code. The bag is then loaded into that ULD. When a passenger has not boarded the aircraft, the boarding gate staff will alert the BRS staff, who will then pass the necessary information such as number of bags and the loading position to the loading staff at the aircraft. The loading staff can quickly retrieve that particular ULD, rather than check in each and every ULD. This is fast and effective. The offloading process mentioned above is an example, but can wary from airport to airport. The common fact is that the bags can be located and quickly offloaded. Some of the basic benefits of BRS system are as follows:

1) Ability to tally the total bags checked in and the total bags received and loaded at baggage build-up section.
2) Ability to know how many bags and all the tag numbers, together with the passenger reference numbers loaded in each ULD.
3) Ability to know the total number of ULDs built-up for the flight and number of bags in each.
4) To locate a bag quickly.
5) Ability to get system-generated baggage manifests and lists.
6) Since the reconciliation system is constantly updated by the check-in system with baggage tag numbers for each flight, it will not accept the bag of another flight, if several flights bags are being received and built-up on the same belt. The scan gun will signal the baggage handler if that bag is for the correct flight before he loads it. So there is no misrouting.
7) Some systems are programmed to give clearance to load bags of those passengers who have boarded that flight only.

These are the main benefits, but airlines or ground handling companies have developed baggage reconciliation computer programs to meet other additional requirements. At airports without automation, manual baggage reconciliation is possible. For this the baggage build-up staff record or write down the baggage tag numbers loaded in each ULD and later reconcile with the final checked-in figure. Even in airports with the baggage reconciliation system, manual reconciliation cards are stored. This is a precaution against any system malfunctions.

Baggage Handling Stages

The main baggage handling stages at an airport are:

1) Check-in
2) Build-up
3) Transfer/interline
4) Loading and unloading
5) Baggage arrival area

1) Check-in

Once the passenger hands over his bag at check-in, the check-in staff tags the bag (system-generated tag) and a claim tag is given to the passenger. In case of no automation, a manual tag is attached. Additional tags such as fragile, heavy, quick transfer at arriving station, etc. are also attached. Now the exceptional baggage such as fragile or heavy bags cannot be sent on the normal conveyor belt system. Each airport has its own method of sending such baggage, such as elevators. Sometimes passengers come for check-in late or after the check-in has counter has closed. So to avoid their bags from being left behind, the check-in staff must always call the baggage build-up staff and inform them of the last bag tag number and what time it was send from check-in area.

Passengers can also be checked-in at the transfer area counter. These are passengers who had come in on a flight, missed their onward connection or some other reason, and are accepted by the airline to travel on their flight. Their bags also will be at the transfer section of the airport. So the passenger and his baggage details, as found on his claim tag or booking reference, are checked-in at the transfer passengers' check-in counter.

Now the tagged baggage is passed to the sorting and reconciliation systems, as mentioned earlier, so that it can be loaded on that particular flight. Since the transfer passenger's bag may not be on the sorting conveyor system, the transfer staff is informed by the check-in staff. He, after security and baggage reconciliation system clearance, moves to the aircraft.

The baggage information (tag numbers) for each flight are passed by the check-in system to the two down-line systems such as the sorting and the reconciliation systems. Please note in some airports, at the same check-in counter passengers for different flights can check-in.

2) Build-up (local check-in)

Once the bags are handed over at the check-in area, that is the baggage is checked in, it is carried by conveyor belts to the appropriate baggage area that sort out and build-up the baggage for that particular flight. The baggage build-up area can be a very large area, where thousands of bags of many flights are simultaneously received, segregated, and loaded into ULDs or bulk loaded for forwarding to the aircrafts. (*See Figures. VI.7.*)

Fig. VI.7.a.

Fig. VI.7.b.

Passenger Baggage Handling

Fig. VI.7.c.

Fig. VI.7: Baggage handling/processing areas in an airport.

In some airports the bags from check-in counters are sent on one or many common conveyor belts, which then branch into a network of conveyor belts that end up at the individual flight build-up area. These bags then pass through the laser scanners of the sorting system, which read the bar codes on the baggage tags and divert them to the separate branching conveyor belts of each flight. *(See figures. VI.8.)*

Passenger Baggage Handling

Fig. VI.8.a.

Fig. VI.8.b.
Fig. VI.8: Baggage sorting and segregation systems.

In some smaller airports this sorting system is not required as they have a common long and winding conveyor belt where the bags of all flights are received from check-in counters. The baggage reconciliation system office and the baggage control office may be one or separate, depending on the handling agents operations. The main activities at the baggage build-up area are,

- Arranging ULDs or transporting trolleys as per requirements for baggage build-up
- Sorting bags as per flight and destination
- Segregating bags as interline, on-line transfer, local check-in, and class of service.
- Reconciliation and dispatch of built-up bags to aircraft for loading.

In this build-up section we are looking at local checked in bags (priority/economy/transfer at down-line station, etc.), in other words, originating from your airport. The load planner or the load controller will ascertain the number of ULDs required for a wide-body aircraft, based on the passenger booking and baggage allowance on the sector. This requirement is passed much ahead of the start of actual check-in, so that the ULDs are arranged and kept ready when the bags actually start coming in. In case of narrow-body aircrafts, the necessary number of transporting trolleys are kept ready. The load planner/the baggage build-up staff will know the airline baggage segregation requirements. For example, an airline will require that its first class baggage is loaded separately from economy class passengers' baggage. The interline bag is separated from on-line transfer bags. So if it is a wide-body aircraft and the load planner has given five AKE containers for baggage build-up, the baggage staff will be advised to load each category in separate AKEs and any overflow bags in the fifth AKE. In case it is a narrow-body aircraft, the load planner will advise the baggage handling staff to segregate the bags as per the different categories into different trolleys as and when they are received on the conveyor belt. This will enable the load planner to issue instructions to the aircraft loading staff to load each category in different locations in the aircraft cargo hold, in the order of priority in offloading at the down line stations. If the bags sent to the aircraft are mix loaded, the loading staff will have to segregate it at the aircraft, thus delaying the aircraft, or if it is loaded as it is in the aircraft, then baggage at down line stations may be delayed or misconnected, causing service delivery failure. As ramp staff, the most important aircraft loading principle that you must know is that *anything loaded first is offloaded last, and anything loaded last is offloaded first from an aircraft hold.* Since baggage has priority over cargo and other loads, it is always loaded last and near the door area, so that it can be offloaded first. IATA resolution 780 states the order in which the different baggage categories have to be offloaded from an inbound aircraft. It is as follows,

First –	interline bags
Second –	on-line transfer bags
Third –	terminating bags
Last –	cargo, mail, etc.

Some airlines give priority to first class baggage, so these bags are loaded last, separately, and near the door area. These are dispatched first from the aircraft to the delivery area. So based on the above principle and order, bags are built-up at the build-up area and forwarded to the flight and loaded accordingly. The segregation, loading, and offloading sequence varies from airline to airline. As baggage handling staff, you must be aware of the requirement of the airlines you handle.

If the aircraft has arrived, then start sending out the segregated and collected/built-up bags to the aircraft side after informing the loading staff at the aircraft. Finally, when the last bags have been received from check-in and the last build-up/collection is complete, it is forwarded to the aircraft with the copy of the baggage reconciliation report/list. This will be required by the ramp staff at the aircraft to locate a bag quickly in case its owning passenger is missing or to forward on board the flight for down line stations or for the station airline/security records. Even the handling agent keeps a record of all the bags loaded in an aircraft by its loading staff.

3) Transfer/interline baggage section

The time between an arriving flight and the scheduled departure time of the next connecting flight can sometimes be very short. This is called connecting time. Airlines have specific minimum connecting time for transferring passengers and baggage between its own flights (on-line transfer) or between flights of other carriers (interline transfer). The minimum connecting time is generally decided by the airlines operating through an airport. For this they take into account the time taken to offload, transfer, and load transfer baggage. The MCT should be realistic, and as short as practically possible. Transfer baggage agreements between airlines or between airlines and handling companies must be made and adhered to, to achieve this. The prevailing facilities/conditions at an airport to transfer the baggage after it is processed must be geared up to meet the MCT. This time can be 30 minutes, 45 minutes, etc. from the time the inbound aircraft comes on blocks, irrespective of what the scheduled departure of the outbound flight. Whatever the minimum connecting time, the airline will also take into consideration that its schedule has minimal disturbance but will try to maximize revenue as much as possible. As mentioned earlier, there will be passengers arriving on a flight transferring onto another flight of the same airline or transferring onto a flight of another airline, together with the joining passengers from that airport. Normally, transfer passengers can reach their next departure boarding gate quiet quickly and faster than their bags. This is because there can be transfer bags coming in from various flights connecting onto many other departure flights. These bags have to be first sorted, segregated (class wise), reconciled, security cleared, and built-up into ULDs or trolleys, before forwarding to the next departure flight. Normally, this transfer baggage processing is carried out by the inbound airline till delivery onto the outbound airline or the whole processing is done by a single ground handling company for all airlines at the airport. The section of the ground handling company that does all this is called the transfer/interline section.

Airline computer systems generate and send Baggage Transfer Messages (BTM) and Baggage Source Messages (BSM) to down line stations. The computer systems at out stations pick-up these messages and their database is updated with tag numbers of passengers transferring at its station, much before the flight actually arrives. This enables the interline staff to make necessary preparations to process these bags quickly in order to meet the MCT. Passengers who are checked in from the origin station right till their destination, although they transfer through several airports, are called through checked in passengers. Their bags will also be checked-in accordingly. This means they don't have to the check-in again at transferring airports again. The bags of these passengers, once security cleared at the transferring airport, go through the baggage reconciliation system. Since the system has already been updated with the BTM/BSM, it will have all the bag tag numbers for the flight in its database. So if a passenger fails to board the connecting flight, the system will not clear the bag for forwarding onto the outbound flight. The activities of the baggage transfer/interline section are more or less like the departure build-up sections mentioned before, some of the main once are as follows:

a) The ULDs for wide-body aircrafts or trolleys for narrow-body aircrafts are arranged for loading baggage as per the requirement for each flight.
b) In case of non-receipt of BTM/BSM, the transfer check-in staff is advised, preparations are made for manual reconciliation based on tags input at the transfer check-in counter. Sometimes cards for each ULD bearing the small peel-off stickers (a part of the baggage tag), containing the bar code, are received on the flight when they come in. The bar codes on the stickers are scanned immediately, thereby the reconciliation system is updated.
c) Physically, the bags are brought from the incoming flights to the transfer area and if the local airport/airline requires it, baggage is x-rayed by security or is put through other security checks, before it is send for reconciliation. Once the reconciliation system has cleared the baggage, it is built-up into ULDs or on trolleys for forwarding to the departure flights for loading on it.
d) Sometimes passengers are required to open their bag by security, if they find anything suspicious in it, for further checks. In this case arrangements are made for it, as ramp area is prohibited for passengers, unless they are escorted by an airport safety and security personnel.
e) Fire arms (only those allowed for carriage in the IATA dangerous good manual or as per airline manual) are allowed only in checked baggage and never in the cabin. In this the airline will take prior permission from the airport security and it must be under guard till it is loaded in the hold of the aircraft.
f) Constant communication is necessary with the loading staff and the aircraft in-charge regarding the baggage handling process, when an inbound flight came in delayed and the MCT has to be maintained.
g) In case of AVI (live animals), as transfer/interline bags are received from an incoming flight, they are given the necessary care and are transferred to the outbound flight in

good time. Other concerned sections such as the load controller/captain/flight in-charge etc. are advised accordingly.

4) Un-loading and loading
We will learn about this in detail in the following chapter.

5) Baggage arrival section
Depending on the baggage handling procedure of a handling agent or airline at an airport, the baggage from an incoming flight is segregated at the aircraft while it is offloaded. At the baggage arrival area, if the baggage is received mix loaded by any chance, it is segregated before it is offloaded onto the conveyor belts. Also, bags of different flights are not offloaded simultaneously on the same belt. As per the requirement of the airline, the bags are segregated class wise and offloaded onto the belt for passenger collection. For example, some airlines require that the first class are received first inside the arrival hall, so these bags are offloaded first onto the belt.

After the all the passenger bags are offloaded, the crew bags are offloaded, unless there is a separate belt only for the crew. This depends on the airport. The interline or on-line bags, if received at the arrival belt area, are immediately sent to the transfer section. Only bags of terminating passengers are offloaded onto the belt. Some items not loadable in the cabin due to security reasons (knives/lighters etc.) or bulky or heavy hand bags retrieved from passengers at the origin airport are loaded in the aircraft hold with a tag called the limited release tag. These items or bags, when received at the arrival area, must be handed over to passenger after informing the airline or security. These items may need special handling and thus cannot be put on a conveyor belt. Nowadays, in their drive for providing quality service, airlines and handling companies are trying to deliver bags as soon as possible. They have set a time within which the first bag must be on the belt and the time for the last bag to be offloaded onto the belt. In previous days passengers complained of long waits of more than an hour to get their bags, but now handling agents boasts the first bags will be on the belt by 10 minutes of the arrival of the flight and by 25 minutes the last bag will be on the belt for the passengers. So the staff at the arrival belt area must keep a record of the time the bags were received, number of ULDs or trolleys, number of flights, etc. Any discrepancy must be immediately brought to the notice of his superiors. Communicate with the ramp staff handling the flight to make sure that the incoming messages regarding the baggage units on the flight was correct, the time flight arrived, and the time they were sent from the flight. If any delay in the bags is anticipated, this must be communicated to the airline and the concerned supervisor, so the passengers can be advised accordingly.

Handling Tips

There are few points to remember while loading baggage on/in a ULD or on transporting trolleys.

- Check if the ULD/trolley is serviceable i.e. it is in good condition, without any damage.
- Open the container or igloo and make sure it is empty before loading anything in it.
- Remove any old tags or markings before using the ULD for loading.
- Do not load suspicious or hazardous items such as leaking bags, flashing lights, or bags emitting any form of noise. Immediately inform your superiors and isolate the bag if you are qualified.
- Load or stack the items with the stronger packing at the bottom and the fragile at the top.
- Load or stack evenly on the floor of the ULD, the weight or volume must not be concentrated on only on one side.
- In the case of containers, the weight should not be concentrated on its contour side. If this is done, there is a chance for the base of the contour side to press down more and the opposite side to be a little elevated due to the weight. This will cause the container to get stuck on the rollers, loading equipment, the rollers in the aircraft hold, and above all, it may not be possible to lock it in place inside the aircraft.
- All load on or in a ULD/trolley must be secure. The netting should be tight on a loaded pallet. If additional securing is required, use lashing belts. Even in the containers the loads must be secure.
- Do not exceed the height limit when building up a pallet.
- Pallet build-up and its subsequent lashing can take time, also its dispatch to the aircraft side for loading can also take time, so the baggage check-in process and the flight

- departure time has to be monitored and considered. Any anticipated delays must be quickly reported to superiors.
- Never mix load different categories of load i.e. baggage, cargo, mail, etc. A ULD should contain only one type of load.
- While transporting, the container/igloo doors should be closed properly and secured. This is because if it is loaded with bags or cargo, etc.. there are chances of the load falling out if the doors and nets are not secured. If the unit is empty, there are chances of it flapping in the wind, whereby it might hit someone or something causing injury or damage.
- It is advisable to load bags vertically rather than horizontally. This is to prevent damage to bags at the bottom, when loaded horizontally and all other bags placed over it.
- Always load the bags with the tagged side facing outward as much as possible. This will enable you to check the tags quickly in case of offloading or finding a certain bag.
- Never forward built-up baggage to an aircraft parking stand if the aircraft is not on stand. This is a security hazard.

****

Chapter VII
Aircraft Unloading and Loading

Introduction

The load controller or the load planner will decide and distribute the load and its amount to be loaded in an aircraft hold, after various very crucial considerations. It is then the loading team who physically load the aircraft. This is no easy job, as there are challenges and various factors to overcome within a set time frame. These challenges and factors can be overcome with proper knowledge, professionalism, experience, and logical thinking. Here loading knowledge means a safe working knowledge of the different aircraft holds, in-plane systems, safety practices and checks, hold limitations, the different types of unit load devices, and preferably as much as possible regarding the nature/volume of different types of loads relative to the aircraft hold volume (in cases of bulk loading), etc.

The whole unloading or loading process involves a collective team effort, to be done correctly, punctually, economically, and safely. The customer airlines priorities and requirements are to be met, after you strictly adhere to the all the safety requirements of the airline, the government safety units, and those of your company. Safety means that of the passengers, crew, the people working on and around the aircraft, the aircraft itself, and that of the servicing equipment. Another major factor is service consideration towards internal customers, which is the airline, and external customers, who are the passengers. The pressure from these two factors together with environmental conditions are a major challenge for the whole loading team. So there are mental and physical pressures that have to be overcome also. Above all, what I always say to the aircraft loading teams, "Ensure to make use of common sense". Aircraft unloading and loading process is in itself a huge subject with various interrelated and combined functions, which will take volumes to fully understand and comprehend.

Chapter Contents

Aircraft hold knowledge
Aircraft hold limitations
Ramp understanding
Ramp safety
Aircraft loading team
Special shipment ramp handling

****

Aircraft Hold Knowledge

Let us familiarize ourselves with the different types of aircraft holds. The passenger aircraft is divided into an upper deck called the passenger cabin and a lower deck. It is in the upper deck where the flight deck, galleys, toilets, and passenger seats are located. The lower deck is where the aircraft holds are located (*See figures. VII.1*].

Fig. VII.1.a.

Aircraft Unloading and Loading

Fig.VII.1.b. Bulk-loading hold

Fig. VII.1.c: ULD-version loading.

Fig. VII.1: Cross section of the aircraft to show upper and lower deck and different type of holds.

It is in the holds that the passengers' baggage, cargo, post office mail, courier, aircraft spares, and any other items that the airline may want to carry are loaded. Basically, aircrafts are designed to have only two types of holds namely, bulk-loading holds and ULD loading holds.

As mentioned earlier, normally smaller narrow-body aircrafts have bulk-loading holds and larger wide-body aircrafts have ULD loading holds, with a smaller bulk-loading hold at the extreme rear of the aircraft for any last minute loads or special load as per airline procedures. This is simply because larger aircrafts have higher capacity and thus would need more time to load all loads, so all the joining load is loaded into ULDs and kept ready. So once the aircrafts arrives, the incoming ULDs can be quickly offloaded and the joining ULDs can then be straightaway loaded, thus saving on ground times and manpower/manual labor. So ground time to turnaround a ULD-version aircraft can be almost the same, even when the load capacity is much higher. This is a big advantage when compared to aircrafts with bulk-loading holds. Further, there is greater possibility for segregating the different loads, such as baggage in separate ULDs and cargo in others, instead of loading all in one hold of a bulk-loading type aircraft hold. Some airlines have now started using narrow-body aircrafts with converted ULD versions, such as the A319/A320/A321.

The biggest disadvantage is the need to have specialized ground handling equipment with additional features and capacity to handle the ULD-version aircraft, such as a high loader, transporter, dollies for transporting the ULDs on the ramp, etc. So the charges for handling will be higher, whereas a bulk-loading aircraft will only need a conveyor belt to get the loads in and out of the hold and trolleys to transport the load on ramp. So handling charges are cheaper.

Also, you cannot and must not bulk load in a ULD-version hold of the aircraft at any time. This is a mandatory safety requirement. Nor vice versa.

Fig. VII.2: An all bulk-loading aircraft hold.

The hold forward of the wing is the forward hold and the one aft of the wing is called aft hold. Most of the bulk-loading aircrafts have one door in the forward hold and two in the aft hold, except MD90, which has two in the forward and one in the aft. Some like the A319/B727/B737 have one in forward and one in the aft. Some airlines further divide the holds into compartments. E.g. the forward hold compartment area will be named as 11, 12, 13, with the door located at compartment area 11 in the case of an A320 aircraft.

Aircraft Unloading and Loading

Fig. VII.3: A typical forward hold of an aircraft.

In the aft hold, there are two compartments, a mid compartment, which is subdivided into area 31, 32 and 41, 42; then comes the aft compartment, divided into area 51 and 52.

Please note compartment areas named as 11, 12, 31, 32, 41, etc. do not signify a quantity, capacity, etc. in any way. It is only a numerical name to identify a specific area within the holds of an aircraft. Airlines or manufacturers can also name the compartments as 1, 2, 3, etc. like in the case of B737, which we will look into next. There are restraint nets that divide some compartments from the next. For example, there are nets between compartment areas 12 and 13 in an A320 aircraft. These are based on the capacities of the holds and are a safety feature from the manufacturers. There must be nets also at the door sill in holds to stop the load from falling onto the aircraft door while aircraft is in operation or on top of any personnel when he/she opens the door. These nets are a mandatory necessity in terms of the aircraft and staff safety. These nets are held in place by special easy-to-install pins, locked onto the locking groves found on the aircraft floor, side walls, and ceiling. (*See Figures. VII.4.*)

Aircraft Unloading and Loading

Fig. VII.4.a. Door net in a bulk hold (protects from load shifting, avoiding damage to door, protects from falling load when door is opened after arrival).

Fig. VII.4.b. Compartment segregation net, protects from load shifting during flight, maintains segregation of loads, etc.

Fig. VII.4: Different types of net placements in bulk-loading compartments.

Door side net (*see fig. VII.4.a*) near the door area inside the aircraft hold protects from load shifting and protects the door from falling loads during the flight, also protects anyone from falling loads when opening the door after a flight arrives.

None of these safety features must be damaged and if they are or if they are missing, then immediately report to the airline's representative, engineers, and the load control staff planning the flight. This is because in these cases certain restrictions apply on how much of or if the hold can be used at all; this information can be found in the airline's ground handling manual. In the case of B737 aircrafts, the forward compartments would be 1 and 2, with the door located between 1 and 2. The aft will be 3 and 4, with the door between them. The net placements are such that a door protection net can be found on three sides of the door inside the hold; one net between the door area and the compartment area 1, another between the door area and the third being the compartment area 2. Similarly, in the aft hold between compartment areas 3, 4, and the door in between (*See figure. VII.5*).

Fig. VII.5.a.

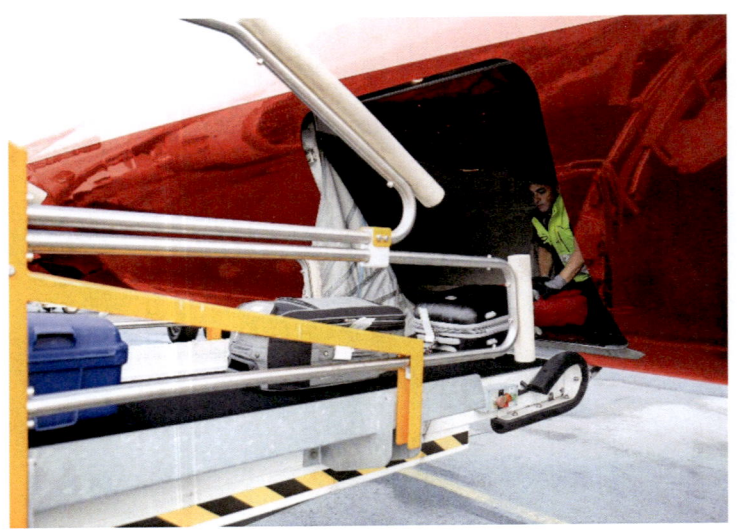

Fig. VII.5.b.
Fig. VII.5: Aft hold compartment and protection nets

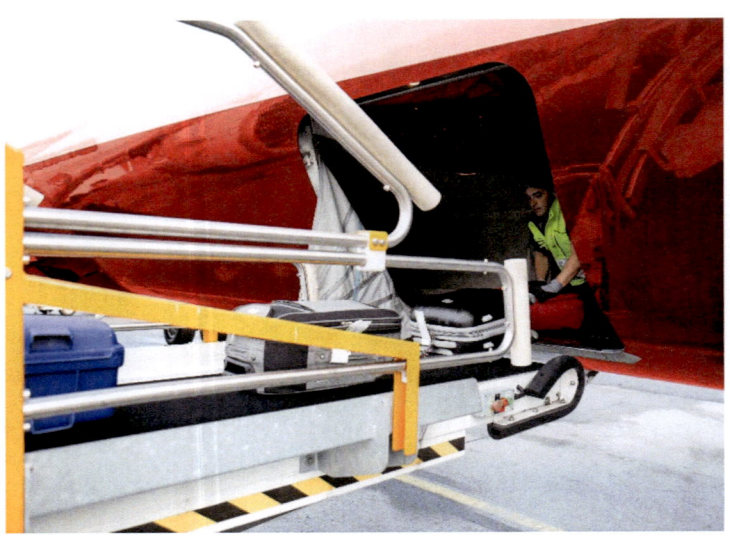

Fig. VII.6.a. Bulk-loading type hold of A320 aircraft type.

Aircraft Unloading and Loading

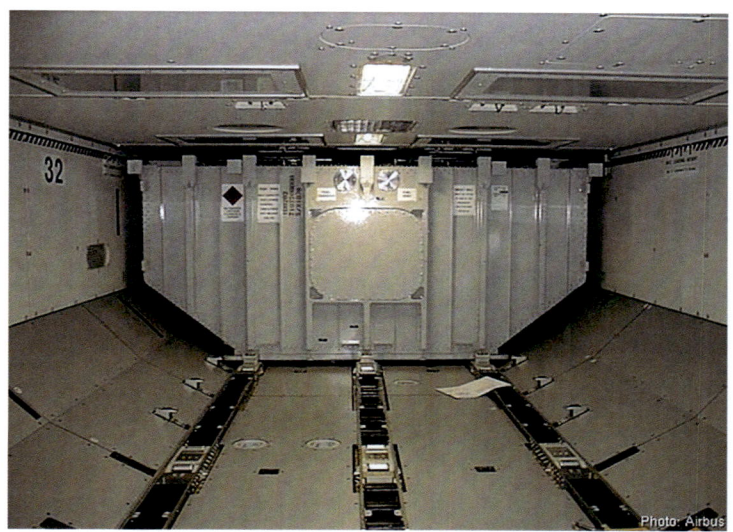

Fig. VII.6.b. ULD-compatible hold of A320 aircraft type.

Fig. VII.6: Bulk-loading type and the ULD-loading compatible holds of A320 aircrafts. It is not possible for both versions to be on the same aircraft simultaneously, unless converted to one or the other.

Other than the ceiling, floors, and sidewalls in the holds of all aircrafts, there are also front and rear/aft bulk heads. These are actually the front and rear walls in the holds. E.g. the forward wall/bulk head is found in compartment area 11, then there is area 12, net between areas 12 and 13 and finally, the rear bulk head. Behind this wall come the wing attachments and all other electrical components. Similarly, there are two bulk heads in the aft hold also. The controls of the ceiling lights are always found near the door of that hold. There are also smoke detectors and air vents on the ceiling. Note below under ULD-version aircraft the reason or necessity for compartmentalization of aircraft holds. It is not always possible to load anything and everything as we wish, in any way we prefer.

The load itself may pose certain difficulties or restrictions in loading it, some of which can be but not limited to:

a) Nature of contents
b) Length and Volume
c) Packing
d) Documentation

Nature of contents – There are substances or items which can pose a potential danger to passengers and crew under certain conditions, also some substances are outright prohibited for carriage on flights. These matters are normally checked by acceptance staff at the cargo acceptance area or the staff at check-in area, against the appropriate manuals. These are then either refused or accepted with proper documentation and necessary notification is given to the load planner and the captain. The load planner will then advises the loading team accordingly. Once such information is received, then appropriate handling and loading procedures must be applied. E.g. items containing liquid or those that may spill need to be loaded upright. Sufficient clearance must be maintained while loading items that may react with each other. Or some animals cannot be loaded together, e.g. cats and dogs and hence, they must be loaded away from each other.

Length and volume – Some load can be long and some may occupy a lot of volume in the hold. Extra care must be exercised to avoid any damage to the hold panels/walls while loading or during flight and also to protect from injury. If a particular load, say some cargo shipments, occupy large volume, then extra vigilance and planning are required to ensure there will be sufficient manpower to load them and sufficient space is left for other maybe more important loads like baggage, courier, etc. If you anticipate a space problem while inspecting the volume of load in reference to the actual volume available in the hold, then always take prior permission from the load planner or the ground dispatcher to keep them on standby or ask for alternatives. Do not load and wait till later to find that there is no room for other must-go load. This will lead to unnecessary unloading, readjusting of loaded load to accommodate other load, and may possibly lead to a flight delay.

Packing – Some load may be of poor packing quality, leading to contents spilling out. In such cases, these loads must never be loaded into the aircraft hold but rather must be shown to the airline representative, airport security, and the ground dispatcher or local security protocols must be followed. If clearance to load is received from them, then it must be properly repacked, to ensure it does not leak while loading, in flight, or while unloading at the other end. All leaking loads, especially liquids, must never be loaded into the aircraft under any circumstances. All offloading and repacking must be properly documented. In case of incoming leaking loads, immediately inform the ground dispatcher, security, engineer, etc., before handling or unloading it. Here the importance is to ascertain if the substance is harmful to the staff, aircraft, if it has already caused damage to the hold, etc. These checks can be done only by the experts.

Once clearance is received that it is harmless and there is no hold damage, then the item must be removed, the holds cleaned, and the concerned department advised. Sometimes the hold damage may not be visible in case of liquids as there are a lot of electric components and wires behind the wall, floor, and ceiling panels. This is why clearance from flight engineers is as must.

Documentation – All load that is to be loaded into the aircraft must have proper authenticating labels, tags, etc. and documentation that gives its category, identifies its nature, origin, destination, etc. Never load anything into an aircraft hold without proper identification stating that it's for that particular flight and is cleared by the local security procedure and also is known to the load planner or the ground dispatcher. E.g. all bags must have a baggage tag stating the tag number, flight number, date, passenger's name (if possible), security screened label, destination, etc. as minimum requirements. In the case of cargo, there must be a cargo label, giving the destination, an air waybill number, etc. and this must be tallied with the cargo manifest of that particular flight. In case of dangerous or special loads, then additional handling labels must be available on the shipment; if missing when checked with the manifest, then replace the missing label accordingly. Hence, never load anything without proper identification.

ULD-Version Aircraft Holds

ULD-version aircraft holds have specialized equipment to load, offload, and lock the compatible ULDs in the hold of the aircraft. Unlike bulk-loading smaller aircrafts, the wide-body aircrafts have huge holds with a large area for loading various loads (*See comparison in figures. VII.7*).

Fig. VII.7.a: Bulk-loading compartment.

Fig. VII.7.b: ULD-compatible compartment.
Fig. VII.7: Two types of aircraft holds (Bulk loading and ULD loading)

Some holds of narrow-body aircrafts like A319/A320/A321/etc. have also been converted to ULD versions, since the holds of these aircrafts can be rather long. If we wait for an aircraft to arrive and then start build-up of load into an aircraft hold, it will take long hours to accomplish; instead, ULDs are build-up with baggage, cargo, etc. and kept ready for the aircraft to arrive.

The incoming ULDs are unloaded and joining ULDs are loaded quickly. So the aircraft is turned around within a short span of ground time. The incoming ULDs with load can be processed without holding up the aircraft, and empty ULDs, after removing the incoming load, can be used for the next flight and so on. As mentioned, using ULDs for larger aircrafts are more suitable; the advantages are:

1) Reduce handling times
2) Increase aircraft utilization
3) Segregation of loads
4) Strengthened support to the aircraft structure.
5) Increased capacity, etc.

The ULD-version hold of the aircraft is physically divided into the forward hold and aft holds, with separation in between due to the presence of the wing root structure and other aircraft equipment. These are behind walls called bulk heads and as thus, not noticeable. All holds have a left and a right side along the center of the aircraft, with locks on the floor to stop left-side or right-side ULDs from moving to either side involuntarily. The left and right side division is possible when loading smaller ULDs like AKE/AVE/etc. The forward hold is situated forward of the wing part of the fuselage in the lower deck of the aircraft. The forward hold is divided (imaginary not physical) into two compartments called compartments 1 and 2. Compartment 1 is further divided into positions, with the first position near the front hold door starting with positions 11L (11 left), 11R (11 right), next subsequent positions behind this will be 12L and 12R and so on. Depending on the type of aircraft and ULD version used, compartment 1 can be from 11 to 14. Further into the hold comes compartment 2, with positions starting with 21L (21 left) and 21R (21 right), 22L, 22R and so on. Again, the total positions depend on aircraft type and versions used. If bigger ULDs such as pallets are used, which occupy both left and right side of each position, then the first position becomes 11P and then 12P, and so on. This is can be clearly understood when comparing the printed layout (refer to aircraft offloading/loading instruction/report under loading team documentation) against the actual hold *(See Figures: VII.8 and VII.9)*.

Fig. VII.8: Hold and versions or combinations of various ULDs possible on board in the hold.

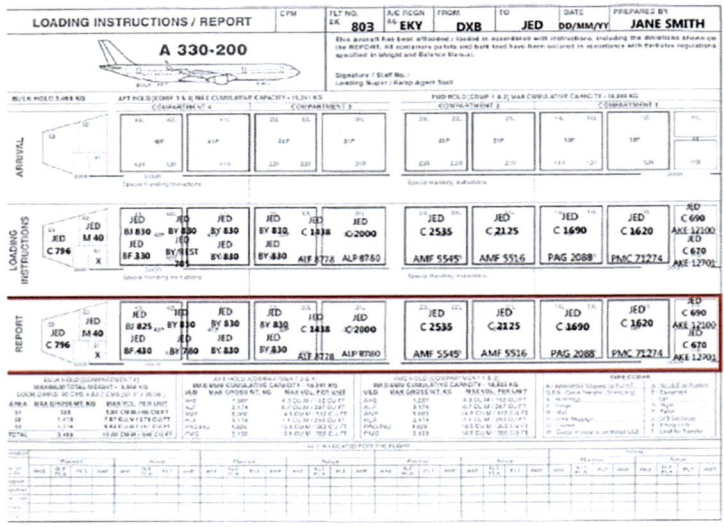

Fig. VII.9: A loading instruction form against the hold layout (Comparing with figure VII.8), to enable planning and depiction against actual positions to be occupied by the ULDs loaded.

Aircraft Unloading and Loading

Also, there are markings on the hold side wall. Each individual position will also have locks on the floor to ensure the ULDs remain locked in position and do not move, unless required for offloading when on ground. Similarly, the aft hold is situated aft of the wing of the aircraft in the lower deck. The aft hold is divided into compartment 3, 4, and 5. The first compartment at the door is 4 and towards the wing will be compartment 3. Compartment 5 will be in the opposite direction, separated by divider netting in between. So compartment 4 at the door will be in between compartment 3 (forward) and compartment 5 (towards the rear). Compartment, 3 and 4 are also subdivided into 31L, 31R, or 31P; 32L, 32R or 32P; 41L, 41R or 41P; 42L, 42R or 42P; etc. The number of positions can vary depending on the type of aircraft, version used, or the airline-specific requirements based on which the aircraft manufacturer had made the changes. Compartments 4 and 5 normally have physical divider netting. Compartment 5 is normally bulk loading and no ULDs are loaded here. Some airlines also have custom-made option to load ULD in compartment 5 also. This can be, however, loaded through the door situated in compartment 4 only. Most aircrafts have a small door to access or load in compartment 5 also. Compartment 5 is normally used for last minute loads or smaller items. The space available and capacity of compartment is limited, due to the narrowing design of the aircraft as compartment 5 is at the tail section of the aircraft. Some airlines use this area for crew bags, aircraft documents bag to keep cargo or other commercial load documents, aircraft equipment like spare tire, etc. Where a specialized equipment called high loader is used to load or offload ULDs from the forward hold and aft holds (compartments 3 and 4), a conveyor belt is used to load or unload from compartment 5. The main operational reasons for these left or right divisions, compartmentalization, and position division are the following:

1) Left and right division is required to control the weight difference between left and right sides of the aircraft. The aircraft cannot have too much weight on one side as it can have higher stress on the wing situated on that side. Also, this will impact structural tolerance and aircraft performance (take-off, flight, and landing). Normally, large differences can have impacts. Bigger ULDs such as pallets that occupy both sides do not have any impact as the complete weight is taken as being in the center of the aircraft, with nil effect for calculation.

2) Compartmentalization and position division: As mentioned, the aircraft is like a balance *(See figure. VII.10)*, with the wings being at the center of gravity or in short, the center along its length.

Fig. VII.10.a. A balance.

Fig. VII.10.b. An aircraft acts like a balance when load is placed at certain locations.

Aircraft Unloading and Loading

Aft   Forward

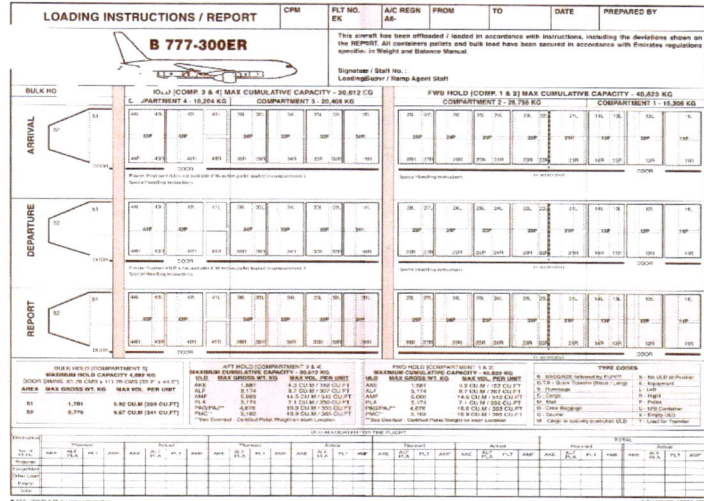

Fig. VII.10.c. LIRF. *An LIRF is one of two documents that enables planning where each load is to be loaded, so the aircraft is in perfect balance/equilibrium within safe limits.*
Fig. VII.10: *Relation of balance, aircraft, and load on board an aircraft.*

Each weight placed along its length at different areas from the extreme ends towards the wing or center can have varying effects on the balance. So, for example, if 1 ton's weight is placed in the forward position in compartment 1, there is higher momentum for the nose of the aircraft to go down. Whereas when 1 ton is placed in compartment 2 at the aft bulk head, which is near to the wing or center of the aircraft, then the effect is much lesser. Therefore, it is important to have a well-balanced aircraft both on ground and in the air. So whatever ULDs or loads are in the hold must be distributed as evenly or equally as possible to ensure the aircraft is in balance along its length, with the wing as its center. Meaning the weight of the front part of the fuselage from the wing and the weight in aft part of the fuselage from the wing should be in balance. Too much weight in the front means a nose-heavy aircraft; after a certain tolerance level it is not safe to operate such a flight and the aircraft may not be able to take-off. Similarly, too much weight aft of the wing means the aircraft is tail-heavy; again, after a certain tolerance level it is not safe to operate and the ground stability will also be compromised. Therefore, holds are compartmentalized and position division is done to derive the actual values of momentum relative to the aircraft's center of gravity when ULDs or loads are placed in each position.

The values of momentum or trim effect are already available for various weights and provided by the aircraft manufacturer. The load control officer plans the flight and determines the values. He will then ensure the load plan is issued and the ULDs or loads are loaded by the loading team in such a way that the aircraft is well-balanced. To enable this, he needs to advise in which location or positions in the aircraft each type of load should be loaded. So this prescribed compartmentalization and division is necessary. A well-balanced aircraft is also necessary for avoiding stress on the aircraft structure and improve aircraft performance, in addition to the most important requirement, which is the safe operation of the flight. This aspect is applicable for both bulk-loading aircrafts and ULD-version aircrafts.

ULD-version aircraft holds typically are comprised of, *(Refer to figures below)*:

1) At the entrance, the hold door and the depressor seals:

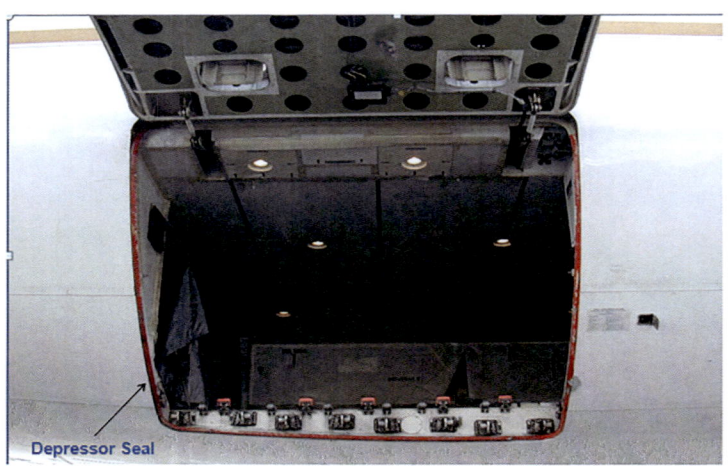

Fig. VII.11: Aircraft door and depressor seals.

Fig. VII.12: Main components of an aircraft hold:

1 = Door sill locks
2 = Powered rollers
3 = Roller mat
4 = Middle guide locks
5 = Dual directional roller tray
6 = Position locks
7 = Side guide locks
8 = Air vents
9 = End locks
10= Bulk head
11= Wall panels

1) Hold doors and depressor seals (Fig VII-11): The doors of the hold can open inwards and sideways, outward and upwards, inward and upwards, etc. Some doors can be opened manually, using a lever on the door; some automatically, using single or multiple switches by activating them separately or simultaneously. Most commonly, hold doors (prominently of wide-body aircrafts) are opened with a combination of first manual and then the automatic method. Some precautions to be taken are:

Aircraft Unloading and Loading

a) Do not attempt to open an aircraft hold door without proper training. As incorrect opening can damage the door control mechanism, rendering the aircraft inoperable.
b) For some hold doors when swinging outward, the lower edge path can go lower than the sill of the aircraft hold door for a certain distance and then continue upwards. So any equipment kept based on the doorsill must always be lower than the doorsill, anticipating the swing of the door when opening and closing. Later, it can be aligned with the doorsill.
c) As the offloading or loading progresses, the aircraft can settle down or lift up, due to the weight of load getting into or out of the aircraft hold. So always monitor and align the equipment positioned against the doorsill accordingly.
d) Ensure the door is fully open, to avoid the ULDs from coming in contact with the raised lower edge of the hold door.
e) There are also door depressor seals along the side edges on the aircraft fuselage or the entrance area, where the door finally comes to rest when closed. These seals (*See figure. VII.11*) are necessary for pressurizing, sealing purposes, etc. They are fragile and extra care must be taken when moving ULDs in and out of the holds to avoid contact with them.

2) The bulk heads, ceiling, and side walls' panels (*See figure. VII.12*): In the forward hold, it is the wall towards the front of the aircraft (in compartment 1), and in the aft bulk head it is the wall at the rear end of this hold (in compartment 2). In the aft hold, there will be a forward bulk head (in compartment 3), and the rear end of the hold will normally have flexible netting that separates compartment 4 of the aft hold from compartment 5. The divider area between aft bulk head of the forward hold (in compartment 2) and the forward bulk head (in compartment 3) is where both wing roots are connected to the aircraft fuselage, and where the center fuel tank, and other aircraft equipment are located. There are critical and highly sensitive equipment and wiring behind the bulk heads, ceiling, and side walls' panels. Therefore, it is important to ensure the ULDs or loads do not hit or protrude against the bulk heads, ceiling, or side walls. ULDs must be built up correctly as per the

contour of the aircraft hold, with sufficient clearance. Checks must be done before, while, and after unloading or loading. Use only ULDs compatible with the type of aircraft hold. Cross-check the offloading and loading against the marking shown on the side walls and offloading/loading instruction form. Ensure to follow the height marking on the side wall to protect the ceiling panels and other accessories fixed on it. Cross-check that the position locks correspond with the marking of the position on the wall.

3) Powered drives or rollers (*See figure. VII.12*): Most aircraft holds are fitted with electrically powered rollers, which have rubber coating for traction. These are used to move the heavy ULDs in the holds. Some at the door area will move the ULDs into and out of the hold, he rest move the ULDs inside the hold towards or from the positions (forward and aft). Care must be taken to avoid anyone being between the ULDs when the power drives or rollers are being operated. Also, the ULD locks must be disengaged. Sometimes, due to excess moisture on the roller heads or wear and tear, the rollers may not be effective. Then manual push and pull on the ULD may be required. Some aircrafts may not be fitted with power drive, then again ULDs need to be pushed or pulled into or from positions. The power rollers in the hold are interfaced with normal dual directional rollers also at regular intervals.

4) Power drive controls (*See figure. VII.12*): These are controls used to activate the power drives or rollers and in some aircrafts certain ULD locks. They can be situated with the door controls, separately, or inside the hold or both. Always get formal on-the-job training before operating these controls, although it is relatively easy to understand.

5) Ball mat floor (*See figure. VII.12*): If we take the forward hold loading, the ULD when it enters the hold, it moves from one side to the other i.e. left to right or right to left (as named by the airline). Then it needs to move inward, for which it has to move backward into the hold. Similarly, for offloading, first it comes out by moving forward, then sideways out from the hold onto the hi-loader. This multi-directional movement is possible with the help of ball mat flooring at the hold entrance. Also, it makes it easier for the loading team to change sides or rotate the ULDs manually if necessary on board rather than bringing it down again to change positions. However, great care must be taken to protect the walls and bulk heads.

6) End locks: There are fortified end locks at the base of the bulk heads to stop the ULDs from moving and hitting against them.

Aircraft Unloading and Loading

7) Middle guide locks: These locks act as guides to enable loading in the left or right side of the aircraft hold and also stop the ULDs from shifting involuntarily from left to right and vice versa. They can be used to align the ULDs for left or right side loading. It is used when loading smaller type ULDs like AKE/AVE/etc. Some of the locks are also designed to stop upward motion, thus giving upward restraint for the ULDs.

8) Air vents / air-conditioning vents: Based on the airline customization, some of the holds may have air vents or air conditioning vents. These may act for:

> a) Continuous air circulation or air conditioning system – This is useful when live animals are carried in the hold.
> b) Temperature control – When the aircraft is flying at high altitude, the temperature is freezing outside, this can cause a freezing atmosphere in the holds. To avoid this hot air from the engine is routed into the aircraft hold, to maintain as near a normal temperature as possible.

These vents can be found at various points in the hold. Availability for an aircraft can be checked in the airline weight and balance manual or handling manual.

9) Dual directional rollers: These are non-powered lazy rollers at regular intervals in addition to the powered rollers. They normally have metallic surfaces and are placed in long trays. They facilitate movement of ULDs, either forward or aft.

10) Position locks: Each position has locks to hold the ULDs in that position, which will restrict any forward, aft, or upward motion of the ULD once engaged. There are various types of such locks, depending on the type of aircraft and locking system used. It is necessary to ensure all locks are engaged in the holds before closing the doors for departure, even if there is only one ULD in the hold. Before engaging the power drives, check that the applicable locks for the position are disengaged. Each position will have multiple locks. If any lock is not operational, immediately inform the engineer and load control officer. Reduced locking ability will have an impact on the weight that can be loaded on that position, so the load control officer will refer to the appropriate manual and advise accordingly, if applicable.

Aircraft Unloading and Loading

11) Side guide locks: These are locks placed at the base of the side walls with sufficient clearance to stop the ULDs from hitting or rubbing against them. These side guide locks also act as guides to enable the ULDs to move into and out of the hold without damaging the walls. Some are designed to act as restraints against upward movement of ULDs.

A pre offloading/loading and post offloading/loading inspection is necessary to check for any damages. If any are found, they should be immediately brought to the notice of the supervisor and aircraft engineer on duty.

ULD Combinations or Multiple ULD Version

So the various ULDs, as explained in the chapter about ULDs, can be loaded. All ULD types cannot be loaded in all aircrafts. It depends on the contour of the hold side walls, height of the ceiling, locking positions, size of the ULDs, etc. It is important to have good understanding of the various ULDs that can be loaded on a particular type of aircraft. Also, various combinations of ULDs can be used as well. The basic aim for using a ULD combination or multiple ULD version is to:

1) Maximize the space available in the aircraft (e.g. sometimes more AKE type ULDs will increase utilization, if there are no oversize shipments; otherwise, a combination of AKE and PMC, etc.)
2) Allow for loading the various types of load (AKE is better for baggage for easy handling, segregation, rather than using a AAP, which will occupy more space if the number of bags is less, so it is better to use AAP for cargo as the cargo may need more space due to bulky cargo loads).
3) Comply with limitations or restrictions at origin or destination airports (e.g. some airports cannot handle ALF at the baggage handling area due to limited space availability), etc.

It is not necessary that only one type needs to be loaded. Normally, the various types loadable and combinations possible are shown in the airline ground operations manual or weight and balance manual or on the aircraft loading instruction/report form (*See Figure. VII.13*).

Aircraft Unloading and Loading

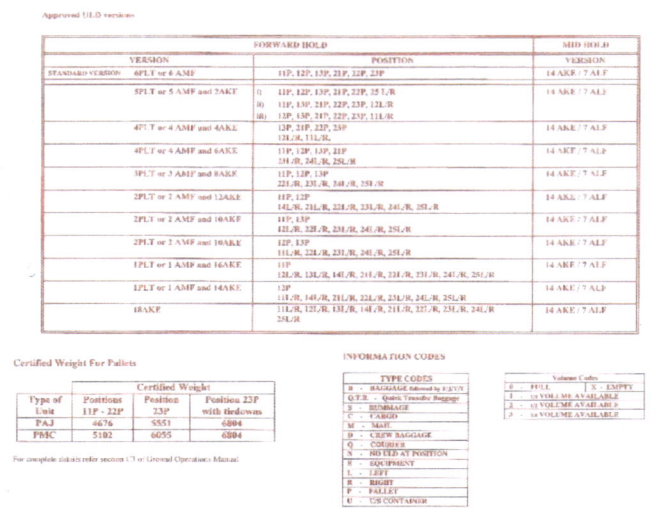

Fig. VII.13: Allowed aircraft hold versions.

Smaller aircrafts mean lesser loads/capacity; the difference would be in terms of manpower and manual labor. Bulk loading into an aircraft hold can be back-breaking and depending on the turnaround time and load change, may require extra manpower. This is because each and every piece of load whether cargo or baggage, etc., immaterial of the weight, has to be moved from the hold door to the appropriate position in the hold, lifted, stacked, etc. in case of loading. But if the incoming load has to be offloaded and then the joining load has to be loaded, it can be a lot of work. All this has to be done in a very confined space (normally in crouching or kneeling or bend-forward position), and in extremely hot or humid conditions (depending on local weather conditions, but higher than outside temperature). Sometimes there can be over 6000kg of load change on these aircrafts within a 50minute to 1hour turnaround time. This puts a lot of pressure on the loading team members, as they have to unload and load each piece that has a different weight, shape, and size within the stipulated time and under the conditions mentioned. Majority of airlines will not offload planned load, increase ground time, or authorize a delay to uplift all load but would insist on loading everything planned within the agreed time, irrespective of the amount of load. Designing ULD versions for all narrow-body

Aircraft Unloading and Loading

aircraft or converting all bulk-loading aircrafts to the ULD version can be exorbitantantly costly, which can remove the advantage for an airline when selecting a narrow-body aircraft against a bigger wide-body aircraft. Also, this would mean a completely new set of equipment to load or offload from the aircraft hold onto the ground and then transport within the airport to various load processing areas. Also, with the confined space availability in the lower deck of these small aircrafts, the advantages in terms of space availability and time are negligible. In fact, more space will be lost when converted to the ULD version.

Aircraft Cargo Hold Limitations

There are several safety limitations that have to be applied while loading in aircraft holds (bulk or ULD-version holds), other than those expressed by the particular airline manual, the main limitations are:

1) *Hold weight limitation*
2) *Floor loading limitation*
3) *Linear load limitation.*
4) *Volumetric limitation*
5) *Combined load limitation / Monocoque limitation*
6) *Door dimension limitation*
7) *Height limitation*
8) *Restraint requirements*
9) *Point load limitation*

All of the limitations are set by the manufacturers of the aircraft, and vary with each aircraft types and must be adhered to at all times. Normally, the door, height, and hold length limitations are checked by the acceptance staff at the different counters (check-in or cargo, etc.) before accepting the load for carriage against the aircraft manuals. All other limitations are also normally checked by the acceptance staff and later rechecked by the load planner while load planning the flight. It's an important aspect to know and understand, since it is a crucial safety requirement of all aircrafts. Also, the loading team, being the last handling team at the origin airport to load, must do the final safety verification or check and hence, their awareness and understanding is important.

Aircraft Unloading and Loading

1) Hold/compartment weight limitation: This is applicable for all types of aircraft. This is the maximum permitted weight of load that may be loaded into a compartment. Also, there is a maximum permitted weight allowed in a hold, that is the total weight in all the compartments located in that hold must be less than or equal to the maximum allowed for that hold. So basically, there is a weight limitation for each compartment and also further for the entire hold. The limits can be found on the loading instruction advice form or in the airline handling manual. Loads can be classified basically on the basis of their density. Some loads, although occupy less area or volume, can be very heavy. E.g. a bag of wool, although more in volume, will weigh a lot less than a similar bag of gold. Now if you get a dense load, the volume may be available but its weight will not allow it to be loaded in one compartment and hence, it may need to be evenly distributed. Normally, the volume of different loads that are to be loaded into the hold will act as a restriction, so the maximum weight will not be exceeded. But when a dense load is expected as in the above example, then careful planning is required. Here obviously, the volume will not act as a restriction, as the load may be smaller in size. Now, the total number of pieces that can be allowed in each compartment must be calculated. For example:

There is a flight XX123 from DXB to IKA, a/c is A320, 110 passengers, baggage of 100pcs weighing 2000kg, and cargo of 25pcs weighing 3000kg. Now we have to find out if the baggage and cargo are dense or not. So we find out the average weight of each piece of baggage and the cargo.

i) Divide total weight with the number of pieces.
Baggage: 2000kg divide by 100pcs equals 20kg.
Cargo: 3000kg divide by 25pcs equals 120kg.

Now we can see that each piece of cargo is weighing about 120kg, which is very high.

If the forward hold compartment area 11 can carry only a maximum weight of 1200kg, areas 12 and 13 say 1300kg each, the total hold weight will be 1200+1300+1300 = 3800kg. Now the cargo must be distributed correctly in the forward hold, because it cannot be allowed to be loaded in a single compartment area. Let's take compartment area 13, which has a maximum allowed weight of 1300kg. If we divide 1300kg with 120kg (weight of each cargo piece), it equals to 10.8pcs. So we can load 10pcs of cargo in area 13, another 10 pieces in area 12, and the remaining 5 pieces in area

11. So now we are allowed to load another 100kg in areas 13 and 12. In area 11, 5pc x 120kg = 600kg. So from the maximum compartment weight allowed in area 11, 1200kg − 600kg= 600kg. Now if required, we can load 600kg of baggage in this area. It is always advisable not to load up to the maximum allowed limit, but to keep a safe limit in between. This is a precaution in case of any weight measuring discrepancy at the time of acceptance and to ensure the safety of the aircraft and its occupants at all times. Now we said earlier that the total weight in the forward hold will be 3800kg, after calculating the maximum from all the three compartments in that hold. But the manufacturer could put a maximum forward hold limitation at 3000kg totally. Now it must be understood that you cannot use the complete allowed maximum in each compartment. Again, this to ensure safety as mentioned previously, to protect the structural integrity.

2) Floor loading or area load limitation: This is the maximum permitted weight of load that can be loaded on a unit area of the hold floor. It is expressed in kg/sqft or kg/sqm. The maximum allowed weight depends on the supporting structure of the aircraft fuselage, the floor strength, and the power drive systems therein. It is basically in consideration of the contact area of the object with direct contact to the surface of the floor. Or in other words, the concentration of the footprint of the object on the aircraft floor. A footprint sometimes is easy to see; for example, when you stand on one foot the weight concentration is more under that single foot. But if you stand on top of a large wooden board, your weight is distributed evenly under the wooden board where its surface is in contact with the floor of the room. If a box has wheels, the bottom panel surface is not the contact surface, but the much smaller area of the wheel that is in contact with the floor surface. This limit is further connected to the next weight limit below.

3) Linear load or running load limitation: It is the maximum permitted weight of load that may be loaded on a unit length of the hold floor. It is shown in terms of kg/inch or kg/foot. In other words, linear load is the weight exerted over a distance of the floor in a portion of the aircraft hold.

The floor or area load limitation is the weight of the object acting on the specific surface of the aircraft floor (the contact area between the object and the aircraft floor), that can have an overall stress impact on the aircraft floor and the structure supporting the floor to the aircraft fuselage. For example, consider a table placed on an aircraft floor, the area of contact is where the four legs of the table come in contact with the floor surface, so the weight of the table is transmitted onto the floor through the four legs' surfaces.

Fig. VII.14.a.

Fig. VII.14.b.
Fig. VII.14: Demonstration of the contact area in two positions.
Aircraft Unloading and Loading

Now consider inverting the table, whereby the entire surface of the table is in contact with the aircraft floor. The weight is the same but the area of contact is increased considerably. So when the table is upright, there is greater stress on the aircraft floor due to limited contact area (*see Figure.VII.14.b*). Similarly, the two aircraft floor loading limitations mentioned above need to be checked when loading heavy items. It is applicable for both bulk-loading and ULD-version aircrafts. **When a heavy item is loaded in a ULD, the base of the ULD cannot be considered as having the ability to spread the weight evenly as required**. So a check must be performed to avoid undue stress or damage to the aircraft floor and structure.

To understand better, the aircraft structure is made with circular metal rings and cross beams (*see Figures. VII.15*), interconnected with rivets, which together become the airframe. So the weight loaded in each area has a direct impact on the capacity of the interconnected structure in the direct area of the hold as well as the adjoining structures.

Aircraft Unloading and Loading

Fig. VII.15.a.

Fig. VII.15.b.
Fig. VII.15: Basic structure of an aircraft fuselage (made of rings, cross beams, and rivets).

Aircraft Unloading and Loading

The manufacturer determines the both the limits or capacity allowed in each part of the aircraft hold, and this can be found in the aircraft ground handling or weight and balance manuals.

For example, to check the floor loading limitation, consider a box with dimensions 6feet length and 4feet width, weighing 2,268kg.

The contact area is length x width = 6 x 4 = 24sqft. Which means 2,268kg weight is exerted on the total contact surface area of 24sqft. So the weight exerted on each sqft area is 2,268kg/24sqft = 94.5kg/sqft. On a B747 aircraft hold, the maximum allowed is about 181kg/sqft. Therefore, the box can be loaded since its weight per sqft is only 94.5kg/sqft, which is within the allowed limits specified by the aircraft manufacturer.

For example, check the linear load limitation by taking the details of the same box. As mentioned, linear load is the weight exerted over a distance (length) of the floor in a portion of the aircraft hold; different portions of the aircraft hold have varying limitations. For a B747, as per the manufacturer, it can range from 38.5kg/inch to 131.5kg/inch. The total weight of the box is 2,268kg and the total running length of the box is 6feet or 72inches. Therefore, the weight exerted by the box contact surface along every inch of the running length of the floor is 2,268kg/72inches = 31.5kg/inch, which is less than the maximum allowed in the portion of the aircraft hold with least value of 38.5kg/inch. So the box can be loaded in any portion of the aircraft hold.

The weight of an oil well drilling head can be 10,000kg and an aircraft can take (based on the type of aircraft) a total weight of over 100,000kg. But even still loading the single piece of 10,000kg may not be possible as it may exceed the floor loading and linear load limits mentioned above. The concentration of 10,000kg in a small area of the aircraft floor can damage the floor and the aircraft structure. To overcome this, the area of contact or foot print of this single piece can be increased sufficiently, so the 10,000kg is spread out along a larger area of the aircraft floor. So, in some cases, the linear load limitation and the floor load limitation can be overcome by spreading the weight of the load evenly on the aircraft floor, by increasing the area of contact, as mentioned above in the example of the table. This can be done by using spreaders or in some places, the term shoring is used. Spreaders or shoring materials are placed under the heavy load to increase the contact length or area of the load on the aircraft floor (*See figures. VII.16*).

Aircraft Unloading and Loading

Fig. VII.16.a.

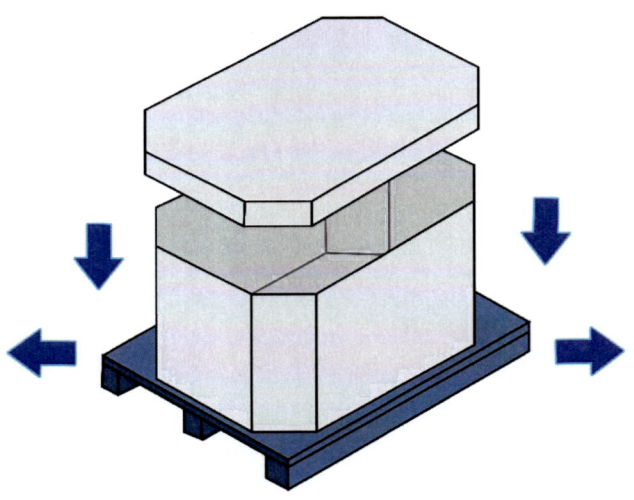

Fig. VII.16.b.

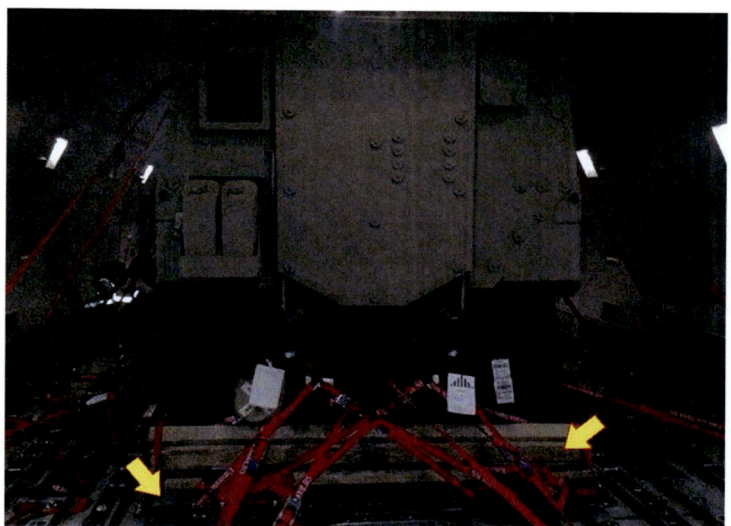

Fig. VII.16.c.
1: Wooden planks spreading weight from the car tires.
2: Airline pallet base.

Fig. VII.16: Spreader

A spreader can be of different types (*see figure. VII.17*). The basic type is a single piece of wood with certain (pre-determined) thickness and length, depending on the weight of the shipment that needs to be spread out on the aircraft floor. There are various types of commonly used shoring materials, for example, wooden custom-made pallets, planks/beams, plywood sheets, steel beams, plastic honeycomb sheets, etc.

Aircraft Unloading and Loading

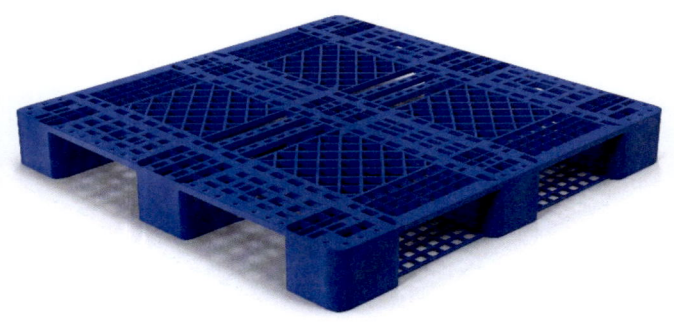

Fig. VII.17: Example of plastic spreader.

The type, thickness, length, number of spreaders, distance between each spreader under the object, height, etc. all depend on the object specifications, such as its dimensions, weight, contact area, packing material used, vulnerability, etc. The primary objective is to ensure the object is safely loaded on the aircraft without causing damage to aircraft floor, safety during transport, integrity of the object, etc. Also, the shoring material used must be strong enough to withstand the pressure impacted on it by the object when loaded on top of it and while being transported in the aircraft hold. Another aspect is that sometimes the lashing belts used to tie down the heavy object may be too tight or the angle of the taut belt can damage the spreader material. So a suitably durable shoring material should be used. Some objects will need specialized built-in spreaders in some unique cases or have in-built base with necessary sufficient shoring properties. In the latter case, the acceptance staff must ensure to check that sufficient shoring is available. The number of spreaders required needs to be carefully ascertained at the time of acceptance, that information must be verified by the load planner and then communicated clearly to the loading staff at the aircraft to ensure compliance while loading the object. Sometimes multiple layers of shoring will be required to achieve the required level of safety. Care must be maintained that too much shoring may increase the height, whereby it may not be loadable in the aircraft hold. Appropriate shoring is required for ensuring the integrity of the ULD and aircraft hold structures.

The floor loading and linear load limitation is important not just in case of bulk-loading aircraft, but also in case of a ULD-. The ULD also needs to be protected against excess strain, that can damage it, make it unsafe while in flight, or even unusable for future. The base of any ULD also has limits.

4) Volumetric limitation: The volume of space allowed in an aircraft hold or a ULD is fixed. The weight of an object may not directly correspond with the volume it occupies. For example, a bundle of cotton may weigh less but need more space or volume. Whereas a bar of metal will occupy less volume or space but will be heavier in weight. So the metal bar will be called dense and the cotton bundle volumetric. There is a well-known formulae to calculate the volume of an object, which is Volume = length x width x height. It may not be possible to get the actual volume of baggage and other load in the planning stage or even at the flight finalizing stage. Also, it may not be possible to measure individual bags, as the numbers are huge and this can be time consuming. Normally, since cargo is accepted and finalized well in advance of a flight, the volume of cargo will be more or less accurate. However, an average volume is normally taken from historic figures for the calculation of load volume expected to be loaded on a flight during the planning stage and compared with the actual volume available in the aircraft holds or the ULDs to be used.

In some cases, the passengers check-in staff or cargo acceptance staff will notify the planners in advance if they come across extremely volumetric or heavy items (out of the ordinary). Volumetric checks are also required by the load planners and load controllers when there is transit load on board a bulk-loading aircraft. They need to know how much space will be available after deducting the volume occupied by the transit load from the actual volume of the aircraft hold to plan their joining load at a transit airport. Sometimes on extremely space-constrained routes, the volume available in transit ULDs are also required, to top-up with similar load at a transit station, in order to maximize the space. For example, consider a ULD-version flight arriving from DXB to BOM and flying onwards to HKG. BOM is a transit airport, where there are joining passengers and cargo to HKG and there are only limited ULD positions available for this load. So excess joining baggage from BOM as per their category (priority, economy, etc.) can be topped up in the transit appropriate baggage ULDs which are in transit on board from DXB to HKG (if required and if allowed by the airline). Similarly, cargo also can be topped up. Hence, it is important to know the volume available in each ULD for a transit station, which is thus shown on the CPM (explained in loading team documentation below). So effective loading can ensure maximum available space is safely utilized, thereby the planned loads are transported to allow the airline to maximize its revenues.

5) <u>Combined load limitation / Monocoque limitation:</u> In simple language, if we take the cross-section of the aircraft fuselage (*See figure. VII.18*), the combined weight of load (passengers/galley/hand bags/etc.) in the upper deck plus the weight of other load (cargo/mail/courier/etc.) loaded in the hold directly beneath in the lower deck should not exceed a certain manufacturer-allowed maximum combined weight.

Fig. VII.18: Weight bearing from different decks on the aircraft structure.

This will vary between aircraft types and different portions of the aircraft. Normally, the extreme forward and the extreme aft (tail section) of the aircraft will have lesser value or in other words, higher limiting combined weights. Therefore, it is important to distribute the weights accordingly.

6) Door dimension limitation: The height and width of the aircraft door is a limiting factor when loading oversize shipment. This is mainly applicable for bulk-loading or freighter aircrafts and to some extent, ULD-version passenger aircrafts (lower holds). In ULD-version aircrafts it is not much of a concern as the loads are in compatible ULDs, unless it is an oversize shipment, its dimensions exceeding the ULD dimensions; for example, if it is a car. It may still be possible to load this shipment into the aircraft hold, with proper checks, build-up, and care.

Fig. VII.19: A car with dimensions within the airline pallet dimensions.

Some cars, although exceeding the dimensions of the airline pallet it is built on, can still be loaded in the hold. This is possible by using spreaders under the tires of the car to lift it, thereby clearing the contoured lower part of the aircraft side walls. For this the vehicle height must be short enough to be accommodated in the aircraft hold after building up on the raised platform of spreaders. Sometimes the car dimensions may be larger than possible for a pre-build-up option at the warehouse, it is still loadable on the aircraft with special and careful handling (if approved by the handling agent and airline). Here an airline pallet will be loaded in position in the aircraft hold, locked, and then the car is pushed manually onto the pallet and lashed down to stop it from movement. For all of the above options, it is important first to ascertain if the car or shipment can pass through the aircraft hold door area and then if it can be turned at the door area to take it to the desired location in the hold. The manufacturer will give dimensions of the aircraft hold door opening, which will be incorporated in the airline weight and balance and the appropriate handling manuals, also a chart is provided to check against various dimensions (height x width to show maximum length possible) to see if an item is loadable based on the hold door dimensions and the turning of the item when entering into the hold (*See figures. VII.20*

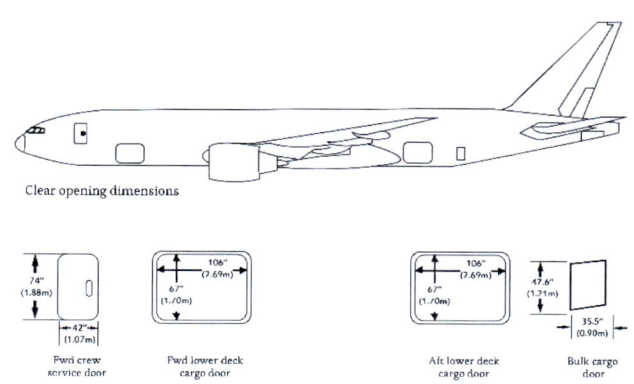

Fig. VII.20.a.

	B777F - FORWARD COMPARTMENT ALLOWABLE PACKAGE SIZES									
	WIDTH IN.									
HEIGHT IN.	10	20	30	40	50	60	70	80	90	101.9
	LENGTH IN.									
64	293	273	253	233	213	193	172	152	130	
60	312	291	271	251	231	211	190	170	149	133
55	328	308	288	268	247	227	206	185	164	146
50	343	323	302	282	262	241	220	199	177	157
45	347	327	306	286	265	245	224	203	181	160
40	347	327	306	286	265	245	224	203	181	160
35	347	327	306	286	265	245	224	203	181	160
30	347	327	306	286	265	245	224	203	181	160
25	347	327	306	286	265	245	224	203	181	160
20	347	327	306	286	265	245	224	203	181	160
15	347	327	306	286	265	245	224	203	181	160
10	347	327	306	286	265	245	224	203	181	160
5	347	327	306	286	265	245	224	203	181	160

	B777F - FORWARD COMPARTMENT ALLOWABLE PACKAGE SIZES									
	WIDTH CM									
HEIGHT CM	25	50	76	101	127	152	177	203	228	258
	LENGTH CM									
162	744	693	642	591	541	490	436	386	330	-
152	792	739	688	637	586	535	482	431	378	337
139	833	782	731	680	627	576	523	469	416	370
127	871	820	767	716	665	612	558	505	449	398
114	881	830	777	726	673	622	568	515	459	406
101	881	830	777	726	673	622	568	515	459	406
88	881	830	777	726	673	622	568	515	459	406
76	881	830	777	726	673	622	568	515	459	406
63	881	830	777	726	673	622	568	515	459	406
50	881	830	777	726	673	622	568	515	459	406
38	881	830	777	726	673	622	568	515	459	406
25	881	830	777	726	673	622	568	515	459	406
12	881	830	777	726	673	622	568	515	459	406

Fig. VII.20.b.
Fig. VII.20: Hold door dimensions and load ability chart.

Aircraft Unloading and Loading

The different hold doors have differing dimensions for each type of aircraft. Sometimes even the same aircraft type of a different airline can have differing door dimensions for a particular hold. This is because of the specific requirements of the airline given to the manufacturer when the aircraft was being made. For example, the lower aft hold of a B767 aircraft for some airlines can load only smaller ULDs, whereas some airlines with the same aircraft can accommodate bigger airline pallets as they would prefer to carry larger loads such as cargo also in the aft hold and not just baggage as preferred by the previously mentioned airline.

7) Height limitation: This limitation is more applicable for bulk-loading aircrafts, freighter aircrafts, and ULD-version aircrafts (only when open ULDs are used, e.g. airline pallets). The hold ceiling has fire or smoke detection sensors, lights, and panel joints. Hence, a certain clearance distance of approximately 10 to 20cm (unless specified by the airline) is to be maintained while loading. Some airlines have clear demarcations along the walls of the hold to show the limit up to which the loads can be stowed in the hold. This will avoid:

- a- Damaging the ceiling panels, lights, or detectors while loading or load shifting during flight.
- b- Smoldering or fire hazard when the item comes in contact with the hold lights which can become very hot when switched on for a long time.

Similarly, it is important that excess weight or pressure is not put on the walls of the aircraft hold as there are air conditioning ducts, electrical wiring, and other critical aircraft components behind these panels.

It is critical that sufficient separation space is maintained between the ceiling and the wall surfaces and the ULDs in a ULD-version aircraft hold. Particularly when open pallets with netting are used. Sometimes the build-up staff can build-up a pallet that exceeds the height limitation. This may not go through the door and can damage the entry area door ceiling or sometimes it may go through but rub against the inner ceiling panels, damaging or ripping them, including the fire detectors or lights. Another impact of wrong build-up is when the load is protruding from the sides of the pallet, then there are chances of damaging the side depressor seals for the door (*See figure. VII.21*), or the inner wall panels.

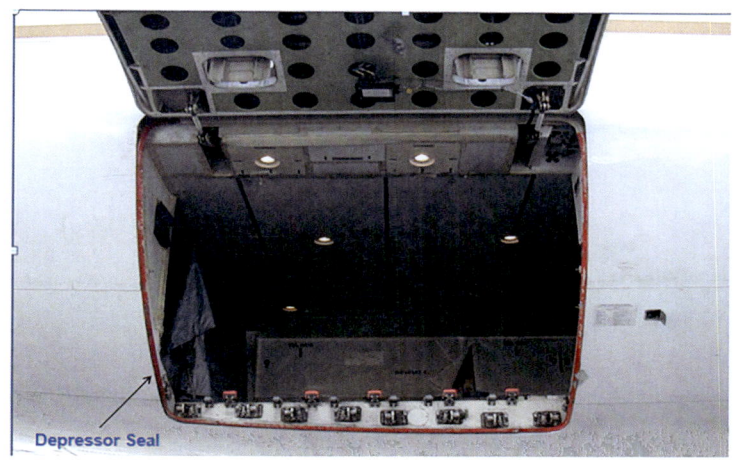

Fig. VII.21.a. Depressor seal.

Fig. VII.21.b. Doorway sides

Fig. VII.21.c. Incorrectly built ULD.
Fig. VII.21: Possible impact of incorrectly build ULD.

An incorrectly built ULD / pallet can damage the depressor seal, or the doorway sides, or the interior side walls or even ceiling of the aircraft hold.

This can happen not only while loading in the aircraft, also while unloading, if the origin station had incorrectly built-up and loaded or if the netting was loose and the item shifted during flight. Therefore, it is important for the loading team to carefully check before loading or unloading to ensure sufficient clearance is available at all times. Also, keep a look out for sharp protruding objects or loose lashing or netting. Do not attempt to load or unload when encountering such situations. Take necessary precautions such as reshaping or re-lashing, tightening the nets, etc., or in extreme cases, where safety of personnel, aircraft, and equipment is in jeopardy, get supervisory help or intervention.

8) Restraint requirement: Every item will have a certain amount of weight, and these weights are categorized into weight classes. Each class will have a minimum and maximum limit. There are various considerations for these categorizations. Any single item more than 150kg in weight must be lashed down to the floor of the aircraft if it is bulk-loading or if loaded in a ULD, to the floor of the

ULD using prescribed lashing belts against the gravitational force or G-force. The number of lashing belts required depends on the weight of the item. The basic aim is to withstand the force of motion in any direction and keep the item in its loaded position during flight. Therefore, the lashing belts used must have sufficient capacity to hold the piece in its loaded position. A loose heavy item in the aircraft hold is like a cannon ball, an aircraft can accelerate rapidly during takeoff and decelerate rapidly during landing, also during flight there can be sudden motion in various directions during turbulence if the weather is bad. So the heavy item can move around rapidly, causing damage to the aircraft hold that can be lethal. So it is important to lash sufficiently and recheck the lashing before completing the loading, to ensure the movement of the item is not at all possible.

Lashing belt or strap requirement calculation:
Shipment tie down to the ULD

Shipment weight x G-force restrain direction = No. of tie-down fittings required

Tie-down breaking strength

Tie down breaking strength of a strap or lashing belt may differ from one manufacturer to another. An airline will select an appropriate model or strap or lashing belt based on its requirements and other factors. All lashing belts used in airline operations will have the breaking strength mentioned on them. For our example, take the breaking strength of a lashing belt as 2268kg (5000lbs)

Example: if the package is weighing 1000kg
(1) $\dfrac{1000\text{kg} \times 3\text{ G (upward)}}{2268\text{kg (breaking strength)}} = 0.66$ strap (rounded up to 1 strap)

(2) $\dfrac{1000\text{kg} \times 1.5\text{G (fwd)}}{2268\text{kg (breaking strength)}} = 0.33$ strap (rounded up to 1 strap)

(3) $\dfrac{1000\text{kg} \times 1.5\text{G (rear)}}{2268\text{kg (breaking strength)}} = 0.33$ strap (rounded up to 1 strap)

Total 3 straps required

Aircraft Unloading and Loading

9) <u>Point load limitation</u>: The ULDs have limitations for taking more than a certain weight, after which it may be possible to load heavier weights, but subject to additional tie downs (as prescribed by the weight and balance manual). Also for bulk-loading holds, heavy items above 150kg must also be tied down. This is to provide additional restraint due to the excess weight. This will be advised by the load control officer if necessary as well as how many lashing belts are required based on the actual gross weight of the ULD or item. To connect the lashing belt end hooks or clips to the aircraft floor, there are specific lashing points (*See figure. VII.22*) that are to be used for extra lashing when necessary.

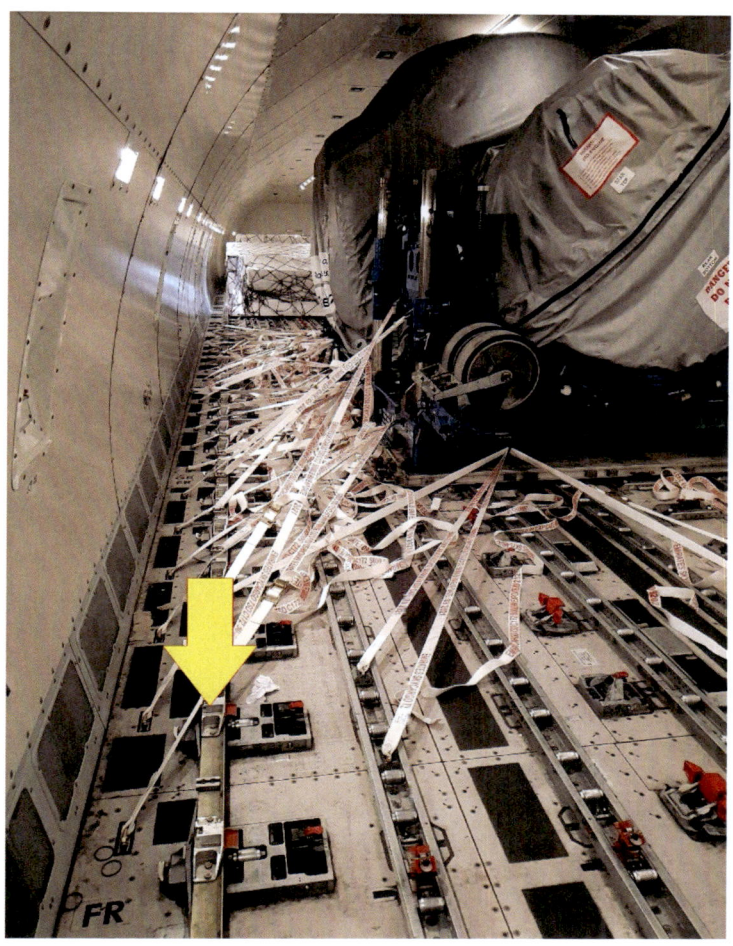

Fig. VII.22.a.

Only these lashing points are to be used for additional tie down requirements. These points have limitations to the weight they can restrain; sometimes multiple lashing points may be used.

Aircraft Unloading and Loading

Fig. VII.23: Shipment loaded with additional tie downs to the airline, and pallet and aircraft floor tie down points for greater securing requirement.

The requirement and numbers will be advised by the load control officer, based on the applicable manual. Some ULD locks on the aircraft floor also have provision for grooves or rings to attach lashing belt pins or hooks that serves as additional lashing points.

Never bulk load loose cargo in ULD-version holds, as the floors and the hold are not designed for bulk loading. This is against regulations.

Ramp Understanding

There are various important concepts in ramp operations that are essential to understand the basic functions of the loading team. The loading teams may not be directly involved in all areas of handling and processes, but form an overall integral part of the ramp handling of a flight. It becomes their responsibility to ensure the safe operation of the flight as they are the last point and first point in handling of a flight in addition to other teams involved in the compounded turnaround of the flight. So an overall understanding will allow critical cross-checks and fill any gaps that may have been left open by the other earlier processing team along the way. The complete handling is a chain of individual handling functions, and it is important to have cross-checks where possible to allow a seamless and smooth operation. Each team supports the others and they are interlinked. Further, it allows for improvement in service standards, empowers staff, improves processes, and increases confidence in staff and customers. Some checks are as follows:

Load – The term load for ramp staff refers to baggage, cargo, and mail. Staff at check-in may use it as the number of passengers. Now for the ramp staff load is identified by the appropriate tags or labels attached to it at the time of acceptance. No load can be handled at the aircraft without a tag or label to show to which category it belongs to. Appearance is not sufficient, because people can send cargo in normal suitcases also. This is because the processing of baggage and other load are different, is done in different sections of an airport, and thus, missing tags can lead to mishandling and security issues. All missing or damaged tags must be reported and the necessary action taken to restore them. No load must be in the hold of an aircraft if it does not have appropriate tag. E.g. a passenger bag must have a tag, basically showing the flight number, date, destination, class of travel (label), and a tag number. Name of the passenger is also preferable. For cargo the consignment number and destination label is must, with the flight number and date shown on the ULD tag. Trollies transporting loose cargo also have tags to show to which flight the cargo belongs. Processing of load is actually all the functions which start from acceptance through to delivery. The ramp staff does only a part of it. For example, check-in staff accepts the passenger and his baggage on the flight that he is ticketed for. He then tags the bags as per the itinerary of the passenger and sends the bags to the baggage build-up section, where it is then segregated as per the destination and class of travel and loaded into specific ULDs accordingly. This is then brought to the aircraft by the tractor driver, where the ULD is again segregated by the loading team and loaded in the aircraft as per the instructions given. At the destination, the ULDs are offloaded by the offloading teams, segregated as per certain airline priorities, and forwarded to the appropriate handling sections such as arrival baggage ULD breakdown area or the transfer baggage ULD breakdown area. At the arrival conveyor belt area the staff again sort and offload the bags onto the conveyor belt, which are picked up by the passengers inside the arrival terminal. The purpose of processing load is to increase the efficiency of flight handling, reduce mishandling, maximize use of available space without exceeding any limitations, and reduce the flight handling time. For processing load, information such as aircraft type operating, its routing, scheduled times, availability of space, etc. are required and can be obtained from different sources.

The concept of first in last out or last in first out is the basic requirement of the unloading and loading process. It means that what is loaded first at an origin airport will be unloaded last at the destination. For more clarity, the aircraft hold will have only one door for access, so whatever is loaded first will be over stowed subsequently with whichever load is loaded next and so on till the door entrance of the hold. Just like filling up a bottle with different items (In *Figure. VII.24, each of the aircraft hold has only a single point of entry or exit*).

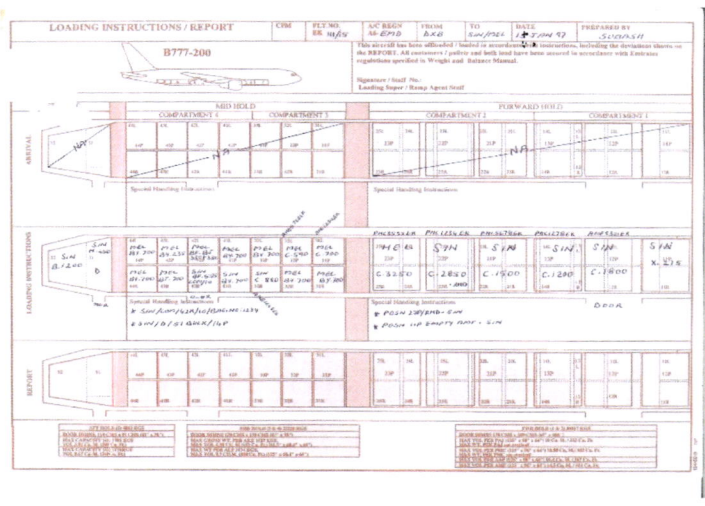

Fig. VII.24: Loading instructions showing position of each load type in the hold from the entrance to the hold. So loads planned near the hold entrance are accessible first, subsequently loads loaded towards the interior of the hold.

So when loading an aircraft hold, this aspect must be kept in mind by the loading team. Why is it important?

As mentioned, various loads will be planned for transportation on a flight from origin to destination, which basically consist of:

    a.   Baggage [priority, transfer (short and long connection), economy class]
    b.   Courier [as express and maybe as cargo]

- c. Post office mail
- d. Cargo [express cargo, special cargo (live animals, perishables, valuables, etc.), other general cargo]
- e. Flight spares, etc. [unless marked as 'to remain on board']
- f. Transit load [if applicable]
- g. Transfer loads [if applicable]

The order of priority for each load will depend on each individual airline's mode of operations. Normally, the order of priority is as per the above list in decreasing priority.

Baggage: Normally, this type of load has the highest priority in handling. Meaning this is required to be offloaded first at the destination, since the baggage needs to be delivered at the arrival hall for passenger collection. Passengers are the highest revenue earning factor for a passenger airline and thus, cannot be kept waiting for long. They need to be cleared smoothly and quickly. Also, it will assist the airport to keep handling the flights that arrive, rather than have a huge number of passengers clogging the terminal and other areas. Baggage is also classified as priority class (first, business), economy, transfer, etc. This is based on the different categories of passengers travelling on board. And hence again, the order of importance in handling baggage depends on the categories accordingly, where priority class passengers bags will be higher priority than economy class passenger baggage. Naturally, due to the higher fares charged by the airline from priority class passengers. Transfer baggage can again have handling priority in order of the connection to waiting connecting flights. For example, the transfer baggage arriving on flight for a passenger who is connecting onto another flight within one hour (short connection) will have higher priority than the baggage of passenger connecting after 2 or 3 hours. So the transfer baggage of the short connection (which will be appropriately tagged as per the airline instructions to the origin station where it was tagged and loaded on the aircraft accordingly) will be offloaded first at the transit airport and sent to the transfer baggage handling area before the other later transfer baggage. Due to the above reason, all other load is first stowed in the aircraft hold and then this baggage is loaded, so that it can be offloaded first on arrival at the destination. Also, at the origin there are passengers who report last minute, but cargo and other loads can be finalized much earlier and brought to the aircraft for loading in advance (unless there are some exceptional cases, like live human organs, critical medicines, etc.). Punctual and smooth delivery of

Aircraft Unloading and Loading

baggage to passengers on arrival is one of the most important aspects of service delivery standards that all airlines try to improve and concentrate on. Therefore, it is important that the loading and unloading teams ensure smooth and efficient handling of all baggage.

Courier: These are courier service bags or extra urgent parcels that will be appropriately marked as belonging to well-known courier companies.

Post office mail: These are post office parcels and bags that are sent by the postal authorities.

Cargo: This load can be classified as special cargo, express cargo, and then general cargo. General cargo is loaded first, then express cargo, and then special cargo). Sometimes courier is under a cargo air waybill, this will be treated as cargo.

Flight spares: Sometimes airlines may send urgent spares for an aircraft. This must be loaded last, so that it can be unloaded first on arrival at destination. Here specific instructions will be given regarding the priority for offloading. There are also spares carried in the aircraft hold that should not be unloaded and will be marked accordingly. These are carried on board in anticipation of some emergency requirement at a transit or destination airport, where the spares may not be locally available. On return to home base, these are unloaded and handed over back to engineering stores or the authorized department.

Transit load: If a flight is planned to operate from airport LHR to airport DXB, and then continue to airport BOM, before finally returning back to airport LHR, then at airport DXB, there can be loads for destination airport BOM also. This load can be baggage of passengers staying on board (in transit), cargo, courier, mail, etc. This load in transit on board is called transit load, which is for final destination BOM. The incoming load messages (LDM and CPM) will show this as for BOM and hence must not be unloaded at DXB.

Transfer load: Similarly, there can be transit loads that need to be offloaded and connected on another flight to a destination on the same day or at a later date. This load is called transfer load. This will be accordingly mentioned in the incoming load messages from the origin airport or advised by the airline handling team.

Aircraft ground stability or trim (balance) concept: An important aspect of aircraft loading is also to ensure the balance of the aircraft while on ground and in the air. Although the prime responsibility of aircraft balance lies with the load control officer, especially during take-off, in flight and landing, it becomes a necessary responsibility for the loading team to have an understanding of the aircraft ground stability trim or balance and ensure to maintain this during the loading or offloading process. An aircraft while on ground or in the air acts like a manual balance found in the local grocery shop. Meaning it can rotate along the center of gravity. Too much weight on one side can increase the tendency of the aircraft to tilt towards the heavier weight area. The rear landing gear (rear wheels assembly) act as the fulcrum. What the loading team must know is that if there is too much weight in the aft hold of the aircraft and too little or no load in the forward, there will be a tendency for the aircraft to tilt backwards and sit with its tail section hitting the ground. Conversely, too much weight in the forward compared to aft hold can also cause damage to the forward landing gear. There can be damage in other areas like the passenger doors getting jammed or damaged against the steps or aero bridges positioned against the aircraft due to the uneven tilt. These situations can happen in the following conditions:

1) The loading team on arrival offloads all or more load from the forward aircraft hold with no load or lesser load removed from the aft aircraft hold. So the aircraft becomes very tail heavy. To avoid this situation, always maintain higher ratio of offloading to be done from aft than from the forward hold. Always keep track of the weight approximation in the forward and aft as the offloading is progressing. If there is transit load or baggage in the forward, to be on safe side, offload sufficient loads from aft hold first, before progressing offloading from the forward hold. The load control officer can be consulted if necessary.

2) The loading team for departure loads more load in the aft and then starts the forward hold loading. Sometimes the load planner may plan baggage in the forward hold and cargo in the aft hold. Since cargo arrives well in advance at the aircraft side, the loading team should keep sufficient cargo load on the ground till the forward hold is sufficiently loaded, before loading can be completed in the aft hold.

Ground stability should be considered as the offloading and or loading process is going on. All aircrafts have a certain level of ground stability, but avoid reaching the threshold. The ratio can be different for various aircrafts. But use a thumb rule to maintain a 60:40 ratio, with 60 always being the forward hold. The load control staff will do the necessary ground stability checks for transit flights or for some airlines, it is a mandatory requirement. However, it is the primary responsibility of the loading team to ensure the correct sequence of offloading and loading is followed, which is:

For offloading: Start with aft hold; when 60% completed, gradually start with the forward hold also simultaneously, and finally finish with the forward.

For loading: Start with the forward hold; when 60% completed, start gradually the aft as well. Ensure to complete the forward first, finally finishing with the aft.

Another important aspect to remember, sometimes a ULD may be extremely heavy, which needs to be loaded in the aft hold, again ensure there is higher weight in the forward. Again, it makes a big difference if the weight is nearer to the wing (wing being the center of the aircraft approximately) or further away. As the effect is much higher when away from the wing rather than near the wing in the aircraft hold.

So ground stability is an important concept for the loading team to be followed.

Ramp Safety

Ramp safety is a general terminology. All personnel, passengers, other airport users, aircraft, equipment, etc. are valuable assets and hence need to be protected. Protection here mainly comes from having the correct safety attitude, correct procedures, hazard awareness, and multi-layered steps or checks to avoid impacts, etc. There are various parts to this, such as:

1) Awareness to create the right safety attitude
2) Use of personal protective equipment – PPE and other accessories to enhance the safety culture
3) Safety briefing / actions
4) Following the correct procedures and instructions
5) Reporting and steps to avoid recurrence

To elaborate further:

1) <u>Awareness to create the right attitude</u>: Training sessions, briefings to include past safety impacted experiences and outcomes, and periodic safety campaigns should be conducted, and posters put up in offices. Recognition should be given for pointing out or

amending incorrect or unsafe practices, averting an unsafe incident/accident, and improvements to current procedures or processes. Since operational handling practices are changing constantly with new technological or procedural improvements, regular review of existing procedures and processes with the view of enhancements to safety aspects of operation is a must. All airports' users must be called to take part in safety awareness and enhancement programs or campaigns as they are all involved in the everyday functioning of the airport in one way or the other.

2) <u>Accessories and personal protective equipment (PPE)</u>: Like all trade, there are certain tools or accessories required by the loading team to do their job safely and correctly. Especially the PPE, which is basically a must for all airport ramp staff all over the world, without which there can be repercussions/penalties from monitoring agencies and most importantly, personal safety is compromised. Some of the PPE are:

1) Safety shoes which have protective front shields, are non-slippery, antistatic, and non-metallic. They give sufficient protection from injuries that can be caused by the foot getting caught between moving ULDs, vehicles, or equipment running over, falling objects, slipping on oil/hydraulic spillage, accidentally stepping on powered rollers in hold or on the hi-loaders, etc.

2) Reflective safety vests: The movement of large number of vehicles, oversized equipment, limited visibility due to climatic conditions, working in a limited space, etc. cause obstructed view or difficulty for the operators. So wearing a reflective vest makes personnel on the ramp more visible to all, during reduced or obstructed viewing circumstances.

3) Gloves: There are moving equipment parts, sharp objects, possible corrosive or other dangerous substances, etc. on the ramp environment and hence, it is necessary to protect your hands appropriately.

4) Noise mufflers: The sound of aircraft engines and other equipment can be very loud and can cause permanent damage in the long term when exposed over a period of time. Thus the necessity for noise mufflers.

Aircraft Unloading and Loading

5) Rain coats and caps: Rain coats are necessary while handling flights during rainy weather. Caps can be useful under extreme weather conditions, this again become a necessity, not in terms of falling or falling objects. Similarly, appropriate company issued apparel for protection against cold weather is also necessary.
6) Appropriate uniform/materials: The use of uniform is a must in all airports for ramp staff, especially in view of the security requirement. But whatever the uniform, the materials used and design should be comfortable in respect of the climatic and working environment of the staff. Wearing of tie when working near moving parts of an equipment is not advisable.

Other useful accessories are:

- Small pen torches: These are useful to read tags or labels during reduced visibility.
- Ropes (preferably nylon, for durable strength) and tie downs pins (*Refer to figures. VII.25)*.

Fig. VII.25.a.

Fig. VII.25.b.
Fig. VII.25: Nylon ropes and tie down pins.

Aircraft Unloading and Loading

- Any heavy item above 150kg or special cargo (e.g. live animals) needs to be secured against any motion during flight using ropes and tie down pins. There are different types of pins which are specially designed to lock into groves made especially for this purpose in the holds of aircrafts. These pins are manufactured under strict guidelines and undergo various tests to determine their capacities. Hence, they are costly and thus must be used appropriately. Lashing heavier items over 150kg or ULDs requiring additional tie downs will be looked into later on in the chapter.
- Safety cones: These are high visibility cones (*See figure. VII.30*) placed to warn drivers and operators to be careful due to the close vicinity of aircraft engines, wings, fuel hydrants, etc. It must be placed in such a way that it is visible as much as possible from all directions. E.g. a cone placed near the starboard engine must be 2 to 3 feet from the front right corner of the engine. This way it is noticeable from the front, back, and sides. There is a high risk of damage to wings of small aircrafts due to the low height; hence, placing these cones under the wing tips can prevent any accidents.

Fig. VII.26: Safety cones.

Although it is forbidden to drive under the wing of any aircraft, some handling equipment such as the transporter need to move under the wing due to space constraints at certain airports. Although transporters are normally used on aircrafts with higher wings, great care must be practiced while operating under the wings of aircrafts. A marshaller to guide the driver while backing is necessary for all vehicles in all operational areas.

3) <u>Safety Briefing / actions</u>: Every department in the airport must have a safety briefing. This can be scheduled based on their area of operation, active deployment times, and level of hazard exposure. For the loading team, there are many, some of the safety requirements to be followed are:

i) Carry out foreign objects / debris (FOD) check before aircraft comes to park and before aircraft is ready for pushback. Remove immediately or report to supervisor for corrective action. This is to avoid any objects from getting sucked into the engine and getting damaged. Also, an oil or fuel leakage or spillage is also to be reported for cleaning, before regular operation can take place.

ii) Always wear PPE and avoid walking under the fuselage of the aircraft as there are sensors and pitots that may be hot that can cause burns or also can get damaged when hit against.

iii) Never approach an aircraft when the aircraft beacon lights are switched on. This means the aircraft engines are about to start or it is still not stopped completely. Also keep well clear of the engine inlet as the engine fan, when spinning, can cause a suction effect. These precautions are to protect against the danger of getting sucked into the engine or encountering jet blast.

iv) Place safety cones under the aircraft at the prescribed positions. This will avoid equipment or vehicles from being driven too close to the aircraft.

v) Avoid driving under the wings of the aircraft if there is insufficient height clearance and strictly avoid driving under the fuselage at all. In the case of small narrow-body aircraft, avoid driving under or near the wings.

vi) Avoid unauthorized access to aircraft areas other than the aircraft holds.

vii) Any unaccounted/ untagged/ etc. objects/ baggage/ cargo/etc. are to be reported to the security department and

viii) Ensure all dolly and trolley brakes are engaged at all times, other than when towed.

ix) All dolly side locks are to be engaged when ULDs are loaded on it and again cross-checks done prior to commencing towing.

x) Any unaccounted ULDs or loads on the aircraft parking after unloading or loading has been completed should be checked, verified, and removed to appropriate processing sections.

xi) Prior to opening the hold doors, check the areas near the door for any damages; after the door is opened, check the edge areas for any damages; and before commencement of unloading activity, always check the integrity of the ULDs and aircraft hold for any damages. Finally, after unloading is completed, check for any damages. Also check for any loads or ULDs that may have been left behind. If there are any flight spares, confirm with engineers or airline if the same are to be unloaded or not.

xii) Similarly, check doors, edges, and holds for damages prior commencement of loading. ULD and load packing integrity is to be checked prior to loading on aircraft. Again, reconfirm after loading is completed.

xiii) Never ride on a vehicle without a seat. And never operate vehicles or equipment unless trained and licensed to do so. Do not offer rides to others if not authorized by the authority responsible.

xiv) Do not stand on the hi-loader when ULDs are being loaded or moved on it.

xv) Do not back a vehicle to an aircraft without a marshaller and always keep a clear exit if necessary to remove it in an emergency.

xvi) Never smoke anywhere on the ramp, vehicle, in the hold, or in the ULD; never sleep anywhere on the ramp, vehicle, equipment, hold, or ULD.

xvii) Always clarify any confusion or doubts; ensure all documents, procedures, and instructions are followed before flight departure or leaving from aircraft.

xviii) Reconciliation with UWS, baggage reconciliation list, LIRF, in addition to debriefing with load controller and flight dispatcher are necessary before the aircraft doors are

xix) closed. Only sign the LIRF, NOTOC, and flight handling check sheet when all of these are completed.
xix) If a passenger baggage is offloaded at the aircraft due to instructions from the flight's dispatcher or baggage services department, cross-check the tag with the dispatcher. Hold the bags at the aircraft till the aircraft is pushed back and then send to appropriate processing area under advisement.
xx) Complete all reports with appropriate suggestions and feedbacks.

As stated, the safety measures and steps needed are many. Above are only the most prominent; again, when it comes to safety, sometimes the most insignificant becomes the most significant. Hence, all are important. Some airports have safety departments who publish safety procedures, requirements, do and don'ts, etc. The loading teams must be aware of this and periodically review them.

4) <u>Following correct procedure and instructions:</u> Each process or function on the ramp needs to be documented and followed. There are standard operating procedures that need to be adhered to by the various teams. These have been formulated after careful consideration and evaluation. The loading teams must be aware of general aviation guidelines, airport, airline, and handling company instructions and regulations. All must be followed and if any deviations are noticed, they must be immediately reported to the superior.

5) Reporting and steps to avoid recurrence: Deviation or discrepancy reports must be made and followed up. Reports must include suggestions or feedback for management to put in place corrective steps to avoid recurrence.

Loading team documents: There are various documents that are used by the loading teams to carry out their functions, some of which are later used for transmitting information and become legal documents. The adherence to the instructions in it and the accuracy of the reports are paramount to safety and providing quality service. It not only helps the loading teams but down line stations also. Some of the important documents are as follows:

1) Flights Information sheet
2) LDM

Aircraft Unloading and Loading

3) CPM
4) ULD weight statement – UWS
5) Offloading/loading instruction form and report
6) Baggage reconciliation report
7) NOTOC
8) Flight handling check sheet
9) Cargo and mail manifests
10) UCM (as mentioned ULD chapter)

Except the last, all other documents must be read thoroughly and understood by the handling teams before the arrival or handling of the flight. Any confusion or ambiguities must be clarified well in advance with the load controller or the concerned superiors.

1) <u>Flight Information Sheet</u>: This typically should be compiled as a brief of the flight with details such as,
a) Flight number, date, routing
b) Schedule, delay, estimate arrivals or departures, delay reason from previous station, ground time available,
c) Special loads incoming, outgoing, in transit, special instructions from load controller, etc.
d) Estimated loads incoming, transit, or departure
e) Key team members such as load controller, dispatcher, baggage handling team leader, etc., with contact numbers.
f) Areas to include loading team members' names
g) Additional columns for reports or feedbacks, etc.

The flight information must be automated and printed out by the loading team allocator. He/she should hand it over to the allocated team leader prior to arriving at the flight and the completed form is to be handed back to the allocator for recording. Nowadays, the flight information sheet and all of the above are automated and are done through handheld portable terminals.

2) <u>LDM or Load Distribution Message</u>: These are sent by the departure station to all down line stations once the flight takes off on its journey. It is a must for all commercial flights. It is system generated or typed manually by the load controller. The information in the LDM is entirely derived from the load sheet (about which you will learn in the forthcoming chapter). It basically gives information of the aircraft, load it carries, the weight distribution in the

holds, any additional information, etc. The information in the LDM is necessary for the down line stations to handle the flight effectively and efficiently. It also allows them to make the necessary arrangements to handle it. E.g. it will tell them how many passengers are disembarking at their station, how many are traveling onward in case of transiting at their station, so that the necessary catering can be arranged or it will tell them the weight and load distribution for that station in the hold. Here you have to be careful because there can be loads for different stations loaded in the same hold and the distribution shown accordingly against each destination in the case of multiple transit stops. With the information on the LDM, down line stations can then prepare the necessary coaches required, and the number of transit cards to be given to transit passengers, who may disembark for duty free shopping or anything else. This information will help in later boarding the transit passengers, and in accepting passengers at that station because now they know exactly how many seats are available for joining passengers after deducting the ones already occupied by transit passengers. The weight of cargo/mail/courier and the number and weight of baggage will give an idea of how many trolleys or manpower will be required to unload the aircraft in case of bulk-loading aircrafts. So even before a flight arrives, the preparations to handle it are started and thus, all the concerned departments are ready when it arrives. The LDM is also used by the airline headquarters for accounting purpose, verification, and recording. An LDM is of particular importance in case of transit flights but also helpful for a turnaround or stopover flight. especially for bulk-loading aircrafts for which there may not be any other message of the load in the hold for the handling teams. The main body format of all LDMs are the same, irrespective if the aircraft is bulk-loading or ULD-version with minimal changes, that may be attributed to the slight variations that will be found on the load sheets of different airlines. These minimal changes are to suit the airline requirements. Let us examine some of the LDMs.

For stopover or turnaround flight arriving at the airport LHR: LDM

```
XH123/20.A6ABC.8F42J304Y.4/16
-IAD.161/130/19.0.T21283.1/2975.2/6058.3/8461.4/3132.5/657
.PAX/1/34/275.PAD/0/1/0.PEA/43R
SI PAX WEIGHTS USED M85 F70 C38 I10
SERVICE WEIGHT ADJUSTMENT WEIGHT/INDEX
ADD
NIL
DEDUCTIONS
NIL
PANTRY CODE D
IAD C 8277 M 0 B 551/ 11114 O 0 T 0
ACT ZFW 223500 KGS
ACT U/L 2332 KGS
```

3) <u>CPM or Container Pallet Message</u>: This message is also sent in addition to the LDM, for ULD-version flights. It is derived from the loading instruction report made by the handling team who loaded the flight, and verified and transmitted by the load controller at the departure station to all down line stations. It gives clear information of the destination and types of ULDs in the hold, their serial numbers (alphanumeric), weight of each (net or gross weight depending on the airline, normally gross), its positions in the hold, the type of load it contains, information of special loads such as live animals in hold, any additional information that may help the handling teams, etc. The main format will remain same, but some information that may not be necessary will not be shown by some airlines, to cut costs, time, etc. E.g. the use of ULD numbers because there is a UCM that is also transmitted containing the ULD numbers exclusively, or the use of destination code may be omitted when the flight is operating to a single destination, stopover, or turnaround from that station. This message is used by the load controller to prepare the unloading instruction and also to help him to plan the flight for departure in case of transit flights. This is because it will tell him how many positions are available for loading the outbound load after deducting the positions already occupied by transit ULDs in the hold. For the handling teams, the necessary dollies and trolley to unload the aircraft hold can be arranged and kept ready. The concerned department can be informed of special load arrival, etc. In some airports to avoid duplication, the CPM

is referred to by the handling teams to unload all stopover or turnaround flights rather than have the load controller make out the unloading instruction form manually or take a printout of the unloading instruction. CPMs are obviously not sent for bulk-loading aircrafts as the LDMs are sufficient and there are no containers or pallets loaded in the hold. The unloading teams also use the CPMs to verify if the actual loading found on arrival is as same as shown. Refer below for an example of a CPM:

XH345/20.A6ABD.DXB
-11L/AKE42006XH/LHR/535/C-
11R/AKE43352XH/LHR/338/C.AVI
-12L/AKE40727XH/LHR/425/C-
12R/AKE17186XH/LHR/97/B/614/BY
-13L/AKE42056XH/LHR/245/C.LHO-13R/N
-14L/N-14R/N
-15L/AKE45104XH/LHR/694/BJ-
15R/AKE40877XH/LHR/325/BF/180/BJ
-21L/AKE11487XH/LHR/710/BJ-
21R/AKE12612XH/LHR/119/B/652/BY
-22L/AKE42941XH/LHR/81/B/540/BY-
22R/AKE16603XH/LHR/100/B/558/BY
-23L/AKE11270XH/LHR/99/B/670/BY-
23R/AKE45670XH/LHR/543/BT
-24L/AKE41191XH/LHR/643/BY-
24R/AKE17141XH/LHR/197/B/596/BY
-25L/AKE40787XH/LHR/662/BY-
25R/AKE15939XH/LHR/713/BY
-26L/AKE45327XH/LHR/714/BY-
26R/AKE18980XH/LHR/765/BY
-31P/PMC35476XH/LHR/1576/C.RNG.ROX
-32P/PMC76223XH/LHR/2410/C
-33P/N
-41L/AKE41990XH/LHR/1126/C.PER-
41R/AKE40407XH/LHR/1053/C.ICE.COL/0.PEP.COL/1.PEP
-42L/AKE43114XH/LHR/1070/C.PER-
42R/AKE11183XH/LHR/1053/C.ICE.COL/0.PEP.COL/1.PEP
-43L/AKE19030XH/LHR/1545/C.COL/1.PES-
43R/AKE17878XH/LHR/1202/C.PEP.EAT

-44L/AKE18223XH/LHR/1089/C.PEP-
44R/AKE12970XH/LHR/1091/C.PEP
-
45L/AKE19339XH/LHR/781/C.ICE.COL/0.PEP.COL/1.PEP-
45R/AKE42573XH/LHR/196/BY
-51.NIL
-
52/LHR/1/B/60/BT/140/B/74/BY/405/D/97/Q.COM/1.VR177
-53.NIL
SI D 52/27/405
1P COM. 27P CRB. 9P BGE IN BLK

4) <u>ULD Weight Statement – UWS</u>. *(See specimen, figure.VII.27)*

ULD/BULK Load Weight Statement

Reprint

Flt No/Date: EK9908 16-Aug-2015 10:00 (STD) Departure: 16-Aug-2015 10:50 (ETD)   : LMC
Routing: MEX-LAX-CPH-DWC   Flt Type: Freighter   Date: 20-Aug-2015
A/C Type: 77XF   Time: 14:49:57

SNo	LC1	LC2	Chng Ind	ULD Code	Cntr Code	Cntr Num	Gross Wt	Net Wt	Pt. of Uldng	Dest	SHC	Remarks
1	C	C		PMC70577EK	AMX	Q5	3302	2627	DWC	DWC	OHG-SPX-E CC-ELI-AXA	58 INCHES W-O BOTH ENDS
2	C	C	U	PMC77206EK	AMX	Q4	2044	1941	DWC	DWC	SPX-HEA	
3	C	C		PMC77054EK	AMX	Q5	3518	3410	MEL	DWC	SPX-HEA-E CC	
4	C	C		PGF08256FF			2572	2000	LHR	DWC	HEA-VEH-R MD-SPX	
5	C	C		PMC07810EK	AMX	Q5	3328	3208	RUH	DWC	SPX	
6	C	C		PMC33241EK	AMX	Q5	3292	3221	DXB	DWC	SPX-HEA	
7	C	C		PMC07801EK	PLD		1438	1327	BAH	DWC	SPX	
8	C	C		PMC35146EK	PLD		1254	1125	MEL	DWC	SPX	
9	C	C		PMC74208EK	AMX	Q4	3112	3054	LLW	DWC	SPX-HEA	
10	C	C		PMC78310EK	AMX	Q4	2078	1955	BAH	DWC	SPX	
11	C	C		PMC77068EK	AMX	Q5	2700	2579	DWC	DWC	ECC-SPX	
12	C	C		PMC78430EK	AMX	Q5	2520	2396	RUH	DWC	HEA-SPX-E CC	
13	C	C		PMC79552EK	AMX	Q5	2396	2322	PER	DWC	HEA-REQ	
14	C	C		PMC34381EK	PLD		398	198	PER	DWC	RFL-ICE	
15	C	C		AKE41302EK			1346	1266	DWC	DWC	BUP-PER-S PX	
16	C	C		PMC79990EK	PLD		3892	3772	DWC	DWC	BUP-PER-S PX	
17	C	C		PMC34094EK	PLD		3234	3114	DWC	DWC	BUP-PER-S PX	
18	C	C		PMC73131EK	PLD		3050	2930	DWC	DWC	BUP-PER-S PX	
19	C	C		PMC75312EK	PLD		2480	2360	DWC	DWC	BUP-PER-S PX	
20	C	C		PMC37350EK	PLD		4876	4626	DWC	DWC	PER-BUP-S PX	
21	C	C		PMC33974EK	AMX	Q5	2250	2129	DXB	DWC	RFL-SPX-H EA-CAO-EC C	
22	C	C		PAG02495EK	AMX	Q4	1510	1479	BAH	DWC	HEA-SPX-E CC-ELI	
23	C	C		PMC35925EK	AMX	Q5	3322	3199	DWC	DWC	SPX-HEA	51 INCHES W-O BOTH ENDS
24	C	C		PMC74209EK	AMX	Q5	3178	1995	CAI	DWC	ECC-SPX-H EA-AXA	
25	C	C		PMC30661EK	AMX	Q5	2236	2115	DXB	DWC	ELI-SPX-EC C-HEA	
26	C	C		PMC75948EK	AMX	Q5	2366	2234	LLW	DWC	SPX-ECC	
27	C	C		PMC78094EK	AMX	Q5	1444	1322	SYD	DWC	SPX-ECC-A XA-HEA	
28	C	C		PMC78584EK	PMD	Q6	3174	3030	BOM	DWC	SPX-ECC-H EA-AXA	
29	C	C		PMC79939EK	PLD		1028	922	DXB	DWC	SPX-HEA	
30	C	C		ALF8081BEK			992	796	BAH	DWC	HEA-SPX	
31	C	C		AKE41482EK			526	445	LOS	DWC	SPX	
32	C	C	U	PMC72935EK	PLD		1492	1383	DWC	DWC	HEA-SPX	
33	C	C		PMC36310EK	AMX	Q5	1188	1126	BLR	DWC	SPX-HEA-E CC	60 INCHES R-T AFT

Total: 33 Units 33DWC 4Q4/14Q5/1Q6/ 77536 71607

Bulk Load:

Change Ind: C = Created, U = Updated, D = Deleted   LC = Load Category, C=Cargo, M=Mail, Q=Courier

Date: 20-Aug-15 14:49:57   Page 1 of 2   ReportID: EXP005R

Fig. VII.27: Sample of a UWS.

The cargo section, after completion of the cargo build-up, will take the trolley or ULDs for weighing. Then they will complete the UWS, giving the list of all the cargo, mail, courier ULDs for the flight, with ULD serial numbers, net weight, gross weight, height codes, and any special loads in the ULDs. Loads for bulk hold loading on ULD-version aircraft will also be given in the same UWS. For bulk-loading aircraft cargo, it will be trolley's reference instead of ULD's, the rest of the details except height code will be available in the UWS. The UWS is passed to the load controller for planning and another copy is given to the loading team as well, for their information and cross-checking with the LIRF. Any addition or deletion subsequently till flight finalized by cargo section will come as edition 1 or 2, etc. and finally, with a final UWS. This process may vary from airport handling to airport handling, based on local set-up. Sometimes there will be only one UWS and no changes thereafter. The UWS forms a consolidated list of all shipments or loads that is planned for the particular flight other than baggage. It will have details specific to that flight only.

5) Offloading/Loading Instruction Form and Report – LIRF (*See specimen, figure.VII.28*):

This is the most important document for the loading team. It is a legal document and as such special care must be taken in reading it, following the instructions, and completing it with all relevant information/details. It is the formal communication between the load control officer and the loading team. It is issued by the load control officer. What is this document? If it is an offloading instruction form, then:

a. It will have the flight number, date, origin, destination, and issued by details.
b. It is itemized information to the loading team of what is in the hold of an incoming flight and what they need to offload in their airport.
c. Based on the diagram or layout of the hold/compartment/position, it will say what was loaded from the previous airport and what needs to be unloaded and what must stay on board (if there is transit load on board). It will state the category of the item, such baggage (priority/economy), cargo, etc. and the location in the hold. The ULD serial numbers, gross weight, and in some cases, volume in each ULD will also be shown.
d. It will give special information if there are special shipments like live animals, dangerous goods, valuables, etc.
e. It will give instructions to be followed, such as steps to be taken to maintain ground stability, etc.

The above details and instructions will be shown in the offloading or arrival section of the LIRF. If it is loading, similar to offloading above, it will give details of the joining load/ ULDs (and of the transit loads if transit load is on board) and where each item is to be loaded Also, if shifting of transit load is required, that also will be specifically mentioned.

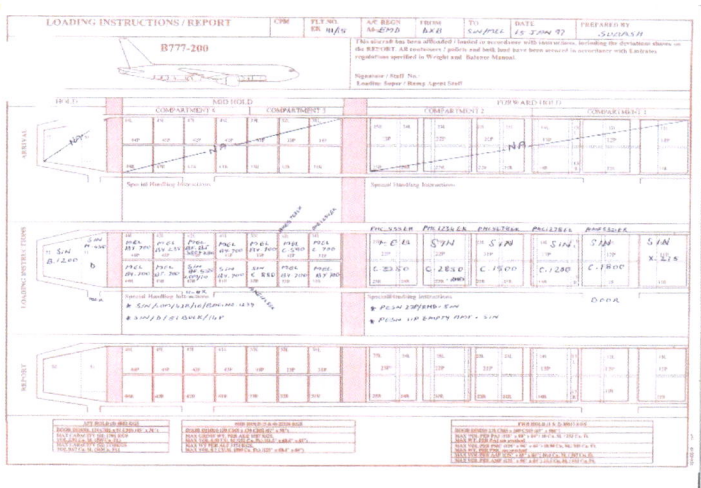

Fig. VII.28: Sample loading instruction copy.

There are manual and automated printed versions. It is important that the language and instructions are clear and understandable. Use only approved abbreviation as much as possible due to space constraints and the need to include all relevant details. The automated versions are usually customized for offloading or loading only or for both, including transit handling. Nowadays, many loading teams use CPM for offloading, as it contains all the necessary information to offload an aircraft. To give greater understanding, it is better to analyze the manual offloading/loading instruction form and report. For convenience, let us use the abbreviations LIRF. All airlines customize the LIRF used for their flights. Some have three parts or sections, first will be offloading (with transit load details, if applicable); the second section is the loading (joining ULDs with serial numbers, weight, destination of load is contains, load category (if baggage, then whether it is priority, or economy, or transfer, etc.), volume, etc. at that airport as planned by the load controller; and the last section or third part of the LIRF is the reporting part, to be filled completely by the loading team leader, inclusive of deviations/changes from those mentioned in the second section by the load controller. It should specify the actual loaded information in the aircraft after completion of the loading process when doors are closing for departure. After the second section is issued by the load controller, there can be changes such as last minute addition or offloading of cargo due to various reasons, increase or decrease in baggage, etc.

Please note, when the load controller issues the LIRF with the first part completed only, it is called the offloading instruction, or in other words, when the LIRF contains only details of unloading at an airport, that official form in which he gives the details is called the offloading instruction. When the first and second part of LIRF is completed and issued by the load controller, then it is called an offloading and loading instruction. When only the second or loading part of the LIRF is completed and issued by the load controller to the loading teams, then the LIRF is called a loading instruction. Finally, when the last or third part is completed by the loading team leader (only) based on changes or otherwise if it is the same as the loading instruction with no change, even then he still has to complete the third part and sign it with his staff number. Now the loading instruction becomes loading instruction report (LIR). Here, for ease of understanding, we will abbreviate and refer to them collectively as LIRF. Nowadays there are various automated computerized programs that are used to plan the loads, check the aircraft trim – or in other words, the aircraft balance, and print the loading instruction.

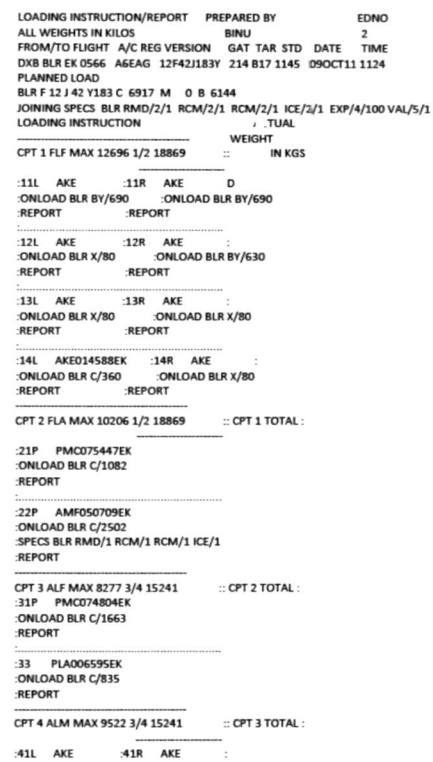

Fig. VII.29: Sample of automated LIRF (loading only).

It is important rule to note the following:
1) Any addition or decrease, or changes in load categories is to be advised by the load controller to the loading team leader, or if the information is received from other valid or authorized sources, then verify with the load controller.
2) Any amendments or changes or deviations to the loading sequences or process, other than those mentioned by the

load controller in the second section, are to be approved by the load controller before applying to the loading process.
3) Once cleared by the load controller and changes completed physically, immediately update in the third report section.
4) The report section is to be completed by the loading team leader, with all details, even if no changes are made to the planning given by the load controller in the second instruction section above.
5) The report should be clear; after completion, signed with the staff number, verified by the load controller in person with proper debriefing, and handed over to the load controller before he gets the load sheet signed by the captain.

Automated LIRF for a departure flight may not have the report section. Here a new LIRF is printed and issued to the loading team leader in case of amendments or changes.

The following are some of reasons for the necessity and importance of the LIRF:

1) It avoids ambiguity and gives clarity to the job to be performed. There will be more than one personnel involved and thus it avoids distortion along communication lines.
2) LIRF gives a tool for the load controller to put down in writing his planning and further instruction to be carried out by the loading team. He must have arrived at the planning based on various factors, such as aircraft ground stability, aircraft balance, loading sequence, load category, airline requirements based on operational, commercial, or customer service aspects.
3) It gives legality to the process completed by the loading team and increases accountability.
4) It allows the load controller to verify if his instructions were followed and if they have not been, corrective steps can be taken prior to aircraft departure.
5) It forms the basis for the preparation of other legal documentation such as the load sheet and trim sheet prepared by the load controller.
6) It ensures safety of flight as manual activity performed and completed is in sync with the operational requirement of the aircraft.

7) It ensures service delivery to customers. The loading teams are able to identify easily the incoming loads segregated based on priority of offloading and then dispatch them to appropriate areas for further handling, e.g. baggage to baggage arrival area, cargo to cargo section, etc. For loading, if any loads are missing, they are able to identify and alert concerned sections.
8) Sufficient resources such as manpower, equipment, dollies for ULD transportation, trolleys for bulk load, etc. can be planned, arranged, and retrieved based on the offloading or loading requirements and progress. This can be verified by the related sections.
9) It is a record as well for future reference and will form part of the flight documents file.

Above are just some of the reasons for their importance and there are many more as well.

6) Baggage reconciliation report:

Baggage checked in for a flight are sent to the baggage build-up area for loading on trolleys to be sent for bulk-loading aircrafts or built into appropriate ULDs for dispatch to the aircraft for loading for ULD-version aircrafts. Prior to loading or build-up, the tag numbers are recorded against the trolley or ULD it is being loaded into. After check-in closes, the final numbers are tallied with actual loaded. This recoding can be done manually by writing on a sheet of paper or recording sheets or automatically if scanners are available and baggage tags are scanned while loading or build-up is being carried out at the baggage area. The baggage reconciliation reports shows the flight number, destination, the baggage tag numbers, with segregation based on which ULD (with ULD serial number) it is loaded in, etc. Some reports will show the baggage check-in sequence number, total bags, time of check-in, time of loading in ULD, etc. The two main reasons for this document are:

1) It forms a record and will form part of the flight file.
2) And importantly, it is used to locate bags if necessary. The final summary list of the baggage reconciliation sheet will also say how many ULDs or trolleys in total were made for that particular flight and sent to the flight for loading and how many empty ULDs were there. The loading team will be able to check if all received against what is loaded on board and on the ground near the aircraft.

So any missing ones can be easily located or the concerned alerted.

It must tally with the load controller's final confirmation of load debriefing before the loading team signs the LIRF.

After check-in, some passengers are not able to travel or go missing in the terminal or elsewhere. As per ICAO security regulation, no baggage should be on board a flight without the accompanying passenger on board. There are some exceptions in case of rush baggage after certain security requirements and screening are completed. So if there are a large number bags, it would be impossible to locate the bags and the flight could be delayed for a long time. Hence, with the baggage reconciliation list, it is possible to pinpoint the exact location of the baggage quickly and retrieve it. Also, at the transit station also it is possible to locate the baggage. It assists with recording for future reference. The automated baggage reconciliation system also records additional information, such as who scanned it, at what time, and at what time the ULD or trolley was dispatched to the aircraft etc. The baggage reconciliation list acts somewhat like the UWS for baggage.

7) Notification to captain / airman – NOTOC. (*See specimen, figure. VII.30)*.

SPECIAL LOAD NOTIFICATION TO CAPTAIN

STATION OF LOADING	DXB	FLIGHT NUMBER	EK 9780	DATE	01/01/2017	AIRCRAFT REGISTRATION	A6-EFD	PREPARED BY	SUBASH			

Station of Unloading	Air Waybill Number	Proper Shipping Name	Class or Division for Class 1 compat. Grp.	UN or ID Number	Sub Risk	Number of Packages	Net quantity or Transp. Ind. per package	Radio-active Mater. Categ.	UN Packing Group	Code see Reverse	CAO (x)	Loading Position ULD	CPT
HKG	1761234561b	BENZIDINE	6.1	UN1885		01	2 Kg		II	RPB		AKE12345EK	

OTHER SPECIAL LOAD

Stn. of Unload	Air Waybill Number	Contents description	Number of packages	Quantity	Supplementary Information	Code see reverse	Loaded ULD	CPT,POS

Container loaded by: (To be signed by cargo staff)
XYZ
There is no evidence that any damaged or leaking packages containing dangerous goods have been loaded.

Aircraft loaded by: (To be signed by ramp staff)
There is no evidence that any damaged or leaking packages containing dangerous goods have been loaded.

Captain's Signature:

Other Information:

Distribution: (1) Aircraft Captain (Original) (2) Loadsheet Ship's Satchel (1st Copy) (3) Station File (2nd Copy)

Fig. VII.30: Sample NOTOC copy.

The aircraft may carry special goods or shipments such as dangerous goods, live animals, etc. These are identified and categorized in the IATA dangerous goods manual. The specifications, location on the aircraft and appropriate description needs to be advised to the operating captain in the applicable format using the NOTOC. It will be prepared by the staff accepting the item or shipment after checking the packing, documentation, etc. as necessitated and prescribed in IATA dangerous goods manual and also whether it is allowed for carriage. Normally, this will be from the cargo section as special shipments fly as cargo predominantly. The load controller will check if this shipment is to be loaded in any particular position of the aircraft hold, based on the property or nature of the shipment and whether the aircraft hold has the facilities available, etc. after consulting the IATA dangerous goods manual and airline weight and balance manual. For example, magnetic material will be needed to be loaded as far away from the flight deck as possible as the magnetic property may interfere with critical reading of the flight instruments located in the flight deck. Or live animals need to be loaded in holds with temperature and air ventilation available holds. Some shipments have tendency to react with each other and have the potential to cause undesirable effects such as fire, explosions, etc. Hence, the shipments are to be loaded separately, with the prescribed separation distance. There can be many such requirements and the NOTOC will give the necessary details and the load controller will advise the location in which it is to be loaded in the hold in the LIRF. There are also quick reference details also given at the rear page of the NOTOC. The loading team is also supposed to check for packing integrity, any leaks, verify tagging, labeling, etc. and then load as instructed. If any issues arise, then immediately inform load controllers or supervisor. When the NOTOC is brought to the aircraft, the loading team leader needs to update it with the actual hold location the item is loaded in the NOTOC and sign with his staff number. The NOTOC is taken by the load controller and given to the captain. It is necessary for the captain to verify the information and also take necessary precautions as necessary. If, for example, there are animals in the hold, he will need to ensure specific temperature settings are set in the flight deck for that hold. If there are dangerous goods and there is an indication of some issue while on ground or in air, then NOTOC will give him the emergency response drill to be undertaken by him. After the captain signs the NOTOC, a signed copy is retrieved for the station by the load controller and is kept on record in the flight file. The NOTOC is basically information to the crew as to what special shipment is carried on the flight and where it is loaded.

8) Flight handling check sheet (*See specimen, figure.VII.31)*:

FLIGHT HANDLING CHECK LIST (Freighters)

Flight No : _____
A/C : _____
Reg : _____
Routing : _____

Pre-flight Checks	Yes N/A		Yes N/A
1. Serviceable ULDs, straps, corner ropes, shoring, and dunnage materials pre-arranged.		**6.** UWS & NOTOC prepared, tallied, and released to all concerned.	
2. Estimate Load Message (ELM) released STD D-10 hours.		**7.** Coordinated with GHA, Catering, Fueler, and other stake holders for provision of resources & service.	
3. Inbound CPM/FFM tallied, in case of deviation, immediate corrective action taken.		**8.** All export cargo checked and arranged under the aircraft, including bulk cargo.	
4. Identified special loads (if any), undertaken prior arrangement to handle.		**9.** FOD check and briefing conducted with the loading team, sufficient resources arranged.	
5. Loading instruction issued by GHA as per airline Freighter W &		**10.** Serviceability check performed on joining units, pallet	

Aircraft Unloading and Loading

B Manual. Ensure loading instruction issued by authorized staff.

On-Ground Checks

1. Provision of GSE equipment on arrival, met and assisted the arrival crew and load master.

2. Handed over UWS NOTOC to the load master and obtained conformation to commence the offloading/loading.

3. Retrieved the inbound document pouch and offloaded incoming ULDs as per sequence on CPM, including bulk.

4. Incoming ULDs and bulk dispatched to the warehouse immediately.

nets, and corner ropes. If DG is planned, same properly loaded, segregated and free from leakage.

5. On-ground delay due to late offloading/loading or other reasons notified to Network Control Center +97147081000.

6. Export cargo document pouch placed on board.

7. Obtained/Retained signed copy of NOTOC, Flight Plan, LIRF (Loading Instruction), Load Sheet, and Freighter Safety Checklist from Captain / Load Master.

Post-flight Checks

1. Sent flight report to Network Control Center.

3. Sent post-flight messages i.e. CPM FFM, LDM, and

2. CPM tallied with FFM and all the Pre-alerts / On Board messages send.

Crew & Grooms
1. Crew HOTAC arrangements and wakeup call done as per the mail received from Dubai.
2. Prepared Gen-Dec and handover to GHA/Captain.
3. Escorted arrival/departure crew and directed them to transport vehicle, cleared immigration and hotel information.

Movement messages to all concerned.
Departed the flight in automated system.

4. Handed over Flight Plan, NOTAM, GD to Captain.

5. Crew/ Grooms bags are secured inside the aircraft.

6. In case grooms on board, they are listed in GD and sufficient oxygen bottles & masks are arranged.

Aircraft Unloading and Loading

Staff Name:_____ Staff No: Sign:_____

To be completed for all freighter flights by an authorized representative and/or cargo personnel at the point of departure.

Notes:

1. Cargo hold doors must not be opened during high speed winds.
2. Special precautions must be taken during inclement weather e.g. rain, snow, etc.
3. Ensure only trained and authorized personnel are involved in flight handling activities with approved equipment.
4. At all times the "Service Delivery" and "On Time" performance must not compromised with Safety/Security Procedures.

Distribution:
White copy: Departing station flight file
Pink copy: Retained with Office
                Version 1: 1st July 2015

Fig. VII.31: Flight handling checklist copy.

This can be manual card type or on automated handheld portable machines and designed based on airline and handling agent requirements and airport features, etc. It is a reminder to the loading team what are the checks to be done and mandatory processes to be followed, etc. For example, check all tags of the ULDs and cross verify against its contents, check and confirm the netting and lashing on pallets are secure and tight as required, check integrity of all ULDs and netting etc. This is to be signed and handed over with the LIRF to the load controller for records in the flight file.

9) Cargo and mail manifest (*See specimen figure. VII.32*):

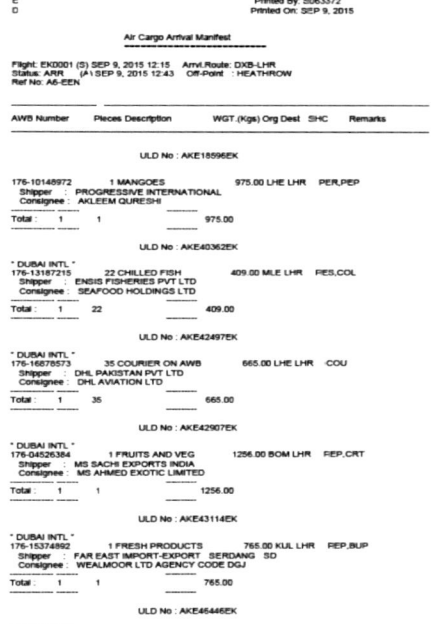

Fig.VII.32: Cargo and mail manifest copy.

In addition to the UWS for cargo, mail, courier, etc., these are separate manifests for each load item with more details of the cargo, courier, and mail being carried. It will basically give the ULD serial number, shipment air waybills loaded in it, number of pieces loaded out of the total, a brief description of the shipment as per the air waybill and weight. With the use of UWS, the importance of the cargo manifest to the loading team has diminished to some extent.

10) ULD Control Message – UCM:
UCM are sent by the ULD section. It gives only the list of all ULDs, with serial numbers, received or sent on board a flight. Even if the ULD is empty, the ULD will be included

in the list. It helps keep track of the movement of this valuable asset of the airline. The loading team can cross-check the ULDs on the flight with the help of the UCM and CPM. The ULD section prepares the UCM based on the report received from the loading team. UCM are sent for all departing flights that have ULD-version holds. The UCM specimen is as follows:

UCM
XH0566/25JAN.DXB
IN
.N
OUT
.AKE11385EK/BLR/C.AKE11686EK/BLR/Q.AKE13714EK/BLR/X
.AKE13757EK/BLR/B.AKE14424EK/BLR/B.AKE15516EK/BLR/B
.AKE16410EK/BLR/B.AKE17099EK/BLR/B.AKE18588EK/BLR/Q
.AKE19350EK/BLR/X.AKE41174EK/BLR/C.AKE42709EK/BLR/B
.AKE46154EK/BLR/B.AKE46184EK/BLR/X.AKE47964EK/BLR/B
.AKE48299EK/BLR/B.ALF80660EK/BLR/C.ALF80969EK/BLR/C
.AMF50531EK/BLR/C.PLA6637EK/BLR/C.PMC30549EK/BLR/C
.PMC30855EK/BLR/C
SI

Aircraft Loading Teams

Ramp knowledge is a very vague/general term because the ramp knowledge required for each function on the ramp is different specifically but is also overlapping. For example, the ramp knowledge of an aircraft pushback operator, a baggage handling team, an aircraft loading team are different, when it comes to their specific area, but are overlapping like when any one of them comes across a baggage lying unattended on the tarmac. They all know the steps to be taken, like informing security, their supervisor, the baggage handling supervisor, etc. They will also be able to read the tag and understand if it is an incoming/outbound bag or cargo, the flight number, etc. Here we will concentrate on the aircraft loading team.

The aircraft loading teams normally consists of four or more members per each flight. Based on function performed, they can be classified as follows:

1) Unloading only (if the flight is arriving and all load is for that airport) or

2) Loading only (aircraft was on ground, all inbound load was previously unloaded, and aircraft is supposed to be empty) or
3) Unloading and loading (flight arriving and then departing with full load change, no transit) or
4) Transit (arriving and departing flight, with transit load).

So they are called aircraft loading teams, in some airports they are given other names and sometimes given additional functions. It is not advisable to change teams unless they complete an allocated task, which would be either unloading all the incoming load for that station from the hold of an arriving flight, loading all the joining load into the hold of a departing flight, and in the case of transit flights, both offloading of inbound load, verifying the position of transit load in the hold (if applicable) and the loading of outbound load for departure. In some airports, in case of long ground times, one team may do the unloading and another may do the loading for transit flights. This practice is not advisable as it can lead to discrepancies and increase the chances of miscommunication. This is because if there is no proper handover between the two teams, then some vital information e.g. the need to unload and handover flight spares to the aircraft engineer before departure of the flight may not be conveyed to the team who will do the loading of the flight.

The members of the loading team complete their function collectively. This is because the unloading or loading process involves various functions such as identifying loads, sorting, positioning load, safety checks, operating loading equipment, operating the in-plane systems, etc. So there would be a team leader among them and the functions are shared or allocated by the team leader. The primary objective is to follow the instructions given by the load controller, complete the allocated tasks as per the requirement, and make a report, within the stipulated time.

The four functions mentioned above are very general, and we will go into it in more detail. Once a flight is allocated to the loading team leader, irrespective of which main function, the team leader needs to start the preparations. He will start by collecting the details, briefing, and planning arrangements, execution, debriefing, documentation, etc. All these can be categorized into three main stages of flight handling, namely:

Aircraft Unloading and Loading

a) Pre-flight: Collecting the details, briefing and planning, making arrangements and checks.
b) Flight handling: Execution of plan, coordination, finalization, and reconciliation, debriefing and checks.
c) Post-flight: Documentation.

The time plan can vary from airport to airport.

1) **Unloading process:**

This is applicable for an arrival flight. All shipments will be destined for the arriving airport and thus, all load needs to be unloaded. So starting with the first stage, the loading team leader action steps are as follows:

a) Pre-flight:
   i. Collecting details: Obtain the flight information sheet to check the origin, schedule, type of aircraft (if bulk-hold or ULD-version aircraft), etc. Next, obtain the CPM or offloading instruction from the load controller to check the amount of load coming in. If it is a bulk-hold aircraft, then LDM as there will not be a CPM. Get the incoming UCM to confirm receipt of ULDs after the flight.
   ii. Briefing and Planning: Check with the supervisor and flight accountable load controller for any special loads, special instructions, etc. Next, communicate the details and the briefing to the rest of the loading team, including the equipment operators allocated for the flight. Form a plan of action with the complete team. The main aim is the quick and smooth unloading of all loads based on priority of dispatch from aircraft to appropriate processing areas of the airport by maintaining agreed service level standards. Plan usage of minimum handling equipment as necessary to expedite release from aircraft as soon as possible, this will allow redeployment at other critical flights and multiple usage, reduce cost of operation, etc. Conduct a safety briefing to include safety checks, ensuring usage of personal protective equipment, etc. Make a plan of action with the team. Allocate responsibilities. Confirm understanding of the task at hand. Advise the plan to the dispatcher and load controller. Take into account all factors, such as equipment availability on

the ramp, ramp congestion, busy schedule, manpower availability, incoming load amount, etc.

iii. Arrangements: Make arrangements with respective sections for resources such as manpower, equipment, dollies/trolley, drivers with special rapid delivery vehicles for transporting urgent/priority baggage, cargo, etc., based on the incoming load. Sometimes based on the load, a parking bay may not have sufficient space for smooth handling. In this case the dispatcher or supervisor is to be informed and asked if possible for a bay change. If possible, then all arrangements are to be made on the new bay.

iv. Checks: Arrive at the parking bay ahead of flight arrival. Check to confirm all required resources are available; if any are missing, then call for the same and escalate if necessary to ensure all are ready prior to aircraft parking. Make FOD checks, remove any and dispose in appropriate FOD disposal collection point. Ensure to follow safety checks. Do not signal the captain or the marshaller when the aircraft is coming to park unless critically important or there is eminent danger. Ensure the dollies and trolley are lined up safely and brakes applied (*See figure.VII.33*).

Fig. VII.33.a.

Aircraft Unloading and Loading

Fig. VII.33.b.
Fig. VII.33: Flight handling area around an aircraft.

b) Flight handling:
   i. Execution of Plan: The loading team should start the plan of action agreed. Start with the correct sequence of unloading, based on aircraft ground stability requirement and priority of load for offloading and dispatch to concerned processing areas. Verify the CPM or offloading instruction information against actual found on board. As soon as the aft hold offloading is completed, check to make hold is empty, with no damages, and release the equipment which as in use for servicing that hold. Similarly, in the forward hold. Inform concerned department if there are any delays in dispatch or any discrepancy and annotate the same in the flight report.
   ii. Coordination: Keep all concerned sections informed of the dispatch of the various loads to their areas. Progress of the unloading is to be coordinated within the team to ensure smooth and expedite handling.
   iii. Finalization and Reconciliation: Verify all loads are unloaded as per the CPM and all holds are empty. Ensure all loads are dispatched from the aircraft.
   iv. Debriefing and checks: Discuss and obtain feedback from the team and debrief the load controller and

dispatcher if there are any matters of concern. Ensure the parking bays are clear of all inbound loads and FOD and all equipment is removed, and hold doors closed after the necessary safety checks.

c) Post-flight:
  i. Documentation: Complete the flight handling sheet and checklist with additional report if any discrepancy was noticed or encountered. Give UCM confirmation to the ULD section, confirming actual receipt of the ULDs received as per the incoming UCM and CPM. All of these are to be filed in the flight file.

2) Loading process:

This is applicable when an aircraft is on ground and departing to another airport or station. All loads are joining. The loading team leader steps of action are as follows:

a) Pre-flight:
  i- Collecting details: Obtain the flight information sheet to check the destination, schedule, type of aircraft (if bulk-hold or ULD-version aircraft), etc. Next, collect loading instruction from the load controller to check the amount and types of load joining and any special information.
  ii- Briefing and Planning: Check with the supervisor and flight accountable load controller issuing the loading instruction for any special loads, special instructions, etc. Reconfirm the ULD version to be used and if any changes are to be made the standard version. Next, communicate the details and the briefing to the rest of the loading team, including the equipment operators allocated for the flight, and allocate responsibilities and checks to be done. Form a plan of action with the complete team. The main aim is the quick and smooth loading of all loads positioned at the aircraft and those received from concerned processing centers based on sequence of loading and priority, in addition to agreed service level standards. Plan usage of minimum handling equipment as necessary and expedite release from aircraft as soon as possible, this will allow redeployment at other critical flights and multiple usage, reduce cost of operation, etc. Give a safety

briefing to include safety checks, ensuring usage of personal protective equipment, etc. Make a plan of action with the team. Allocate responsibilities. Confirm understanding of the task at hand. Advise the plan to the dispatcher and load controller. Take into account all factors, such as equipment availability on the ramp, ramp congestion, busy schedule, manpower availability, incoming load amount, etc.

iii- Arrangements: Make arrangements with respective sections for resources such as manpower and equipment to be available at the aircraft at the agreed time. Reconfirm the parking bay of the flight to the concerned departure load processing centers such as the baggage build-up area, cargo dispatch area, etc. Majority of the cargo will be at the aircraft earlier than 1hour of the schedule time of departure. This is because cargo, mail, etc. other than baggage are finalized well ahead of baggage. Whereas passenger check-in process normally closes about one hour prior to departure, after which the baggage is released to the baggage build-up area for build-up and dispatch to the aircraft side. Sometimes urgent last minute cargo can be expected with prior information from the load controller or the dispatcher.

iv- Checks: Based on the joining load, ascertain the amount of time required for the loading and arrive at the parking bay accordingly. Check to confirm all required resources are available; if any are missing, then call for the same and escalate if necessary to ensure all are ready prior to aircraft parking. Make FOD checks, remove any and dispose in appropriate FOD disposal collection point. Ensure to follow safety checks. Verify the availability of joining load or ULDs at the aircraft against the LIRF and UWS. Normally, approximately 60% of the baggage and all other load should be at the aircraft approximately 01hour and 15minutes before planned departure. The last remaining baggage should arrive at the aircraft from the baggage build-up area a minimum 30 to 40minutes before the schedule departure time. Any missing are to be followed up immediately with the processing sections, and keep the flight dispatcher advised.

Confirm the holds are empty and there are no damages. Start the handling checklist. Check the serviceability and integrity of the ULDs, lashing, netting, and other accessories before loading. The contour of the ULD and compatibility are also to be checked against the hold lay out. Check and reconfirm serviceability of locks in the hold, their alignment against the positions are to be in conjunction with the LIRF.

b) Flight handling:
   i- Execution of Plan: The loading team should start the plan of action agreed. Ensure the ULD or loads are lined up correctly in the designated area near the aircraft side for commencement of loading.

Fig. VII.34: Joining ULDs lined up near an aircraft.

Start with the correct sequence of loading based on aircraft ground stability requirement, priority of load for loading (with least priority in offloading at the destination to be loaded first). Sometimes the flight may be operating to multiple destinations; in this case, the loads for the next immediate airport will have priority and hence will be loaded last, near to the door area. The load controller will plan and advise accordingly. As soon as the forward hold loading is completed, and if no baggage is loaded in the forward hold, then release the equipment which is in use for servicing that hold. Unless there are no ULDS with other loads to be kept standby in the forward hold anticipating increase in baggage last minute. If we need to load the excess baggage ULD, which maybe received last minute for loading in the forward hold, then do not release the equipment. This plan would have been mentioned in the load plan by the load controller initially, if anticipated. Normally, the aft holds are used more for baggage loading as the baggage come later, and based on the sequence of loading, the load controller will plan all cargo in the forward. In this case it is sometimes possible to handle a flight with only one hi-loader. Complete the forward hold loading first and then reposition the hi-loader to the aft hold for commencing the loading there. Follow the loading based on the LIRF, the loading instruction section. Any special loads must be stowed accordingly and may require additional lashing. Verify the contents of the ULDs against the ULD tag, to be sure. All loose loading in compartment 5 is to be checked, counted, and confirmed. The bulk netting must be fully latched before closing doors. Maximization of space is important for loose bulk-loading aircraft, proper stacking and stowing of load will allow for sufficient space saved. This can avoid last minute issues due non-availability of space and then intervention from airline or others concerned to make space. Also, there will pressure due to insufficient time available. Never mix load different types of load in the hold or in an ULD.

ii- Coordination: Keep all concerned sections informed of late or missing loads, if any. If anticipating long delay, coordinate with the dispatcher and load controller to swap existing ULDs or loads at the aircraft with missing ones. This way the loading can be completed as much as possible and when the late or missing load (unless authorized by load control to offload) is received, it can be subsequently loaded later. All this should be done in coordination with the load controller. Progress of the loading to be coordinated within the team to ensure smooth and expedited handling. Although it is important to ensure safety of operation and commercial benefit to airline by loading all load as planned, it is also important to ensure the punctuality of schedule is adhered to. For this the loading activity must be completed with sufficient time for finalization and reconciliation before planned departure. If any issues are anticipated, keep the supervisor and dispatcher advised, if the same is beyond your control as well as when solutions by you can be administered. Delays can cause loss in revenue to the airline, additional charges, etc. Hence, it is important to ensure the loading is completed as planned before the schedule time. The airlines have a time path for each activity done and so loading is also included. Any baggage offloaded due to missing or offloaded bags must be done expeditiously after consulting the baggage reconciliation sheet or the appropriate reconciliation team for ascertaining the location of the bags. Reconfirm the tags after offloading with the dispatcher and keep away from other joining bags. The same is to be sent to appropriate processing area after the flight.

iii- Finalization and Reconciliation: The baggage reconciliation sheet will be send to the aircraft with the last bags. Once the loading is completed, verify all loads or ULDs against the UWS, baggage reconciliation sheet and the LIRF. Next, do a physical check of the parking area near the aircraft so as to ensure all joining loads for the particular flight are on board and a reconfirmation is done. Complete the LIRF report section with loading details, with any deviations, even if there is no change. Update the NOTOC and sign if there are any special loads, as applicable, and handover to the load controller.

iv- Debriefing and Checks Handover the completed LIRF report after signature to the load controller and summarize the same with the load controller. Particularly emphasize on any deviations between the initial instructions and the final. Discuss and obtain feedback from the team and debrief the load controller and dispatcher if there are any matters of concern. All these are to be done before the load controller takes the load and trim sheet to the captain for signature. Ensure the parking bays are clear of all loads / ULDs and FOD, and all equipment is removed and hold doors closed after the necessary safety checks.

c) Post-flight:
    i- Documentation: Complete the flight handling sheet and checklist, with an additional report if any discrepancy was noticed or encountered. A copy of the LIRF report can be given to the ULD section for sending the outgoing UCM, unless the same is automatically sent when the CPM is dispatched. All documents used are to be filed in the flight file.

3) Offloading and Loading: This is applicable when a flight is arriving and departing with full unloading and full loading.

Here the process will be a combination of the above for offloading and loading. Only for the pre-flight data or details collection, both the incoming offloading details and the joining loading instructions and other documents will be collected simultaneously. The ground time may be more constricted, especially if the flight is operating off schedule. Then some airlines tend to reduce ground time to make up for the delay. But they will also at the same time insist on loading all joining loads. The tasks involved are more and thus, due to the compounded requirement, additional manpower and resources may be arranged.

4) Transit handling: In this case too, it involves arriving offloading and departing with joining load handling, as mentioned above. Here the flight is arriving from an airport with load for your airport and also has load for the next airport or airports it is going to. Meaning, there will be transit load on board. In addition to the above three processes, the extra point to be noted is that the transit loads must be carefully handled to avoid missing any. It should be separately kept if necessary to unload and reload after loading joining loads. Sometimes the load controllers plan to keep the ULDs or load on board only, without the necessity for unloading and reloading. Reconfirm contents also. Care must be taken to avoid dispatch to inbound load processing sections. Sometimes due to space constraints, joining baggage may be topped up in transit baggage ULDs as per the load controller's plan. Ensure that the tags of baggage topped up and the category of baggage is also the same. Do not mix load different types of loads.

The above four are the main core functions of the aircraft loading teams.

In some airports the equipment operators are a separate team altogether.

Loading Equipment: The height of the aircraft hold is higher than the ground, for some aircrafts over 20 meters. So specialized equipment are required to reach that height to unload or load any load or ULD from or into a hold. A conveyor belt, with height adjustable front and rear ends, is required to unload or load a bulk-loading aircraft *(Ref to figure. VII.35)*.

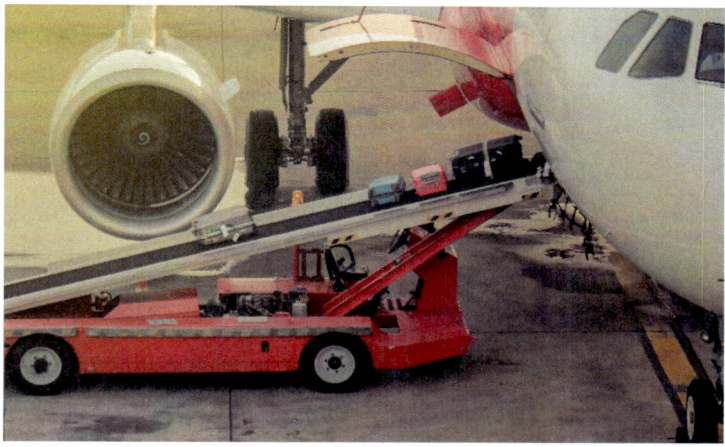

Fig. VII.35: Conveyor belt.

These are relatively easy to operate. If self-powered to move it from one aircraft to another, then only a licensed operator should drive it.

The other two equipment are more complex. First is the Hi-Loader, which is used in the unloading and loading of ULDs from or into the aircraft hold. It basically has a high platform (less area) and a lower platform (bigger area) *(See figures. VII.36)*.

Aircraft Unloading and Loading

Fig. VII.36: High loader or ULD High lift.

Both platforms have multi directional powered rollers on them. Only trained personnel should operate these equipment as they are positioned very close to the aircraft hold opening and must be aligned correctly so that aircraft doors do not come into contact with them while opening and also the ULDs can be moved in and out of the hold without them coming into contact with the edges, sides, and ceiling near the entrance to the hold *(Ref to figure. VII.37)*.

Fig. VII.37: Hi-Loader operation.

Aircraft Unloading and Loading

There are different hi-loaders with varying capacities. For freighter aircrafts and combi aircrafts, cargo can be loaded in the main deck also, which is higher than the lower holds and can also accommodate very heavy cargo. For this there are large capacity main deck hi-loaders *(See figure.VII.38)*.

Fig. VII.38: A main deck hi-loader on a freighter.

Next is the transporter *(See figures.VII.39)*, again a specialized equipment and the operator must be authorized to operate it.

Fig. VII.39: Transporter.

The ULDs for loading are brought to the aircraft on dollies and then are transferred by unlocking and pushing them onto a transporter. The transporter is basically a movable platform with powered rollers. Once the ULD is on it and is locked in position, it can then be driven to where the hi-loader is to discharge the ULD onto the lowered platform of the hi-loader. Similarly, vice versa for unloading. There are different types of transporters with varying capacities. Most of them can take a maximum of two ULDs with base dimension code K/P/V or one ULD with A/M/L/Q codes. The bigger ones are normally for G base code ULD but can also be used to accommodate four K/P/V or two A/M/L/Q ULDs. Its availability at an airport depends on the type of flights and cargo handled at an airport; again, it can be substituted by using appropriate dollies. There are equipment that perform the functions of a hi-loader and a transporter. The area near the holds of an aircraft can be very congested (Refer to figure. VII.40). with very little space to maneuver; it can be a beehive of activities. In some airports the tractors position the dollies directly adjacent to the lowered long platform of the hi-loader for unloading or loading ULDs to and from it.

Fig. VII.40: Aircraft handling area around an aircraft.

Hence, this equipment is not an absolute necessity. There are advantages and disadvantages of not using a transporter. Some of the common disadvantages are:

- The tractor driver must be sufficiently trained and capable of positioning the ULDs correctly, due to the space constraints caused by the catering service hi-loader trucks that may be positioned on either side of the hi-loader. If not properly trained, a lot of time may be wasted trying to position, remove, or reposition the dolly to reduce the gap, or for proper alignment between the dolly and the hi-loader.
- If the dolly is not properly positioned, the ULD may fall off or tilt when while moving from or onto the dolly and hi-loader. This can cause damage to the ULD and its contents, which potentially dangerous for the staff around it, and it is also time-consuming to rectify the problem.
- While loading there is the danger that the ULD or the contents on a pallet may cause damage to the aircraft engine or the catering equipment due to the close proximity.

Aircraft Unloading and Loading

The advantages are:

- Reduced costs of not procuring these expensive equipment and hence, their maintenance. Also, tractors are cheaper than transporters.
- The operator can be used elsewhere if necessary. Since there is always a need for a tractor at an aircraft site for transportation or repositioning of load appropriately, there is maximum use of a tractor.
- The loading or unloading process can be expedited using a tractor in some cases.

Special Shipment Ramp Handling (VAL/Vehicle/PER/DGR & RRY/AVI)

There are special loads, usually cargo (in some cases can be as baggage, e.g., falcons) that are carried by airlines. The loading teams handling these special loads need to take extra care while offloading or loading and making arrangements. Each will have separate handling requirements. Some of the frequent shipments are:

1) Valuables – VAL: These shipments can be of high value, like bank notes, gold bullion, etc. Some of the special handling features are as follows:

i. If incoming, then the shipment needs to be offloaded immediately and handed over to the security escort after verifying the total number and air waybill against the manifest. Get signature of handover from the security escort.
ii. These will be brought under security escort closer to the departure time for loading.
iii. Should be loaded last near the door area, after verifying the total number and air waybill number against the manifest and LIRF. The escort will ask for signoff on appropriate documentation.
iv. The quantity will be normally small and may be loaded in appropriate security boxes for loading in bulk-hold or lockable ULDs, based on the airline specification.

      v.   Since these shipments can be dense, heavy lots will need appropriate securing with lashing, even if loaded in ULDs.

     vi.   Ensure to annotate on the LIRF, and verify details on the NOTOC, and update with loading position on aircraft.

2) Vehicle: Sometimes customers send cars on the flight. Most cars come under the category of restricted miscellaneous dangerous goods as per IATA dangerous goods manual. If the load ability check is carried out against the load-ability chart for the aircraft hold, the chart will probably show that it is not loadable due to exceeding the door dimension allowed. However, most cars are loadable due to the maneuverability of the cars. The acceptance will do the necessary checks if loadable and process other mandatory compliance requirements, as prescribed by IATA dangerous goods manual and airline manual. At the aircraft the loading team will need to make advance preparation for handling, in addition to processing special unconventional handling capabilities as well. This will need additional manpower and support from senior loading team leaders initially or if handling for the first time. Some of the handling aspects are as follows:

      i.   If loading on the flight, plan to start early loading process at least 30mins in advance, consult the load controller, and check if one or two positions are required, arrange for empty pallets and lashing belts (two for each wheel) at the aircraft. The car may come to aircraft palletized, but may not be possible to load as it may not be able to go through the door in the palletized condition. If any other ULDs are planned beyond the planned car loading position, complete the loading of those ULDs. First load the empty pallets on the planned position as per the LIRF, then engage the locks. Also load additional empty pallets till the door. Now take the keys of the car, which will be attached to its air waybill, and insert in the ignition without switching on the engine. This is only to free the locked steering. Load the palletized car onto the hi-loader, lift and bring to the door area and remove the lashing. Next, with sufficient manpower slowly roll the vehicle into the hold with one experienced driver steering.

Aircraft Unloading and Loading

Extra care must be taken to avoid the tires or body of the car coming in contact with the aircraft floor or the walls at any time. You may also need to push back and forth to get sufficient clearance when turning into the hold. Position sufficient look outs around the car to warn the driver and others. The driver can operate the brakes in addition to the steering. Once rolled onto the allocated position as per the LIRF, lash each wheel tightly with two belts (one towards the forward and one towards aft of the car) onto the pallet. Use the wheel spokes and only certified lashing belts. Remove the excess pallets not required, switch off the ignition completely, and attach the keys to the air waybill. Recheck the lashing again before closing doors, and ensure lights are switched off. Update in LIRF and NOTOC and sign.

ii. If unloading from flight, remove all ULDs in front of the car, if any, and then load empty pallets and lock them. Then similar to loading, but now in reverse order, unload the vehicle. Once the vehicle is out of the hold, rebuild it on an empty pallet and lash it for transportation to the cargo handling area / terminal.

3) Perishables – PER: These can be fruits, vegetables, newspapers, etc. that are time sensitive and can get spoiled or lose value with time elapse. ULDs loaded with perishables can be heavy and difficult to unload at times due to the dense nature of these shipments. Also, a huge amount of fruits and vegetable in the hold can cause a steamy atmosphere that can cause the power rollers to slip under the ULD base. These shipments will need to be dispatched as soon as unloaded from aircraft, before other general cargo. Some airports have cool dollies that are air conditioned for transportation of perishables on the ramp. When loaded in the aircraft, some shipments like fresh meat will need extremely cold temperatures. The captain will be informed through the NOTOC to set the temperature accordingly; however, the loading team must try to complete the loading as soon as possible and close the doors to keep the temperature cold in the hold. Sometimes perishable items such as vaccines need extremely cold temperature and may have dry ice loaded with it in the packing. Avoid touching or staying in close proximity of it, especially in the hold for a long time, as it is carbon dioxide in gaseous form.

4) Dangerous goods – DGR and Radioactive Material – RRY: Some items (as part of baggage or as cargo, courier, etc.) may pose a potential risk or danger to the environment around it, the aircraft, crew, airport employees, etc. These may by itself be dangerous or become dangerous if they interact with other categories, etc. IATA has categorized approximately 3,000 items known by its committee of experts as such. There are specific requirements for their packing, marking, labeling, storage, transportation, handling, stowing, etc. when carrying by air. The main aim is safe handling, storage, and carriage. Many types of dangerous goods and radioactive material can be transport by air, in prescribed quantities and packing, as specified by IATA dangerous goods manual. They are categorized into various classes. The main aspects to be followed by the loading team are:

    i. When mentioned in the CPM or LIRF, check physically the location and verify shipment orientation if applicable; make sure it is tagged and labeled correctly, which should tally with the documentation.
    ii. There should not be any leakage, damage, or other issues. If otherwise, immediately inform your supervisor and clear the area.
    iii. If it is on a ULD, it must be accessible for checking.
    iv. Some DGR shipments may react with other DGR shipments due to chemical properties, and hence, sufficient separation, as mentioned in LIRF and NOTOC, must be followed while loading.

5) Live animals – AVI: Live animals when carried must be planned in hold with air and temperature controlled atmosphere. Some of the handling aspects for the loading team are as follows:

    i. If loading, then load last near the door area and lash to avoid movement.
    ii. If there are chances of leakage from cages or containers with animals, first place plastic sheet and absorbent material under before lashing them down. Ensure to arrange these in advance before proceeding to the flight for loading. The lashing belt may also need latching pins as these may not be available in the hold.
    iii. At the aircraft do not try to feed, talk to, or try to attract the attention of the animal. Keep them at a shaded area

if there is any delay in loading. Avoid contact with the animal.
iv. Ensure the cage or container is properly locked or door secured on receipt at aircraft. If inbound CPM shows AVI, open the door gradually, anticipating a possibly open cage, then check to confirm the cage door is locked.
v. Follow segregation requirements shown in NOTOC when loading AVI and other special loads.
vi. When handling live bees, always wear protective clothing as there are chances of bees escaping from the cages.
vii. All labeling, tagging, and details must correspond with the documentation. Ensure to reconfirm the destination of the AVI before unloading at an airport; if there is any confusion, reconfirm.
viii. AVI can be transported as baggage and cargo. So ensure to check the correct load type before dispatching from the aircraft as the processing of baggage and the cargo terminals may be far apart and the AVI may be difficult to retrieve if sent to the wrong terminal. If it is transported as baggage, its anxious owner may be waiting for it at the baggage arrival area.
ix. Some airports have specialized transportation vehicles for AVI. Ensure to arrange for the same when expecting inbound AVI. Expedite dispatch to the appropriate area on arrival to avoid it trying to escape and to reduce the undue stress on the animal, since the ramp environment may be distressing for it.
x. If AVI is not received for loading at the aircraft latest by 40mins to departure, immediately inform the concerned section and supervisor.

The loading team forms the physical presence of the load controller. All that is planned and required by the load controller is brought into reality by the loading team. They are the inseparable two sides of the same coin. Therefore, it is important for both to be in tandem and work in close cooperation. This makes perfect symbiosis for mutual benefit and smooth operation that will be safe, commercially beneficial, and punctual, with minimum utilization of valuable resources. The innovative, professional approach and tireless efforts of the loading team can make the biggest positive impact on the handling capability and efficiency of any handling company, enabling it to give world-class quality services to customer airlines.

****

Chapter VIII
Aircraft Weight and Balance (Load Control)

Introduction

The primary objective of the load controller can be summarized as the planning of the flight in such a way that the safety of operations is enforced at all times, maximum commercial benefit is derived through the maximum utilization of space, minimum utilization of resources and time occurs, within the applicable governing rules and regulations of his or her company, the airline, affiliated global body regulations, and the country. So, in short, it is an all-encompassing function to ensure operational, commercial, and punctual handling of a flight. An aircraft has certain maximum capacity regarding how much can be accommodated on a flight. On ground or in the air, it acts is like a manual weight and balance scale that you would find at the local grocers or supermarket. Put a heavier item in the pan on one side than the weights in the pan on the other side, and that side will tilt down. The speed at which the tilt takes place depends on the distance from the center and the weight difference. So the weights are adjusted to attain equilibrium (trimming) in relation to the center of gravity of the scale. The center of gravity of the aircraft usually lies in the area between the wings. Therefore, all aircrafts will have a center of gravity, and based on where each item is loaded in the aft of the wing and forward areas, the balance of the aircraft shifts accordingly (trim effect). Also, each position will have a certain limit to the amount of load that can be loaded based on the structural limitation of the material and design used to build the aircraft. All of this can be understood to be the basic functions of the load control.

These limits are set by the manufacturers of the aircraft. In addition, there are various other limitations, restrictions, requirements, regulations, etc. that need to be considered while loading anything on an aircraft to ensure its safe operation. It is, therefore, the prime responsibility of the load control staff, or in other terms load controller, to ensure all these factors are considered while planning the allocation of loads on an aircraft. His instructions and finally, the documents prepared are legal and necessary for the operation of flight. To function as a load controller, formal training and licensing from a recognized training provider is necessary. In addition, some airlines also need load controllers to undergo their customized licensing as well before a load controller can handle their flights. In addition, it is necessary for the load controller to complete the IATA dangerous goods familiarization training as well. Another highly preferable requirement is for the potential load controllers to have loading team background as well. A good understanding of the preceding chapters will be necessary for progressing in this chapter.

Chapter Contents

> Commercial and operational plan
> Principle aim
> Aircraft upper deck
> Weights and load sheet.
> Aircraft balance (trim), index, and trim sheet
> Factors for load planning
> Load Planning (LIRF, coordination, verifying, finalizing, and post-flight).
> Automation and centralized load control.

****

*Aircraft Weight and Balance
(Load Control)*

Commercial and Operational Plan

The commercial team of the airline will analyze commercial benefits of operating flights to a station. The main commercial factors that are analyzed are: potential interest in the market, the possible revenues that can be generated, cost of operation, competition, and their load factor and pricing, etc. In addition, commercial risk factors and peak and off peak periods, holiday trends and other aspects that can cause revenue fluctuations, etc. are considered. For example, in the Middle East, there are many countries that rely on economic migrant workers from the subcontinent and Far East for working in their construction and hospitality industries. The school vacation season starts in the month July till August in the Middle East and it is the peak of summer as well, so there is huge outflow of the population during the first week of July and return by the last week of August or first weeks of September. So during these times, the airlines increase the fares due to high demand. Here what must be noted is that migrant expatriates tend to carry lots of huge baggage when they go on holidays due non-availability of quality household items in their home countries, availability of cash at hand, cultural requirements, etc. And on return, they bring almost negligible baggage or small bags. So as a planner, during these months, depending on the sector, greater capacity should be allocated for the baggage and less space for other loads in the holds. On the return, more space can be allocated to other load and to attract cargo customers, special low rates can be given. All this is to maximize the revenue. Another example is that during other times, since the Middle East region is situated almost in the middle between the west and the east plus Australasia, the airlines in the region are better placed to convey passengers between these regions with the least operational cost. So there is high potential for transit passengers as well. In this case, the baggage size and weights are more or less standard in both ways, as the passengers are tourists.

The operational analysis takes the resultant data from the commercial analysis for scrutinizing the operational plan; for example, based on anticipated load, revenue, and cost, which is the most preferable type of aircraft available in the airline fleet that can reap the highest commercial benefit for the company, what are the reciprocal traffic rights and bilateral agreements between the country where the airline is registered and the country to which the operation is planned or whether it between two other foreign countries, etc. (freedom of air transport), does the destination airport have any restrictions, and does it have sufficient infrastructure to handle the flight, what is the political climate of that country (safety of aircraft and crew), etc.

After all these analysis, if the results are positive, the airline will start operations after the necessary approvals and agreements are in place. Flights schedules will be published and opened for bookings. So that potential passengers, cargo customers, courier companies, etc. can start buying tickets or space on the flight accordingly. This can be done as soon as the airline publishes the schedule and is open to take bookings. Most airlines have a reservations system which can be accessed by travel agents (for cargo through freighter forwarders/agents) or otherwise directly through online internet access, which gets updated in the airline reservation or cargo system accordingly.

Passenger and Cargo Load Relations

What must be noted is that traditionally, for a passenger airline, its first priority are passengers and their baggage, cargo and other loads are incremental revenue that are added bonuses. However, lately, passenger airlines are also upgrading and giving more attention to their cargo solutions as well, since the potential is huge. Cargo and other load revenue supplement the passenger load revenue. Many a times, even in slack passenger load seasons, or in low demand sectors airlines are able to maintain a profitable schedule due to cargo revenues generated. Another reason is that transfer cargo brought in from one sector maybe for another sector destination, depending on the airline network, so one sector may act as a feeder for another sector. Similarly, if an airline has both passenger and freighter aircraft network, then both can complement each other and loads are transferred between them to ensure an overall profitability increase. Cargo from multiple passenger flights can be consolidated to fill up one freighter aircraft. Also, cargo customers benefit due to greater accessibility to otherwise inaccessible stations/markets when the airline network is vast.

As a load controller, you must be aware of the different requirements when loads are transferred between different aircraft types, although these are normally handled by the cargo planning sections. Different aircrafts have different hold specifications. For example, all ULDs from a freighter cannot be loaded on a passenger aircraft and vice versa. Passenger seat numbers and configuration will vary from aircraft to aircraft types.

Hence, all the sales efforts, promotions, bookings, negotiations, preparations, acquiring of resources, etc. involve months of efforts, intelligence, planning, initiatives, commitments, and huge investments from various departments, internal and external service providers, all of which culminate in and are put into reality when the load controller derives all the accumulated data and plans the flight, gets the loading team to load all planned loads, when the aircraft finally departs and arrives safely at its destination. The commercial and planning team may overbook the flight and excess space may be released, anticipating last minute cancelation from customers (both passengers and cargo). The idea is to maximize the load on the flight. This may cause a very tight and pressurized atmosphere when the load controller plans the flight. The spotlight may be on him to ensure all loads are accommodated. Thus, careful planning and full cooperation from the loading team can mean success in uplifting all load safely. The success of a flight is when the planned loads are uplifted safely.

Principle Aim

The load controller's main aim is to accommodate all the planned load on the flight after careful analysis of the load, by satisfying all the applicable regulations, requirements of the airline and authorities, invoking the correct organizationally accepted procedures, and utilizing minimal resources.

Here analysis of load would mean the priority of loading and offloading, special handling requirements for the special shipments, avoiding mix loading of different loads or categories, etc. he must avoid over-stowing with less priority load of high priority loads. Another important part for the load controller is that he must find options to safely load all planned load if possible, within the safety and procedural realms of planning and handling. This is to avoid offloading of planned loads last minute. There are many regulations that govern the carriage of load on a flight. Civil aviation is a highly regulated industry, with many agencies involved; for example, ICAO, IATA, the civil aviation authorities of both the departing airport country and the destination airport country. And all have applications in load control functions.

The customer, such as passengers, cargo customers, etc. have requirements when they pay the airline for services. For example, when a passenger buy a ticket, he expects the airline to transport his bags also. This is his requirement. Now he may have 50kilos, but the airline will put in place a condition that only 30kilos will be the free allowance, anything above will be charged. So the airline will streamline that requirement. The passenger may have a requirement to get his bags as early as possible on arrival. Here the airline will translate the requirement to ensure the first-class bags reach the arrival carousal within 10mins of aircraft arrival. So the load controller will plan the bags near to the door area, so that they are unloaded first at the destination and are able to be delivered as per the airline requirement. Such requirements are set by the airline. Similarly, the handling company may say that only one hi-loader will be provided for a flight during peak times. So the load controller will plan with all cargo in the forward and bags in the aft hold, so that the loading can be completed quickly and then the high loader can be repositioned to the aft hold. The airport authorities, including aviation governing agencies like the ICAO and IATA, require all changes to the load on board an aircraft to be depicted in the load sheet prior to departure and for the crew captain to indicate approval for same in the form of his signature. This automatically also becomes an organizational requirement as well. Further, the organization of the load controller may require him or her to check the cargo load before planning to get an idea of the space required to load it, considering the priority is for baggage loading. This is applicable for bulk-loading aircraft, which allows for more accurate planning, gives more options, and will avoid last minute changes or offloading. Resources, even if in excess, are to be used sparingly, as minimal use also reduces cost and protects the environment against pollution. Aviation manpower have specialized knowledge and skills and equipment are specific and expensive. So their use also should be controlled. The staff should have sufficient rest between flights, as the external conditions can be stressful and their jobs are critical in regards to safety.

Aircraft Weight and Balance
(Load Control)

Aircraft Upper Deck

The lower holds of the aircraft was extensively covered in the previous chapter. The load controller needs to have an understanding of the deck above. It is worthy to mention the A380-type aircraft, where the upper deck has an extended double upper deck as well. The upper deck is normally divided into various sections in a passenger aircraft. Some airlines have various classes of travel, like priority class, which is divided into first and business classes. Economy may be further divided. These are based on the level of services and comfort required by the passengers and the amount they are willing to pay for it. Some airlines have only a priority class and an economy section or only economy and so on. It all varies from airline to airline and their mode of operation, sector flown, market demand for a particular class, type of aircraft in its livery, etc. The class or number of classes in the upper deck are collectively called configuration. So the configuration can vary from airline to airline, aircraft type to aircraft type, and within the same aircraft type as well. It is possible for an airline to change from a single class configuration to a multi-configuration in a short time by making changes to the seating and other interior fittings and amending the in-flight service provided. There will not be any necessity to make any change in the lower holds. The upper deck typically comprise of, from front to aft, the following:

1) The flight deck, with seating for operating crew and additional two to three seats for engineers or additional crew.
2) The galleys (catering carts, amenities, food, drinks, plates, duty-free goods, pillows, blankets, etc.)
3) Overhead stowage compartments along the full length of the aircraft above each seat
4) Crew seating
5) Priority class cabin or area (seats will be more comfortable, with more leg room, which means fewer seats and occupants)
6) Toilets
7) Mid Galleys
8) Economy class seating
9) Toilets
10) Crew seating or crew rest cabin

11) Finally, the passengers who are on board in various classes, their hand carry bags and their checked bags (which after check-in, are not accessible for passengers till the destination arrival hall and are loaded in the lower holds during the journey).

The airline personnel or crew on board a flight normally are:

1) The flight deck crew
2) Cabin crew
3) In case of some airlines or sometimes there can be an engineer or load master on board. This is because of some special reason or mainly due to non-availability of certified engineer or load master at the en-route airport.
4) Some airlines may position crew in advance to operate the next flight back (either the same flight or a later flight). Crew duty times are governed by a strict set of regulations, which must be adhered to by all airlines. Sometimes on long sector flights, there can be additional crew on board due to crew duty time limitations. The duration is applicable differently for the flight deck crew and the cabin crew.
5) On sectors with increased safety threat, the aviation or security authorities will require airlines to send an air marshal or security staff.

When there are engineers or load masters on board, they will be marked as Engineer or as LM in the General Declaration. Additional crew operating on a flight are shown with all other crew as one set. When there is crew positioned to operate the same or a later flight, they are referred to as dead heading (DHD) crew in the General Declaration. It is mandatory that all on board a flight must have a proper certified seat with seat belts. The operating crew and if any engineer or load master are operating on board, then there are crew seats available; otherwise, for the excess crew, passenger seats will be blocked off. Also, for positioning the DHD crew, passenger seats will be blocked off. This will be communicated by the crew operations team to the reservations team, so that these seats are not sold to passengers, and priority will go for accommodating the crew as it is necessary they travel for operational purposes. If a seat is blocked for an engineer, the seat in the allocated class will be

Aircraft Weight and Balance
(Load Control)

blocked off in the reservation system as well. Depending on the sector, crew may carry crew bags. Some airlines have a fixed location in the lower hold compartment 5 for stowing the crew bags, while others use a specific ULD. In the case of bulk-loading aircrafts, it would be a specific compartment in the lower hold.

The relevance of the location and weight of all of the above in the upper deck, and the allocation of loads in the various lower holds as specified in the earlier chapter are the main area of analysis and interest for the load controller. Therefore, for our study, load (commercial) will be a collective term, which will stand for:

Load Types:

In the upper deck, passengers and their hand bags, together with the lower deck passengers' checked-in baggage, cargo, mail, courier, and any other load that brings commercial benefit to the airline will be the traffic or commercial load.

All others such as crew, galley fittings, food, duty-free goods, etc. are operational load and are considered separately for calculation purposes. An exception is when there are aircraft spares or additional crew travelling as DHD. Here special analysis in terms of their weight and location is undertaken as these are non-standard and their location on the aircraft may change. Thus, these will be under consideration with the commercial load analysis for some airlines. Still others will make only aircraft spares part of commercial load. The ULD weight is added to the load contained in it. So the gross weight includes the weight of the load and that of the ULD in which it is loaded. If there is an empty ULD, then only the weight of the ULD is accounted for while making calculations and shown as additional (e.g. as EIC – equipment in compartment).

Each and every load (traffic/commercial or operational), meaning personnel, items, fixtures, baggage, etc. has a direct relation to the total maximum weight an aircraft can carry and the center of gravity of the aircraft, meaning it can influence the balance of the aircraft. For example, a car can carry only a certain maximum weight, a truck can carry higher weights comparatively and this is specified by the manufacturer; similarly, an aircraft also has limits to how much weight it can carry. The aircraft can carry only prescribed the total weight as specified by the manufacturer, any weight in excess means the aircraft is overweight and hence cannot take-off or operate. Also, a full load of first-class passengers and less number economy class passengers can cause the aircraft to be more nose heavy. This is because the first class cabin is located in the forward extreme of the aircraft, near to the front. In addition, the total combined weight has a direct influence on the maximum allowed operational capacities of the aircraft. Therefore, both the aircraft balance or trim and the weight must always be accounted for when planning and must fall within the allowed range for a safe operation of flight at all times. Therefore, it becomes the most important aspects of the load controller's considerations.

Weights

Maximum Structural or Operational Weights

The different hold weight limitations were discussed in the earlier chapter, and the load controller needs to check against the applicable manuals when planning heavy loads or ULDs in the aircraft hold during planning and issuing the LIRF. Everything in this world has limits above which it cannot function normally or safely. A vehicle manufacturer will conduct analysis based on the targeted commercial market, and the cost of development and manufacture. The structure, engine capacities, performance under various operating conditions, and fuel efficiency will be the major considerations. Later, prototype models will be made for tests to finalize the maximum possible capacity that can be carried safely in terms of volume and weight and of course, the fuel efficiency as well. Therefore, maximum weight for a vehicle is more or less standardized when delivered. Even if the weight is more than the maximum suggested on a vehicle and the vehicle is stalling or showing signs of unsafe handling, there is an option to park it and remove some load. In the case of aircrafts, there is no option to do this. An aircraft operates at high speed, after take-off flies at high altitudes, and lands at great speeds, with lots heats generated by the brakes, etc. The velocity and other forces are greater. Therefore, there is only one chance to get it right, that too when the aircraft is on the ground, so it is imperative to calculate the weight distribution correctly at the planning stage. There is no margin for error. Every kilo of weight makes a difference. For aircrafts, maximum allowed operational/structural weights provided by the manufacturer for operating the flights safely are for three different operating stages. Such as

    i)   When aircraft is on ground,

Aircraft Weight and Balance
(Load Control)

ii) While taking off,
iii) At landing time.

This is because at the various stages of flight, the forces acting on the flight are different as is the engine capacity (thrust provided by engine against the drag), and also the aircraft responds differently to these forces. Also, the stress on the structures are different at various stages. The actual total gross weight of the aircraft differs at various stages of flight as the fuel carried on board gets used up / burned off, although all other weights remain constant during each flight. Thus, the actual weight on a flight has differing effects at various stages of the flight. For example, when the aircraft is loaded, it has its own weight plus the commercial and operational load, next fuel is added for the flight, so at departure time the weight includes aircraft, loads, and fuel. At commencement of take-off run some fuel is used up / burned off during taxying to the runway from the parking stands. Again, when it is landing at destination, a major portion of the fuel is burned away during the trip. If the weight is more than maximum allowed when aircraft is on the ground, it can damage the landing gear (wheels and structures) and the aircraft air frame due to excess stress. If the weight is more than allowed during take-off, then the aircraft cannot take-off as the thrust provided by the engine will be insufficient to lift off and can damage the wings; if the weight is more than maximum allowed at landing, it can damage the landing gear. Thus, most importantly, the maximum structural weights are different figures. The three maximum structural weights are as follows:

1) Maximum zero fuel weight (MZFW)
2) Maximum take-off weight or regulated take-off weight (MTOW or RTOW)
3) Maximum landing weight (MLW)

1) MZFW: It is the maximum allowed gross weight, excluding the fuel required for operating the flight and including all load (traffic and operational) and the aircraft weight. If the aircraft weight is less than or equal to this, the flight can operate safely.
2) MTOW: It is maximum gross weight of the aircraft allowed including the fuel at the commencement of the take-off run. Sometimes the MTOW is restricted by the

dispatcher or captain due to operational conditions such as the prevailing or forecasted weather at origin, en route, or destination, etc., so extra fuel is carried, another reason for the restriction can be due to shorter or wet runways so weight is restricted to aid in braking action, etc. When the MTOW is restricted, it is called regulated and restricted take-off weight (RTOW). The load controller must always check with the dispatcher if there is any anticipated restriction on the MTOW and later confirm with the captain when the fuel figures are finalized by him closer to departure. This limitation protects the wings and allows safe lift from the ground.

3) MLW: It is the maximum gross weight of the aircraft at touch-down time at the destination airport. This limit protects the landing gear.

Therefore, the most initial stage of flight planning starts with checking the booked loads, calculating the estimated gross weight of the aircraft at various stages of flight, and comparing it with maximum allowed structural weight of the aircraft. If it is overweight, then options must be considered for standby or reduction (will be further discussed as we progress).

Quick reference file/folder (QRF): It can be cumbersome to refer to the weight and balance manual of an airline every time the weights are calculated or a flight is being planned for each departure. These manuals can be huge as they contain a lot of data, details, and they can also include all aircraft types of that airline as well. So a QRFs is used, which only has the most relevant load planning data. Basically, it contains the weight of the empty aircraft, and each operational load and its effect based (on its planned location on the aircraft) on the trim of the aircraft. Such as:

1) Aircraft weight and trim (point where its center of gravity lies along the trim or balance index line) for each aircraft registration
2) Crew weights (operating and additional) and their effect on the trim
3) Catering weight and its effect on the trim
4) Maximum allowed structural weights (max zero fuel weight, max take-off weight, maximum landing weight, etc.) for each aircraft registration

Aircraft Weight and Balance
(Load Control)

5) Weight of flight spares and trim effect (there are permanently fixed flight spares or kits on some airline aircrafts)

The maximum allowed structural weight for a certain type of aircraft may remain the same, ensure to verify each time against the QRF. Ensure the most recent QRF is used at all times and discard any previous QRF.

The actual total gross weight of the aircraft will vary from flight to flight. This due to various factors such as changes in the operational load (crew, catering, etc.) and commercial load, which will be different on each flight. Therefore, it is imperative the applicable weights at various stages are calculated for each flight at the initial stage of planning. Do not memorize weights for an aircraft to avoid errors, especially since aircrafts are reweighed after every periodic check. So always refer to the quick reference guide (QRF) published by the airline when starting the weight calculation. Also, weights can differ from aircraft to aircraft within the same types. To understand more, the various important applicable weights required for calculations for the load controller are as follows:

1) Basic weight (BW)
2) Dry operating weight (DOW)
3) Traffic load
4) Zero fuel weight (ZFW)
5) Fuel weights
6) Operating weight
7) Allowed traffic load
8) Take-off weight (TOW)
9) Landing weight

These weights assist the load controllers in checking how much commercial or traffic load can be carried safely by comparing with the maximum operational weights specified by the manufacturers, what is the actual weight once the flight is finalized, and how much more capacity is allowed for any last minute additions, if any. Details are as follows:

1) Basic weight (BW): It is the weight of the empty aircraft (*See figure. VIII.1*).

Fig. VIII.1.a.

Fig. VIII.1.b

Aircraft Weight and Balance
(Load Control)

Fig. VIII.1.c.
Fig. VIII.1: An empty aircraft (Cabin and holds).

This is the weight of the aircraft with the seats and galley fitting only, no crew, food, duty-free items, or commercial load. It is provided by the manufacturer when the aircraft is delivered and later updated after each service check by the engineering or the concerned airline department. The weight can change after a service check due to repainting or new modified component replacements, etc. The latest BW is to be taken from the current QRF only.

2) Dry operating weight (DOW) (*See figures: VIII.2*):

Fig. VIII.2.a.

Fig. VIII.2.b.

*Aircraft Weight and Balance
(Load Control)*

Fig. VIII.2.c.
Fig. VIII.2: Components of DOW.

When the weight of the crew and pantry (food, duty-free items, drinks, etc.) are added to the basic weight, this weight is called dry operating weight. The DOW needs to be calculated by the load controller for each flight. Here crew consists of both flight deck and cabin crew. Each sector will have different number of crew operating the flight, short sectors use less crew, long sectors use more crew, etc. And they will have their areas of working; for example, the flight deck crew will be based in the flight deck, part of the cabin crew in forward area, some in the middle, and some in the aft cabin. Each will have allocated crew seats accordingly. On some sectors the crew will operate with crew bags and on others they may not. The weight and the effect on the aircraft balance in terms of their location on the aircraft will be published in the QRF for each sector. For example, like DXB-TRV 2/8 (2 flight decks and 8 cabin crew) weighs 900kg (without bags), index –0.2 (stands for the effect of their weight and location on the balance of the aircraft). Another example, DXB-LHR 3/10 (3 flight decks and 10 cabin crew), weight 1300kg (with crew bags), index –0.3 (trim/balance effect). Airlines will set standard weights for the crew (separately with or without crew bags); similarly, they have identified the effect of the crew weight based on their location in the aircraft and accordingly, the crew data is prepared for inclusion in the QRF. The DHD crew or the engineer or the load master, etc. when occupying a passenger seat, holding an air ticket, will be checked in, and calculated along with the passengers (weight and trim effect). Similarly, the catering equipment (food, drinks, etc.) also varies from sector to sector for each type of aircraft. The weight and its location have an effect on aircraft capacity and trim of aircraft. This is simply shown on the QRF as DXB-HKG 200kg/–0.04. There are airlines who use the DOW straight off. They have the DOW calculated for each sector in the QRF. Therefore, the DOW is the weight of aircraft, crew, and pantry/catering.

3) Traffic load/Weight: As advised earlier, it is the weight all commercial load on the flight, passengers, hand bags, checked bags, cargo load and part of the commercial load such as flight spares, DHD crew, etc. If any of the

components are estimates, then the traffic load weight will be an estimate only. When all are finalized and no change is expected, it will the actual traffic load weight.

4) Zero fuel weight (ZFW): When the weight of the traffic / commercial load is added to the DOW, it is called zero fuel weight. Here too if an estimated traffic load is used, then the ZFW arrived at will be estimated ZFW, and if actual, then Actual ZFW. Meaning all weights are included except fuel. When ballast fuel (as explained below) is uplifted for trim proposes, it is added to the ZFW. Therefore, Basic Weight (BW) + crew + catering (operational weight) = DOW + flight spares (if any) + additional DHD crew (if any and when not added with passengers) + total commercial / traffic load (passengers + hand bags + checked bags + cargo + mail + courier + etc.) = Zero Fuel Weight. When the flight check-in closes and all the weights are finalized, the load controller calculates the actual ZFW and passes it to the captain. He needs this to calculate the fuel required (total fuel, taxi fuel, trip fuel) based on consumption, weather, altitude, and other factors. This fuel is then given to the load controller for completing the load and trim sheets.

5) Fuel weights: Once the bookings are made and the aircraft finalized by the appropriate commercial and operational departments, the flight operations dispatcher will plan the estimated fuel required for operating the flight. These depends on many factors, such as:

i) Type of aircraft and capacity of the tanks
ii) The fuel required by the engines to carry the total gross weight for the route.
iii) Fuel required for taxying from parking stand to runway at the origin airport and from runway to parking stand at the destination airport.
iv) The weather at the origin airport, en route, destination airport, alternate airport (including distance of alternate airport from destination airport, contingency if any last minute restrictions arise at the destination).
v) Aircraft limitations, etc.

Aircraft Weight and Balance
(Load Control)

Based on all these and many others, the dispatcher will calculate the fuel required at various stages. Some of the common fuel terminologies are:

i. Total fuel: It comprises the fuel required for taxying at both origin and destination airports, fuel required for use/burn to operate the flight, contingency fuel, additional fuel for the on board power generators (for lights, air conditioning, etc.), and any other additional the dispatcher feels is necessary for the safety of flight. Although an aircraft fuel tank will have certain capacity, it may not be necessary to carry full tanks; also sometimes, it may not be possible to load all cargo as the fuel required is more and thus after filling up the fuel, the total permitted structural weight will not allow for all loads to be accommodated (will be clarified further in this chapter).

ii. Taxi fuel: It is the amount of fuel required or used by the engines to move on the ground or in other words to create thrust so that it can reach the runway from the parking stand for departure and on arrival at destination from runway to the parking stand. Some airports have a short taxi distance, where fuel required will be less, whereas others can have long taxying time due to distance or airport congestions, so more fuel will be required.

iii. Take-off fuel (TOF): It is the amount of fuel remaining after using up some of the fuel for taxying from the parking stand to the runway for departure at origin airport. In other words, it is the fuel remaining in tanks at the commencement of the take-off run. Therefore total fuel − taxi fuel (origin) = take-off fuel.

iv. Trip fuel: It is the fuel required for flying the aircraft. The amount depends on the total weight of the aircraft − the greater the weight, the more fuel is required for the engines to create more thrust, route distance, en route weather, etc.

v. Contingency fuel: Sometimes at the destination there may be restrictions, such as delay in landing clearance due congestions, weather, etc. or if the aircraft is not able to land, it then needs to fly to the nearest possible airport as an alternate, so some fuel will be carried additionally.

vi. Ballast fuel: All fuel on the aircraft has an effect on its balance or trim, based on which tank it is in. Normally, the center tank fuel has no effect on trim as it is at the center, whereas tanks on the outer wings and in some aircrafts in its tail area create significant effect on its balance. Sometimes the loads are such that it may not be possible to evenly distribute the loads. Then it becomes necessary to load extra fuel in the appropriate tanks to bring the aircraft center of gravity (CG) within the safe operating limits. For example, if the forward hold of the aircraft is heavy with heavy cargo and baggage and also full first-class passengers, then the aircraft will be very nose heavy. So we need more weight in the aft section of the aircraft. So then load controllers can calculate how much amount of fuel is required in the tail tanks to bring the aircraft CG within limits. The charts will be available in the weight and balance manual. The ballast fuel is not useable and is often added to the zero fuel weight.

vii. Fuel tankering: Some airlines carry fuel for the return flight due to higher cost at destination or non-availability of fuel.

The most important fuel amounts required by the load controller are total fuel, taxi fuel, trip fuel, and in case of any requirement due to trim, ballast fuel. Here except the ballast fuel, which is determined by the load controller, the remaining estimated fuel figures are provided by the dispatcher approximately 4 to 6 hours in advance of the flight departure time and the actual by the captain approximately 1 hour before departure. It is necessary to get the actual fuel figures from the captain before finalizing the flight by the load controller.

6) Operating weight: When the take-off fuel is added to the dry operating weight, it is called the operating weight. Meaning the weight of the aircraft when operating the flight without commercial load on that sector. It is just the aircraft, crew, catering, and fuel added together for the flight. This makes up the base operating weight of the flight.

7) Allowed traffic weight/load: At the initial stages of planning, we need to how know much commercial load can be taken on a flight; this is the basic knowledge required for a load controller to start planning. To do this, the operating weight figure is significant since it is this weight that needs to be deducted from each of the three maximum structural weights after adding the fuel amounts accordingly to get the weight of commercial load that can be loaded on the flight, or in other words, the allowed traffic load. The manufacturer gives us the three maximum structural weights (MZFW/MTOW/MLW) as the limiting conditions. For example, let us take the maximum zero fuel weight as 250,000kg, the maximum take-off weight as 340,000kg maximum landing weight as 260,000kg for an aircraft. The DOW is calculated as 141,600kg for the flight and by adding the take-off fuel as 30,000kg, which is specific to the flight being planned, the operating weight will be = 171,600kg (DOW+TOF = Operating weight). By checking against each of the maximums:

MZFW + take-off fuel for operating the flight = allowed total weight for operating. So 250,000kg + 30,000kg = 280,000kg. From this we need to deduct the operating weight, which was calculated specifically for this flight. So 280,000kg – 171,500kg = 108,500kg. Here in regards to the MZFW limitation, to operate safely, the total traffic load allowed is 108,500kg gross. Anything above can damage the aircraft and so such an aircraft is not allowed to operate.

Next, MTOW already includes the total maximum weight allowed, including the fuel, so 340,000kg is the allowed total weight of the aircraft for it to operate safely without damaging the wings and for it to take-off safely.

Lastly, the MLW + trip fuel = allowed total weight for operating. So 260,000kg + 25,000kg = 285,000kg. From this we need to deduct the operating weight which was calculated specifically for this flight. So 285,000kg – 171,500kg = 113,500kg. Here in regards to the MLFW limitation, to operate safely, the total traffic load allowed is 113,500kg gross. Anything above can damage the aircraft and it is not allowed to operate. Further in comparison, 108,500kg is the least allowed and by

Aircraft Weight and Balance
(Load Control)

restricting the gross allowed traffic load to equal to or less than this weight, all other maximum limits will also be satisfied, thus ensuring safe operation of flight.

At the planning stage, only the estimates will be available, although the cargo load will be finalized, the passenger check-in only closes about 1 hour to departure time (normally). So it is possible to get the estimated gross allowed traffic load, which is useful for planning purposes. However, after the flight check-in closes, that is the flight is finalized, it is possible to get the actual allowed traffic load since all loads are final and weights are accurate.

8) Takeoff weight: DOW + traffic load + take-off fuel = take-off weight. It is the weight of the aircraft at the time of commencement of the take-off run. It will include all the weights together on board the aircraft, including fuel (except taxi-out fuel). Again, it will be estimate TOW if any component is an estimated total.

9) Landing weight: It is the weight of the aircraft at touch down. It is calculated by deducting the trip fuel from the take-off weight. So take-off weight – trip fuel = landing weight.

Load Sheet:

This is an important legal document and will be part of formal load control training in regards to its preparation (*See specimen. VIII.3*).

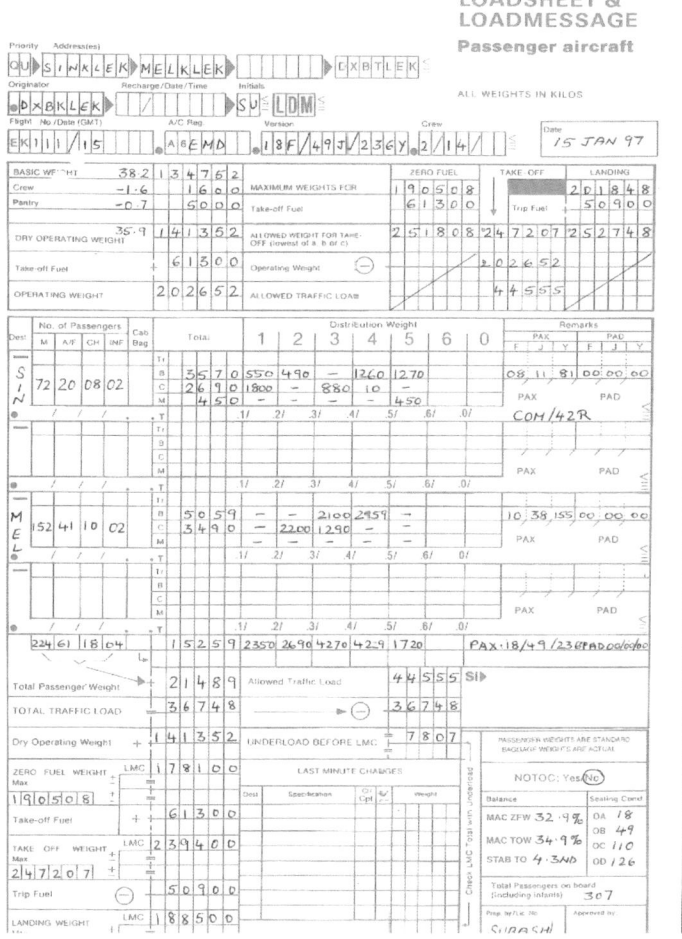

Fig. VIII.3: Load sheet specimen copy.

*Aircraft Weight and Balance
(Load Control)*

A load controller must pass the necessary proficiency test and be licensed to prepare the load sheet for a flight. It is a document which will have all the important details of the flight in terms of the flight number, routing, date, aircraft registration, etc. It is prepared by the load controller allocated for planning the flight. There are appropriate columns for each of the loads and its balance effect on the aircraft's center of gravity. When completed, it is a tool that will allow the load controller to calculate the weight of the aircraft, with the addition of operating loads, traffic loads, etc. It allows the load planner to allocate the number of passengers in each of their designated classes of travel and annotate the total weight, segregate the loads, distribute the weights by allocating their locations on the aircraft, etc. Even transit loads can be accounted for. Once the total weight of each load is updated, the grand total can be derived to check against the limits column. And finally, this confirms if all traffic load can be accommodated for safe operation of the flight after comparing with the maximum limits of the aircraft. Special loads and the balance effect of the loaded aircraft are mentioned in summary. The load sheet, when completed and signed by the load controller, becomes a legal document, which is counter signed by the captain before departure. A copy is retained by the load controller and another by the captain on board. The captain needs the details on the load sheet for operating the flight, it tells him of the weights on the aircraft and helps him accordingly determine the fuel required and other operational functions to be done. The load sheet, together with the trim sheet, forms the most important document between the load controller and captain. It is a confirmation from the load controller that he has planned the flight as shown after considering all the parameters of safety in regards to it and that the aircraft has been loaded accordingly. A load controller uses the details on the load sheet to transmit the LDM for the flight to the next station. As it summarizes the load details and positions, so sufficient preparations can be made. The load sheet is filed for records with the other flight documents.

Aircraft Balance (Trim) Index

Every object has a center of gravity. It is the average point or location on the object at which the gravity acts equally. The object is able to rotate freely about its center of gravity. Take for example a dancing doll toy *(See figures. VIII.4)* with a circular base and tapered towards the upper part.

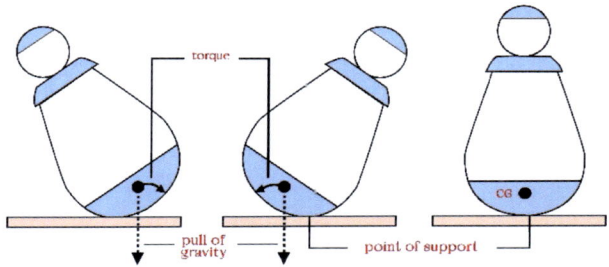

Fig. VIII.4: Dancing doll toy due to shifting center of gravity.

We would imagine the center to be somewhere in the middle. Yes, in terms of the length it will be in the center, but in regards to overall weight of the complete object, the concentration of gravity will be approximately more towards base. In other words, it is the average equal point between heavier and lighter regions of the object. So for an object in space to be in equilibrium, it needs to be supported along its center of gravity. This enables equal rotation along an imaginary axis along this center of gravity, irrespective of its shape. The center of gravity or CG of the doll can change if a heavy item is placed at the top.

Similarly, an aircraft in air is also very much influenced by gravity, and its rotation should be predictably accurate along its center of gravity. We had looked at how an aircraft flies and said that the airflow, together with the design of the wings, creates lift on the wings. So the aircrafts are built in such a way that the center of gravity lies somewhere closer to the wing root area. So depending on the weights of load at different areas on the aircraft, there is an effect or rotation along its center of gravity axis. To explain better, consider a manual weight balance and an aircraft with a line drawn along the center, marked from +10 to –10, with zero being the center of gravity of the aircraft *(See figure. VIII.5)*, negative numbers towards the nose, and the positive numbers towards the tail.

Aircraft Weight and Balance
(Load Control)

Fig. VIII.5.a.

___-10_-9_-8_-7_-6_-5_-4_-3_-2_-1_0_1_2_3_4_5_6_7_8_9_10___

Fig.VIII.5.b.

Fig.VIII.5: Comparison between a conventional balance and an aircraft based on center of gravity.

Now place some weight on the right pan of the manual balance (*See figure. VIII.6*),

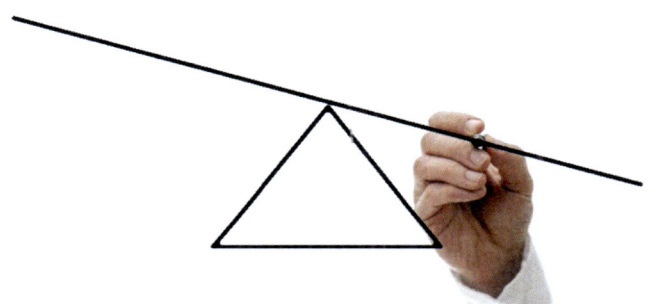

Fig. VIII.6: Effect of weight on the balance/trim based on the position a load is placed.

The left side will start to come up and the needle at the center will move towards the right side, indicating the right side of the balance is heavier. This is because the center of gravity or (CG) of the balance arms have moved due to the weight from its base reference point. Next, place the same amount of weight on the left pan, then both left and right side will become balanced and the needle will come to zero. It is in equilibrium. Instead of the same weight, if you place a lower weight on the left pan, the right pan may come up slightly but not align completely with the left side, but at an angle and the needle will move slightly to the left. The tilt depends on the weight difference. Next, with the same manual balance try to place weights at different distance intervals from the center or needle, first on the left and then on the right side. You will notice that the speed of rotation and the effect decreases as we move closer to the center of gravity, with no rotation at all when the weight is placed on top of the center. The amount of weight difference between left side and right side and the distance from the center are the main factors that influence the rotation. An aircraft acts in the same way when any form of weight is loaded in it.

Here consider a weight (load) placed in the forward hold compartment 1, there is rotation towards the front and can be balanced by loading equal weight in the aft hold compartment 5 or 4. Again, the tilt depends on which compartments are used in the front or aft of the wing, weight difference, and what is the desired tilt or balance level required by the load controller. The above diagram of the aircraft showing positive (+) numbers for aft of wing rotation and negative (-) numbers for the forward of wing rotation that is applicable in reality. For aircrafts, when a load is placed forward of its CG, the effect is a negative movement and an aft of wing is a positive movement. The movement is measured as index. The whole CG and index of the aircraft needs to be within a safe range. Safe range is otherwise a tolerance area with in which the aircraft CG must be to operate safely. The aircraft can fly safely with or without load, only when its CG is within this safe range. Even an empty aircraft will have its CG at a point, which will be advised by the aircraft manufacturer and after each service check by the concerned airline department, too see if there has been any change due to repainting or other aircraft component change or additional fittings, etc.

Therefore, every item (aircraft, operational and traffic loads), including fuel on the aircraft, has an index effect, except for some aircrafts where there is minimal or no index effect in the center of the wing box area. So it is the load controller's responsibility to find out the basic index of the aircraft (empty aircraft) and then plan the loads in such a way that the aircraft balance lies within the safe range. This is in other words called trimming the aircraft or balancing the aircraft. We need the aircraft to operate upright or in other words, in equilibrium in regards to the front and aft of wings or be balanced in relation to its center of gravity.

We mentioned basic weight, crew, pantry, dry operating weight (DOW), traffic load, etc. All these weights are added up to check the possibility of loading all the planned loads on a flight. Similarly, we also need to add up the index effect of all items to see how best to plan their locations in the aircraft to make it well-balanced for safe operation. Indexes of the operational load (crew, pantry, flight spares), including that of the aircraft, are standard and will be available in the W&B manual or the QRF. Whereas those of the traffic or commercial loads (based on location planned by the load controller) need to be derived from the trim chart after adding the operational load indexes. The weights mentioned and have corresponding indexes as each weight placed on the aircraft has a corresponding index effect. They are as follows:

1) Basic index
2) Dry operating index (DOI)

Aircraft Weight and Balance
(Load Control)

3) Traffic load indexes
4) Fuel index
5) ZFW index
6) Take-off weight index (TOW)

1) Basic Index: It is the index of an empty aircraft. The manufacturer provides this at the time of delivery and thereafter the concerned airline department calculates it. It will be available in the W&B manual and the QRF. It will be specific for an aircraft.
2) Dry Operating Index (DOI): Just like the DOW, the crew index and the pantry index is added to the Basic Index to get the DOI. The crew index and the pantry index will be available in the QRF against the crew compliment (crew number, with or without bags) and catering sector being flown.
3) Traffic Load Indexes: Passenger cabin in an aircraft is divided into zones. Passengers in priority class are in the forward of the aircraft, economy class in the middle and aft, etc. But all will be divided into zones. Each zone will have certain number of passengers shown in the trim chart and that number will have a unit value index. So on for all zones. When the passenger numbers are distributed as per seating in each zone, the load controller will derive the index effect in each zone. Next, after adding individual indexes to the DOI, he will know where the aircraft CG lies, when all passengers are seated. How it works is that airlines allocate average weight for passengers. When they are grouped into zones, the total weight will have an index effect in that area of the aircraft. Here to make it easy instead of calculating the weights, the number of passengers, when allocated, correspond directly to the applicable units for the zones. Similarly, the weight in each compartment (may include baggage, cargo, etc.) will be translated to index units in the appropriate column on the trim chart. Here the category of load is not important, the total weight in each compartment is what is required. Thus, all the indexes of the compartments are to be derived. The final graph drawing will show if the loaded aircraft CG is lying within the safe range of the trim limits. The load controller is the only person who, through his planning and

decision, can ensure the load locations are such that the aircraft CG is within the safe trim limits or envelope.
4) Fuel Index: Fuel in the aircraft fuel tanks also has index effect. The main center fuel tanks are located within the wing box center area (*See figure. VIII.7*); however, other tanks are located inside the wings.

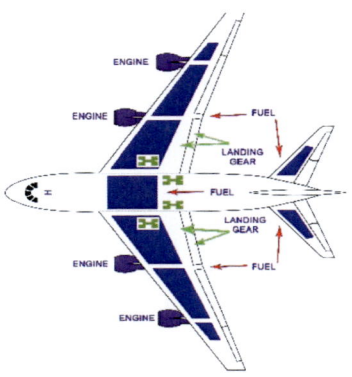

Fig. VIII.7: Fuel tanks on a typical commercial aircraft.

The curved design of the wings means the weight of fuel in the outer tanks on the wings will have a positive index effect as they lie towards the tail part of the aircraft CG. Some aircrafts have inner tanks near to the center tank on the wing, which give a positive index effect. Normally, when the fuel is pumped, the center tanks get filled up and then the other tanks starts getting filled up at as per the standard sequence designed by the manufacturer. This is standard fueling. In standard fueling, the trim chart will give the total fuel index effect for the total fuel weight given, that needs to be taken into account for aircraft trimming, in addition to other loads. The individual tank index need not be taken. Sometimes, due to a technical fault or some other reasons, the aircraft will be fueled by the captain or engineer out of sequence or through non-standard fueling. In this case take the weight of fuel in individual tanks from the captain, obtain the index from the weight and balance manual for individual tanks with fuel against the weight of fuel it contains, and add them up to get the total fuel weight index for aircraft trimming.

Some aircrafts have tail tanks as well. These tanks are used when fuel requirement is high for that sector and all tanks are full. Again, if it is standard, this will be part of the fuel index chart shown in the trim chart. Sometimes, as explained in weights, the load controller may need more weight in the aft holds due to very heavy load in the forward, resulting in a nose heavy aircraft. Then he can calculate how much index is required to obtain safe trim range, can check the W& B manual for tail tank fuel index effect, and then ask the captain to fill up accordingly. This fuel will not be used for operating the flight but will be only as ballast for trim purposes.

5) ZFW Index: It is the actual point where the CG of the loaded aircraft is when the CG line is derived after adding or plotting from the basic index, then DOI, and through to traffic index against the ZFW (*See figure. VIII.8*).

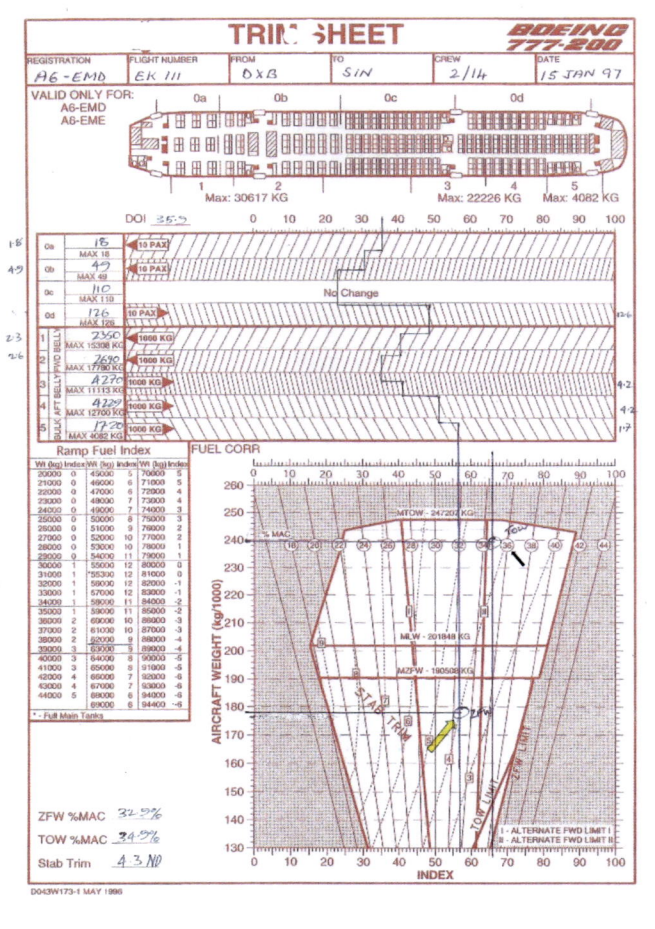

Fig. VIII.8: ZFW CG (big yellow arrow) on a trim sheet.

It must fall within the allocated ZFW safe range envelope.
6) TOW Index: When the ZFW index is adjusted with the take-off fuel index, the new CG line is then plotted against the corresponding TOW. This is called the Take-Off

Weight Index (small black arrow). So at take-off, this is where the CG of the loaded and fueled aircraft will be.

A few other important aspects of aircraft trim:

Ideal Trim: For load controllers, there is term called an ideal trim. It does not mean when the aircraft CG is zero or when the front and aft are perfectly aligned or balanced. When the aircraft flies with a slight tilt towards the aft, or in other words, with a slight nose up alignment, it is called ideal trim (*See figure. VIII.9*).

Fig. VIII.9: The relevance of ideal trim.

Aircraft Weight and Balance
(Load Control)

Fig. VIII.9.a

This has a cushioning and upward effect on the aircraft fuselage when the aircraft moves forward and also gives greater stability. So it saves slightly on the energy or thrust required to be produced by the engines. This translates into fuel saved. Fuel is a major cost factor in airline operations, and any fuel saved can be valuable for the airline. This also forms part of the consideration for the load controller when planning the flight. Some airlines specify the ideal trim range within the safe trim limits or it can be obtained in the W&B manual.

Lateral Imbalance: Similar to the front and aft rotation, there are left and right rotations along its wings (*See figure. VIII.10).*

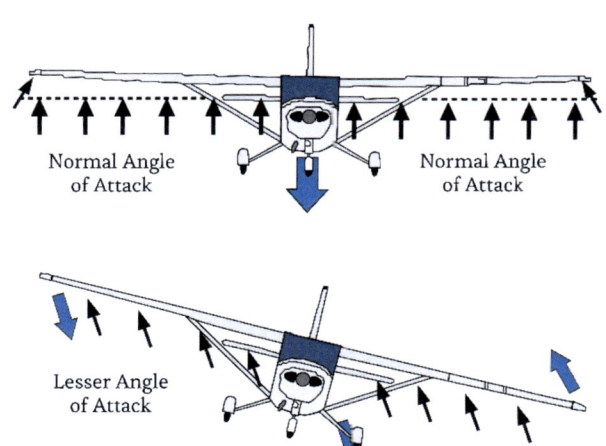

Fig. VIII.9.b.

Aircraft Weight and Balance (Load Control)

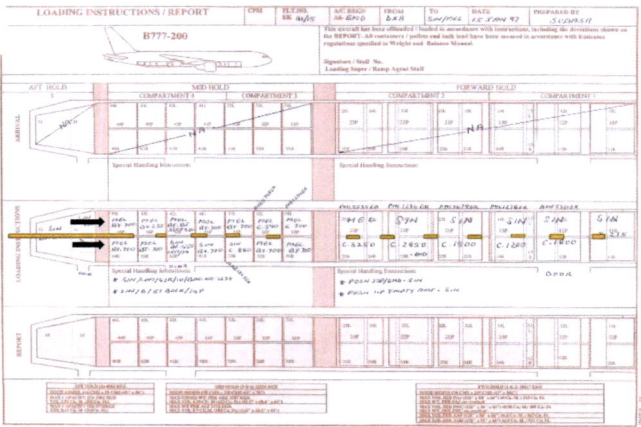

Fig. VIII.10.b.

Fig. VIII.10: Lateral imbalance due to variance in the sum total of load weight between the right and left side of aircraft (effect is pronounced in larger aircrafts). Figure is for illustrative purpose only

This is more applicable in the case of large wide-body aircrafts. Here it is important to have a balance of weight between what is loaded on the left side of the aircraft against the right. However, this rotation is not major a concern usually and is applicable only if the differences of the total weight on left and the total of the right side loaded weights are higher figures, e.g. above 1000kg, depending on the aircraft. The W&B manual can be consulted as applicable.

Aircraft Weight and Balance
(Load Control)

Trim Chart:

The whole concept of aircraft CG movement or index change has been developed into a simple graph (*Refer to figure. VIII.11*) called the trim chart.

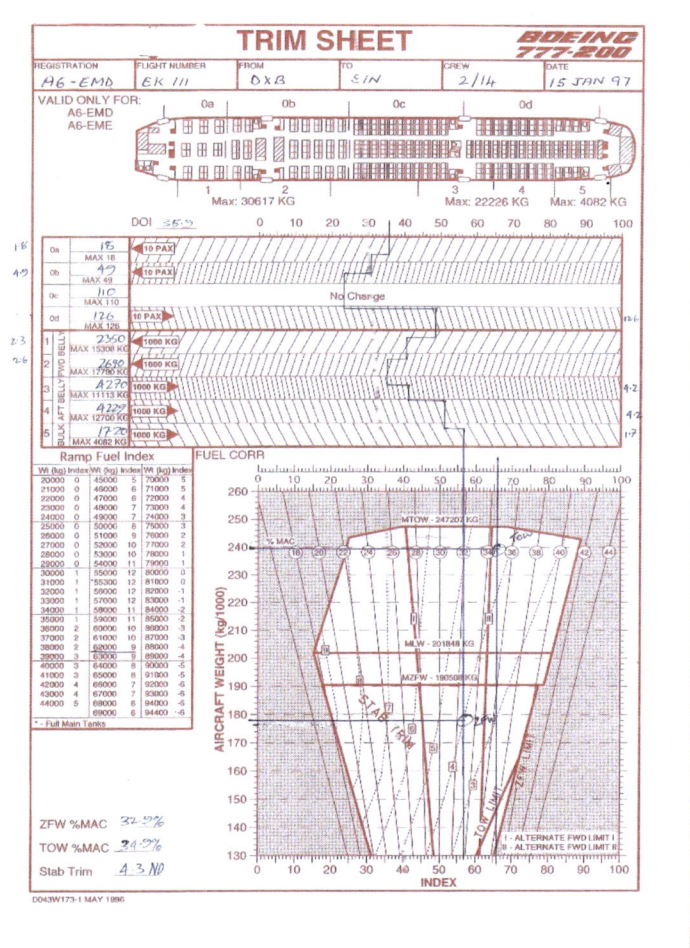

Fig. VIII.11: Sample trim sheet/chart.

Aircraft Weight and Balance (Load Control)

Professional training will be required for completing a trim chart. Some of the important steps and facts to understand will be explained here. Trim charts used will vary from airline to airline. Some will use a combined load sheet cum trim sheet in one, while others separate the two. Start by entering the empty aircraft index (which will be in the QRF) and then record the index effect of each individual item, personnel, operational and traffic loads based on the loading plan by the load controller of the location in the aircraft that they are to be loaded or located, then the CG of the aircraft can be determined using the trim chart.

A typical trim chart will have flight number, route, date, aircraft registration, crew compliment, fuel index, etc. It is a tool for the load controller to check the trim of the aircraft. In the load planning stage, the load controller does a trail trim with all the estimated weights to see if the aircraft will be in trim. After the flight is finalized or closed for check-in, he will complete a load sheet in parallel with a trim chart with actual data and indexes. The resulting details need to be entered in both the load sheet and trim sheet. So based on the actual ZFW, actual TOW, and actual landing weight, the corresponding actual aircraft indexes at ZFW, TOW, and landing weight can be drawn on the trim chart. The ZFW index and TOW index in the trim gives the percentage of MAC (mean aerodynamic chord) for each of them. The captain uses these percentages to set his stabilizers. There are horizontal stabilizers on the tail section of the aircraft (Refer the previous chapter on basic aviation knowledge). These need be adjusted based on the aircraft trim effect. The incline of the horizontal stabilizers at the tail has an effect on the nose alignment. When the horizontal stabilizers with the desired incline cut through the air current, the nose area of the aircraft can get a nose up or down alignment. This is pitching or adjusting the pitch. A completed and signed trim charter by the load controller who planned the flight is a legal document, which is required by the captain, then signed by him and at least a copy retained by each, before the aircraft can depart.

Factors for Load Planning

There are important factors to be considered when planning a flight. These can mean success and smooth operation towards the last part of flight handling. It can vary flight to flight and airline to airline. Each flight can be unique. Sometimes it is simple and at other times complicated. The main aim of load planning is to maximize loads or ensure to uplift all planned within capacity available for a safe operation. At times innovative and creative thinking and decision making will be required. Never compromise on safety, whatever the pressure or consideration. Do not rush through, but ensure careful consideration of all facts and details. Consideration of all factors while planning gives a strong base for handling and bringing out options for improvement if changes are necessary later. Earlier a few of the factors were mentioned. There are various factors; the most important are as follows:

1) Capacity: Compare the booking or planned loads against the capacity available. If there are more passengers booked than capacity, it is rather simple, plan with a full passenger load as per capacity available. If both other traffic load and passenger load are high, check with the cargo department to see what is the least priority cargo that can be kept on standby. So in case of a drop in passenger numbers, the baggage also will drop, which may give space last minute for loading the standby cargo. If the booking suggests no drop at all and the cargo loads are too high and will need to encroach onto the baggage space, then ask for offload plan and a standby plan from the cargo section.

2) Trim: The balance of the aircraft can be brought within the safe range by planning the loads in the appropriate holds for bulk-loading aircrafts. However, for ULD-version aircraft, it is important that based on weights expected for the baggage, the cargo ULDs are allocated. Sometimes the cargo can be dense, meaning more heavy than volumetric; in this case, baggage ULDs may need to be distributed in both forward and aft without over-stowing the baggage ULDs with cargo. It is important to do a preliminary trial trim to check the trim when allocating ULDs for baggage or cargo on critical flights with high or unpredictable loads fluctuations. Sometimes in extreme cases, the tail fuel tanks can be used for nose heavy trim adjustments, but this is not preferable due to fuel cost, etc. It is possible to achieve safe trim range with proper planning. Always start with planning heavy loads from the wing area and work away from it with lighter loads. This is because the aircraft fuselage is much stronger near to the wing box area and

another reason, as mentioned earlier, is that since the aircraft CG is near the wing box area, the index effect is lesser or in some aircrafts almost negligible. For example, if you have a pallet weighing 3,000kg and another weighing 1,000kg, then plan the heavy pallet in compartment 2, position 22P and the other lighter pallet in compartment 2, position 21P or maybe in compartment 1. Similarly, for the aft hold as well. It is advisable not to leave vacant positions in between two loaded positions. The reasons for this are that there can be locking issues, it may create a bending effect on the aircraft structure if the weights are heavy, can be misleading for the loading team, etc.

3) Hold versions: ULD-version aircrafts can accommodate various types of ULDs, pallets, containers, etc. in various combinations. The available versions approved by the airline can be found in the W&B manual or are sometimes shown at the rear side of the LIRF. Using different versions allows for flexible planning to obtain preferred trim, accommodate maximum load, and segregate load based on requirements. E.g. containers for baggage as they are easier to handle, pallets for cargo, since the space on these ULDs are more, etc.

4) First in last out and last in first out: As mentioned in detail in the previous chapter, since the forward and aft hold access is only one each, when anything is loaded first and subsequently other loads or ULDs are loaded, then for unloading, all the loads in front of the door have to be unloaded first before the first loaded item can be removed. So when planning, ensure the least priority load not wanted on an urgent basis at destination is loaded first. Normally, these are general cargo. Usually, priority baggage and quick transfer baggage (or ULDs with them) are loaded near the door area for urgent retrieval at destination. Also, first destination loads should not be over stowed by last destination loads, as much as possible. Then on arrival at the first destination, the loading team will need to unload, keep it on ground, remove their destination's load, and reload transit again. This can cause unwanted additional work, missing load, delay in their inbound load delivery,

etc. Each airline will have its own order of priority list and this must be followed when planning.

5) Origin and destination restrictions or congestion: Some origin or destination airports cannot handle certain ULD types. So do not plan those. Again, there may not be sufficient equipment or none at all. If manpower is not sufficient, do not plan too much in bulk compartment 5. There can be many such restrictions.

6) Payload restriction: Sometimes due to weather or runway conditions, flight operations/dispatch section or the captain will restrict the amount of load (weight) that can be carried. This could be to uplift more fuel or to reduce the weight while landing, etc. Meaning the payload is restricted. Therefore, the aircraft will have to operate with a restricted ZFW or TOW. Then it is not possible to utilize the maximum weights allowed. But the aircraft and other operational weights are necessary for operation. So the only option is to reduce the commercial loads and so this is called payload restriction (*See figure. VIII.12*).

Fig. VIII.12: Understanding payload availability and fuel requirement.

Consider a glass with some rocks at the bottom, then some sand, and then top up with water till the brim. If we reduce the amount of rock and soil, then the amount of water can be increased or vice versa. Payload restriction is somewhat of the same principle to an extent. Up to a point within the limits of each, that is maximum ZFW and maximum capacity of the fuel tanks, the ratio of traffic load, in other words, the payload and fuel weight can be adjusted. Higher payload uplift would mean lesser fuel uplift and the other way around too is applicable. This is allowed, as mentioned, if it is within the limits and also after taking the necessary fuel for safe operations. Additional fuel can be increased or decreased, subject to approval from flight dispatcher or captain.

7) ULD stock equalization: ULDs must be required at an airport for future flights and hence, may be transported on the operating flight, these need to be accommodated as EIC – equipment in compartment and accounted in the load weight and trimmed as any other loads. Similarly, when an airport has excess stock, the airline may bring some back to its base airport. The order of priority needs to be checked with the airline planning department as it can change due to the stock conditions and requirements.

8) Special loads: There are can be special or dangerous loads, although allowed to be transported by air, but need to observe certain conditions for safety or handling reasons. For example, some dangerous goods cannot be loaded next to each other due to the potential for them to react with each other. Live animals like dogs are not to be loaded near human remains, etc. Thus, these special requirements are to be considered when planning. Some of the requirements will be in the NOTOC, while others in the airline W&B manual. Still others are common knowledge; for example, live human organs and valuable shipments are to be loaded near the door area for easy and quick retrieval. Hold air conditioning is required for animal carriage.

9) Locks: If there are locks missing or not serviceable, then there can be restrictions on the load that can be loaded on that position. The amount of weight penalty can be obtained from the W&B manual.

10) Heavy or volumetric loads: Heavy shipments, if loose for bulk-loading aircrafts, will need to be tied down with additional lashing (this needs to be advised to the loading team) and other cushioning loads should be planned around it, especially in front and aft of it. Similarly, if rigid heavy

load is in ULDs, then they should be tied down inside the ULD and planned with cushioning other loaded ULDs in front and aft of it. Details of which loads are considered as rigid and cushioning will be available in the airline W&B manual. This is to protect against any unwanted movement and damages to the aircraft.
11) Ground stability check: The load controller needs to check when the aircraft is loaded if there will be any impact on the ground stability of the aircraft or if the sequence of hold loading needs to be different from that normally followed by the loading team. Normally, when planning starts, it will be with a view of ensuring the aircraft is well balanced. However, exceptions are when there is transit load on board or if during the loading process, there will be a need to load more cargo in the aft, with more bags in the forward hold. Then a trail trim check is to be done and appropriate instructions given in the LIRF to the loading team to follow accordingly. Similarly, when preparing the offloading instructions, the ground stability check is to be done.

As mentioned, there are many considerations and the ones listed above are not limiting, since each flight, airport, aircraft, airline, etc. will have varying requirements and restrictions.

Load Planning (LIRF, Coordination, Verifying, Finalizing, and Post-Flight)

The airline's route planners would have done their preliminary assessment and released the flight for bookings. However, this would be much in advance and are subject to fluctuations in the market/demand. Also, there are other departments who need a near accurate average or estimates to start preparations. For example, the cargo department will need to start build-up of cargo, dispatch will need to plan the route analysis and fuel estimates, etc.

Load Planning: Load planning is allocating planned operational load and booked traffic loads to appropriate locations on the aircraft, within the parameters of available capacity, safe trim range, and in consideration of all applicable factors of load planning.

So based on and with a strong understanding or application of the various factors of load planning, there are seven basic levels of load planning or handling that can be categorized as follows:

Aircraft Weight and Balance (Load Control)

1) Pre-flight preparation (normally 24hrs to 12hrs in advance of departure, depending on airline and airport)
2) Pre-flight load planning
3) Issue loading instruction
4) Coordination
5) Finalization and documentation
6) Verification and debrief
7) Post-flight messaging and recording

1) <u>Pre-flight preparation</u>. At this stage the preparation for the flight would start generally 24hours from departure time or at some airports 12hours before departure. There are generally two steps involved:

    i- Estimated ZFW calculation: Next the planner will calculate the weights. Airlines allocate average weights for adults, children, and infant passengers and an average weight for bags as well. This, for example, can be taken as 80kg, 30kg, 10kg for passengers respectively and baggage at 30kg each. So based on the booking figures, the estimated weight of passengers and baggage can be made, inclusive of the ULD weights required for build-up. Similarly, the cargo weights will be given by the booking by the cargo section along with the ULD weights required. Next, based on the aircraft and route planned, the DOW will be calculated and added to the estimated traffic load to obtain the estimated ZFW. This is passed onto the flight operations team. The flight operations team will use the estimated ZFW and other data to prepare a flight plan to determine how much fuel will be required for operations (in regards to the load control) and other functions. The estimated fuel figures (total fuel required, taxi fuel, trip fuel), any restrictions on the maximum structural weights especially the TOW, all will be advised by the operations dispatcher to the load control when he finalizes the flight plan about 4 to 5 hours before departure.

    ii- Advanced space allocation: Allocate space on the flight for the build-up team of baggage and cargo sections. Normally, about 24hrs in advance of the departure time, the airline planning department will release the flight to the load controller chief planner with estimated loads (passenger and cargo bookings, etc.). If the passenger booking is more than the available seats, then only the actual seat availability is used and any over-booking is ignored, as there are no more seats. He will check the historical data or average baggage numbers to determine the space required or ULDs required (depending on the aircraft type) for baggage on the flight. He will cross-check the cargo loads and ULD allocation plan with the cargo section. In consideration of the applicable load planning factors, he will coordinate with both the baggage control section and the cargo control section (it is normally the cargo control sections that control all loads other than baggage in an airline), to provide a preliminary baggage ULD allocation to the baggage control section. This will give a build-up plan for the baggage team and an estimated build up requirement to the cargo teams.

For transit flights the above will still be applicable. However, the transit load estimation will need to be obtained from the airline planners, in addition calculate the seats available for joining passengers. This needs to be coordinated with the check-in supervisor (he will need to coordinate with the previous station as soon as flight check-in is closed at the previous station on the day of operation), then an estimated total transit load figures is derived, to which the joining or booked loads are added for departure load planning.

For bulk-loading aircrafts, advanced space allocation is not required; however, based on the passenger booking and cargo booking, inform cargo section to provide standby or offload priority if passenger loads are higher and space required for bags is more than available capacity. Estimated ZFW calculation is still necessary.

2) <u>Pre-flight load planning</u>: The actual load planning starts when the load controller is allocated the flight. In some airports this is done by the officer in charge when the load controller comes on duty. A load controller would normally start the load planning about

6 to 8 hours before the scheduled departure time of flight. There are several steps involved, such as:

iii- Pre-flight preparation verification and confirmation: The flight estimates or bookings are more or less clear or accurate about 6 to 8 hours to departure. The operational loads would be final at this juncture, even the aircraft planned for the flight as well. Which means the aircraft registration and flight spares (if any) are known and confirmed. Based on this, the load controller will recalculate the actual DOW and DOI. Next, he will recheck the estimated ZFW and advise the flight operations dispatcher if the difference is more than the agreed range. The preliminary confirmed data for the load sheet (flight number, date, registration, DOW, DOI, and maximum structural weights can be entered in the appropriate columns). The passenger check-in would start in 3 – 4 hours, although some airlines allow for 24hrs check-in as well. So some of the bags would start to arrive at the baggage build-up area for build-up. Cargo ULD space or ULD allocated previously are to be checked as well from the previous allocation with the cargo section, for any changes. Transit load details are also to be verified. This stage is basically the background details or basic data gathering of the flight by the actual allocated load controller planning the flight and further issuing the LIRF, executing the load sheet and trim sheet through to completion.

iv- Load calculation and trail trim: Approximately 3 to 4 hours to flight departure, the cargo and all other loaded ULDs, except baggage or load (for bulk-loading aircrafts) will be finalized, check-in would start and baggage flow to baggage build-up area would be in progress. At this time, based on the finalized cargo ULDs, other load ULDs allocation and planned baggage ULDs, the appropriate version can be decided and a preliminary load plan on the LIRF can be prepared by allocating positions based on the factors of load planning. Subsequently, about 3 to 4 hours to departure, the flight dispatcher will also give the estimated total fuel, taxi fuel, trip fuel, and if will advise if there is any restriction on structural weights and thus enable the load controller to prepare a preliminary trim sheet to check where the trim or CG of the aircraft will be when the aircraft is loaded with the planned loads. This will be based on the preliminary load plan considering estimated loads and allocating booked passengers in the appropriate zones. If there are areas of concern in regards to the aircraft trim and if the allocated baggage ULDs utilization is less or more, based on prior agreement with the baggage section, the baggage ULD allocation or type of ULDs to be used can be amended. Another aspect is that if the anticipated baggage ULDs or space will be more and will encroach on the space allocated for cargo, then based on the standby or offload details provided by the cargo section, the appropriate cargo load or ULD is to be planned for offloading or standby, subject to loading once the flight check-in closes and baggage space requirement is confirmed.

Sometimes cargo and loads other than baggage need to be planned on standby or offloaded due to payload restrictions (structural weight restrictions). This will be known when the flight dispatcher provides the estimated figures; in this case, it will be the captain who will provide the maximum limits that can be used (usually it will be on the maximum take-off weight or the landing weight). This is possible only after the flight closes for check-in and all load actual details (weight and space) are available, which happens approximately one hour to departure. Then the load controller is able to calculate the actual ZFW. The crew will then calculate the possible payload uplift based on the actual ZFW provided and the operational requirements. But an indication will be given in advance by the flight dispatcher when he provides the preliminary fuel figures, based on which the loading team would have kept some general cargo on standby subject to payload release by the captain. This accordingly can be loaded or offloaded last minute.

For a transit flight, during this time the origin or previous station needs to be contacted or otherwise will be advised by the previous station or the airline through the operational messages of the transit loads, which also need to be accounted for. That would be number of passengers, including breakdown into adult, children, infant, and classes, weight of baggage, cargo, etc. The passenger details are to be coordinated with the check-in team, unless already done by the airline planners or previous station directly. This is to avoid accepting more passengers than seats on board, as they may not otherwise know how many passengers will remain on board in transit. If there are special shipments that come under provisions of the NOTOC, check and verify as per the appropriate manual and IATA DGR manual regarding handling, loading, and stowing requirements.

For bulk-loading aircrafts, it would be desirable for the load controller to physically see the cargo and other load (if possible) before planning. This is advantageous as he will already have an understanding of the hold space available and the expected baggage space requirement from experience (or overtime this can be gained). Now when he or she sees the cargo (could be oversized, heavy, volumetric, or normal but more in quantity, thus requiring more space), there is a clear understanding and he will be able to make a more accurate load plan and instructions. This will avoid surprises last minute, avoid offloading to make space for baggage, etc. This is part of creating a strong background check of the flight, or in other words, doing the homework. It may not be necessary for all flights, but only when the flight is fully booked and a large amount of cargo planned or if there is bulky or heavy cargo planned on critical flights.

3) <u>Issue LIRF (or in other words Loading Instruction)</u>: The LIRF is an official written communication from the load controller to the loading team leader in a document form. The load controller, after careful analysis and aircraft trim check, will decide what needs to be loaded, what not to be or to be kept on standby, will allocate the locations or positions for loading each load based on various load planning factors, on which flight number and which registration, on what date, from where to where, etc. In addition, if the flight is operating to one more than two airports, each position should clearly mention the destination in addition to the ULD serial number, weight and load type, and if any special handling is required. He then needs to put all of this into written format that can be easily understood by the loading form. This is called as the loading instruction. Verbal loading instructions should not be given nor taken. If verbally given, then it is immediately to be followed

up by a written document. When changes are needed to a loading instruction that was issued, then all subsequent issues should have a version number. As mentioned in the previous chapter, when an aircraft is to be offloaded, an offloading instruction is given to the loading team leader. When the aircraft needs to be loaded, a loading instruction is issued; when both offloading and loading of a flight is to be done, then it is an offloading-loading instruction. When the loading team leader completes the loading of the flight, he needs to update the loading instruction and sign it, then it becomes the loading instruction report (LIR). Collectively, for ease we have mentioned it here as LIRF. The planning of the load controller is carried out physically by the loading team, and this report becomes the confirmation of the same, that the aircraft has been loaded as instructed. This was a brief introduction of the LIRF.

In continuation to load planning level, approximately 2 to 3 hours to departure, the load controller will receive the UWS (ULD weight statement) for the flight with actual cargo, mail, etc. details (gross weight, ULDs with serial numbers, destination, contour if applicable, etc.). Do not issue a loading instruction based on incomplete or incorrect UWS or verbal information. Re-verify the information on the UWS with the cargo, mail, courier manifests. The load controller will then check the BRS (baggage reconciliation system) or with the baggage build-up team for the flight regarding the baggage build-up progress. How many build-up or bags have been checked in and how many more to be build-up or if any changes, addition, or reduction in ULDs is required, etc. Then based on all these details and the trail trim, and in consideration of the factors of load planning, he will prepare the loading instruction. All the necessary instructions, special handling requirement, etc. for the loading team will be included in easily understandable language and decipherable recognized standard aviation abbreviations. This loading instruction will be edition one or version one. The next step is to conduct a briefing with the loading team leader and the aircraft ground dispatcher, before they go off to the flight for loading and handling process commencement. Discuss all the specifics of the flight, summarize the loading instruction, provide clarity if required, etc. This is a good process as it gives clear understanding of the background of the flight, what is expected, and all are clear of any areas of concern, if any. Finally, issue the loading instruction (edition one or the latest) to the loading team leader, with copies of UWS and the current BRS list or baggage ULD list (planned and

Aircraft Weight and Balance
(Load Control)

currently loaded) or in case of bulk-loading, number of bags checked in. Another set of copies, including a loading instruction copy can be given to the aircraft ground dispatcher as well as he will be responsible for the overall handling progress at the aircraft site. The load sheet can be updated as they progress, as soon as each load is finalized (except passenger and baggage details), the weights can be entered in the appropriate columns. Only wait for the finalization level for updating the location/compartment columns for each load type.

4) Coordination: Once the loading instruction is issued and the loading has commenced at the aircraft, a periodic check would be desirable. This can be with the check-in team, baggage build-up team, and the loading team at the aircraft. This will be in regards to the progress so far and if there are any concerns, if any changes required can be done without impacting the flight planned schedule. If it is a necessity, then appropriate escalation to the ground dispatcher should be done for decision-making. If changes required are for safety reasons and there are no alternates, then they must be done after informing the ground dispatcher. Also, during this time there can be a Last Minute Change (LMC) UWS from the cargo section. These will not be major changes, only a small amount of additional cargo, mail, or other load, approximately in the range of 500 – 1000kg. Normally, LMCs are kept to a minimum due to the fact that the LIRF was issued and changes can impact the load plan, which need to be revised, which can affect the flight schedule. In rare cases, there can be offloading from previous or initial UWS or amendment in weights. Sometimes decisions can be taken at this level if any standby cargo is kept due to space constraints, then depending on the baggage build-up conditions to offload some cargo due to lack of space or payload on the flight. Also due to trim purposes, if any fuel is required in the tail tank, then the captain is to be advised of the amount approximately 01hour to departure.

5) Finalization and documentation: At this level, there are basically three stages:

    a- Space finalization: The last part of the puzzle to fall in place will be the actual passenger numbers (adults, child, infants, and numbers in each class) and the baggage weights with numbers. This will be known as soon as the check-in closes and no more passengers are accepted. This is normally 1 hour before departure time. Now the passenger details, including their weights, can be taken (standard), BRS will give the number of ULDs built, how many bags are to be loaded in each ULD, and the actual total weight. For calculations or the load sheet preparation, remember to include the ULD weight as well as the baggage weight. Some airlines have a standard weight for each type of ULD. With the baggage space requirement finalized, it is now clear as to how much space is available if any cargo is kept standby due to space constraints. So a decision is to be taken immediately to offload or look at the possibility for merging less full baggage ULDs (of the same category) to make space for the standby cargo ULD. Time permitting and if agreeable to the baggage team, this can be done at the baggage build-up area or at the aircraft if the airport authorities permit it and loading teams have sufficient manpower. This decision to be taken in conjunction with the ground dispatcher. Any change is to be amended on the load plan and the new loading instruction to issued and sent across to the loading team leader with verbal advice to both ground dispatcher and loading team leader. All changes must be done with a view of the aircraft trim. To avoid a last minute situation (either due to standby load uplift or otherwise), where a change in load plan can cause the aircraft to go out of safe trim range, careful analysis during the load calculation and trail trim should be done. There should be options in the plan to load smoothly, without making major changes that can derail or delay the loading process at the aircraft at the last minute.

b- <u>Payload Finalization</u>: Next is to calculate the actual ZFW, including any cargo that on standby due to payload. That is if the there is a drop in passengers and baggage and the drop in weight allows to uplift the standby cargo weight without exceeding the structural limits or RTOW provided earlier by the flight dispatcher. If the drop in passenger and baggage weight is not more than the standby cargo weight, then offload or if the cargo section has agreed previously to part shipment uplift (if bulk loading) then go ahead and uplift only the weight possible. As mentioned in the earlier paragraph regarding space standby, follow the trim effect process check and procedure also for this. Pass AZFW to the captain operating the flight at least 30 – 40 minutes to departure. He will calculate and advise regarding the actual total fuel, taxi fuel, trip fuel, and if any change is required to RTOW. If any change is to be made to the RTOW, then loads are to be checked to ensure the actual AZFW, ATOW, and ALW are within the limits.

c- <u>Documentation</u>: Next is to input all the remaining data, including the passenger and baggage details and location/compartment allocation of all the loads, on the load sheet. Verify the NOTOC details and update details in brief in the appropriate columns on the load sheet. Prepare the final trim sheet with the details as required as well. Complete it, recheck the indexes taken and plotted, and sign it. Transfer the MAC percentage to the load sheet and sign it. Recheck all the information from the UWS, LMC UWS, final BRS list, NOTOC, and compare derived and calculated data between LIRF, load sheet, and trim sheet.

6) <u>Verification and debrief</u>: This takes place at the aircraft side, not later than 20 minutes to departure time. Ensure the loading team was following the latest edition of the loading instruction, has clearly written down all the loading positions with the load details as planned by the load controller, and if all deviations (if any) were as authorized by the load controller himself. Verify the UWS and BRS details against the LIRF. Confirm special load stowage positions. Get the NOTOC signed by the loading team leader after he has verified and acknowledged the loading positions and special load types. Obtain the completed and signed loading instruction report from the loading team leader. Check if all safety checks have been carried out and if there are any other comments during the debrief. All of these, including the debrief, can be done in the presence of the ground dispatcher as well, to save time and avoid duplication.

Now there may be last-minute changes; for example, a missing passenger (may not have reported at the boarding gate after check-in and the airline cannot delay the flight) and so he and his bags will need to be removed (it is mandatory to remove bags as per ICAO regulations due to security reasons). This offloading will be organized by the ground dispatcher, and he will inform the load controller to do the Last Minute Change (LMC) in the load sheet. Then the load controller will make the LMC in the appropriate column of the load sheet. LMCs are allowed only up to certain weight changes, after which a new load sheet and trim sheet need to be prepared with the changes. The LMC limit range will be known to the ground dispatcher and load controller from the W&B manual as it varies from airline to airline. Some airlines allow the ground dispatcher to perform the LMC amendment on the signed load sheet if the weight difference is within the allowed tolerance limits. The last process at this level is for the load controller to present the completed and signed load sheet, trim sheet, and NOTOC to the captain. He will verify, take the relevant details, and sign off all of them. Since all of these documents are in multiple copy form, he will keep one signed copy and the rest will be returned to the load controller. A copy may also be required to be kept in the aircraft documentation bag, this varies from airline to airline. As per IATA/ICAO regulations, a signed copy of these documents must be retained in the airport of departure.

7) <u>Post-flight (messaging and recording):</u> In the final level, the load controller will take the data from the final details column of the load sheet to send the LDM. Basically, the total of the main figures. Total passengers, passenger classification, total load weight, distribution of the weights in the holds, etc. and the CPM with details from the LIRF (only for ULD-version aircrafts). A copy of the LIRF is given by the loading team to the ULD department for updating records and for sending the UCM. The messages are copied to the concerned department of the airline and the onward stations, particularly the next arriving station for their preparation for handling and so on. All the documents, copies, or messages, etc. are to be filed for each flight handled. This is a mandatory regulation.

The load controller is one of the most important links in the flight handling chain or process. His or her expertise, knowledge, and skill in planning are important to ensure accurate load planning to enable smooth handling, maximum commercial benefit, and punctual flight.

Aircraft Weight and Balance (Load Control)

Automation and Centralized Load Control

In today's technology driven world, aviation is at the forefront of new processes, innovative ideas, and cutting-edge automated solutions. There is a tendency to automate processes to reduce or ease human intervention as much as possible. Therefore, airlines and airports in many advanced countries have IT systems that are interconnected or integrated. Travel booking on the airline website or through a travel agent is connected to the airline reservation system, which is connected to the airport check-in system. Similarly, the cargo booking and documentation is also almost fully automated. These systems track and initiate processes as the commercial load progresses till the flight is finalized and beyond. Similarly, load control documentation such as issuing LIRF, load sheet, trim sheet output, NOTOC, etc. are also automated. All the other systems, like reservation system, check-in system, cargo system, baggage system, etc. feed data at the prescribed time or by initiation into the load control system. Which is then verified, analyzed by the load controller, re-assigned if done automatically by the system, and the loading instruction is prepared based on the factors of load planning, etc. The system will also show the trim effects continuously, so tail trim is not required, weight limitations, so weight calculation is not required. Some airline systems will not even give a load sheet output if the aircraft limits are exceeded or if it is out of the safe trim range. So there are safety checks in place at all levels, which have been built into the system. The messaging (LDM/CPM/etc.) are automatically transmitted by the system in the required format when the load controller initiates the flight close in his system. The addresses to be copied are also updated based on the flight route.

Although a lot of manual work has been automated, the basic processes mentioned above still need to be performed as complete automation has not yet been applied or is not possible currently. A level of human intervention is necessary as there are logical comparisons and complicated decisions to be taken at various times of flight handling by load control. As mentioned, each flight will have some unique requirements or situations that need a unique solution. Another fact is sometimes there would be need for options depending on the anticipated situations as they develop and decisions must be taken accordingly. So an automated solution by including all parameters of consideration usually done by a load controller, although not possible at the moment, can happen in the future.

Another concept used by airlines today is centralized load control. Earlier, airlines needed to send trainers to teach and certify load controllers to each and every airport they operated to. Later follow up training and recurrent training was also required. Even if there was only one flight a week or more, the requirement was still necessary. The cost involved and proficiency levels were also a concern. With the facilitation of new technology, it is now possible to have load controllers perform load control functions at a centralized location. These locations are normally where the proficiency is high, sufficient numbers are available, and cost is less. So it is possible for a load controller in DXB to prepare a load plan and perform all load control functions for a flight operating from LHR to JFK. There are agreed processes, with timelines for each process and clear communication guidelines and equipment provided to do this. The data for load planning and LIRF, load and trim sheet is made available in the load control system or through email messages at the prescribed times. This is used by the load controller to prepare the load plan based on the factors of load planning, complete the safety and limit checks, pass AZFW to the captain in the flight deck (as the flight communications system is also connected). After which the captain will respond with the fuel figures. The Final LIRF is faxed or scanned and sent to the load controller. The load controller, after verification with the actual load plan, will transmit the load and trim sheet data to the flight deck for the captain to take a print and sign it. Although the load controller will not have a signed copy, the electronic version copy which he transmitted and will take for his record is acceptable by the authorities concerned. The departing station will ask the captain to sign a duplicate copy for their records as required. All the messaging is done automatically in the required format when the load controller closes the flight in his system. The biggest drawback in this method is that there is higher chance of communication gap between the load controller and the loading team. Transfer of knowledge, skill, and expertise is lost between them. The multiple layers of safety or cross-checking are reduced. All these can give rise to errors that can have safety impacts. In terms of cost, the airline will need to send a trainer to train the loading team anyway, as each aircraft handling will have some special features e.g., aircraft loading systems and locking, etc. along with specific airline requirements as well. So cost difference is negligible. It sometimes is more important to have a load controller handling flights in the airport as depending on the level of proficiency and understanding of loading teams at certain airports, they would need assistance and clarification from the load controller. Another important benefit is the ability to make quick decisions if the load controller is at hand.

Overall, it is desirable to have a load controller at a station with the assistance of an automated system to assist in his function. However, the basic functions of the load controller will still need to be done, whichever the method employed.

****

Aircraft Weight and Balance
(Load Control)

Chapter IX
Aircraft Ground Dispatch

Introduction

It is expected that once each team with the required knowledge, expertise, and skill are given a set of instructions or functions to perform based on the standard operating procedures applicable, they would do it. This can happen in a perfect world or almost always, meaning not all the time. Well, we don't live in a perfect world, and we need to ensure every time there is 100% accurate, reliable, safe, and customer service oriented performance within the framework of the applicable regulations. This is possible if there is a binding and guiding force or prime leader to ensure order is maintained, and each team's aim corresponds with the organizational goal. The aircraft ground dispatcher is just that person. He is the flight manager at the aircraft. He manages, coordinates, guides, and monitors all functions and personnel working on the aircraft. He is the person most responsible at the aircraft to ensure the flight departs safely, punctually, with the planned commercial load, all within the applicable state, international governing bodies, airline, and handling company regulations.

If there were no ground dispatchers, each team can amend or follow their own set of processes that is most convenient and suitable for them. They may not have any regards for the other teams. As mentioned, the complete aircraft or flight handling is a long chain of interconnected and sometimes overlapping functions performed by different teams in the airport. All these need to be synchronized well for the whole machinery to function smoothly. E.g. the loading team may take more time than required for loading the flight, this can delay the load controller and subsequently, the flight. Here the ground dispatcher's role sets in to check what the issue is for the hold-up and take necessary steps to bring the process in line. He becomes the management representative at the aircraft site. The flight operations dispatcher is different from the aircraft ground dispatcher. The flight operations dispatcher prepares the flight plan, flight routing, etc., whereas the ground dispatcher is responsible for ramp handling of the flight at an airport.

Chapter Contents

Knowledge, expertise, and skill
Area of responsibility
Precision timing schedule
Dispatch card and checklist
Functions of ground dispatcher
Delay analysis and allocation

****

Knowledge, Expertise, and Skill

The ground dispatcher should be proficient in aircraft loading and load control, with check-in and baggage services exposure as added bonus. He must also possess sufficient experience in the fields mentioned. This knowledge and experience is necessary for him or her to comprehend and understand different requirements and scenarios that will be faced during the course of the job function, thus enabling him to make the correct decision when options and time are limited. He may not have the luxury to analyze all the facts, but job knowledge and expertise will act as the ideal tool in these tight situations. For example, if he needs to explain the loading progress on the flight to the load controller, he must have a good idea of the hold layout, ULD types, and other load planning factors. Another example is if the loading is held up due to missing cargo ULD, he can coordinate with the load controller to re-plan the load plan with ULDs already existing at the aircraft to continue the loading without stopping and plan the missing ULD, if received, near the door area. Another important quality is that he should be able to anticipate potential issues that will be detrimental to the safety and punctuality of the flight handling and take necessary steps to avert an impact. He must devise innovative solutions that are within the provisions of applicable safety and security regulations. E.g. if the loading on a flight is to be started and the loading team is held up at another spot, he can coordinate with the loading supervisor and shift another loading team to the flight, if available nearby and conduct the briefing as well. Or if there is a passenger number reconciliation issue on board the aircraft, where the boarding staff is unable to get the correct number of passengers boarded against those checked in, while this is being verified, he can simultaneously ask the crew to do a manual head count on board. The dispatcher may start the flight handling about 01hour and 15minutes to departure, and the most critical time is the last 20minutes till departure. As you can see every activity will be conducted in minutes from then on and so the response and decision-making capability of the ground dispatcher will be critical and would mean the difference between punctuality and delay. He has to be 100% accurate in terms of safety and security, there is no margin of error. So there is tremendous pressure and responsibility on the dispatcher to ensure the flight departs safely and punctually. Hence, it is paramount that the dispatcher is equipped with all the critical knowledge, understanding, and skills.

Communication

In addition, communication skills are an added necessity. He must ensure to transmit information clearly and understandably in all forms of communication. Avoiding and reducing heavy accents, talking in even tone, etc. He must ensure the communication equipment is serviceable and has sufficient battery life. Never joke, avoid inappropriate comments, insults, or shouting when transmitting information or communicating in a professional environment. Always be precise and to the point. All reports must be legible and in professional language. Note down important aspects, issues, solutions, times of these, etc. for conflict management, later analysis, and reporting if necessary.

Presentable

Grooming standards for a dispatcher are particularly important, as he will be exposed to outside environmental elements, will need to be in the aircraft cabin, and, at the boarding gate, may need to even communicate with the passengers as well. So he or she must have appropriate smart and clean uniform. Refer to grooming standards mentioned in the chapter for ramp staff.

Aircraft Ground Dispatch

Area of Responsibility

The ground dispatcher's area of responsibility is in and around the aircraft. He is responsible above the wing (i.e. in the upper cabin and boarding gate) and below the wing (aircraft holds and ramp area around the aircraft). The main responsibilities can vary from airport to airport and airline to airline. They can be categorized but not limited to the following:

1. Operational responsibilities
    - Check if crew are boarded on time for departure and follow up if there is any delay. For arrival crew, check if transportation from aircraft is available.
    - Ensure crew bags are loaded as per LIRF. If they are for an arrival flight, ensure that they are sent with the crew or to the arrival hall. If transit, ensure the same remains on board.
    - Confirm if crew are having all necessary flight operations documents such as flight plan, weather charts, etc. If not, arrange to obtain the same minimum 01hour 15minutes to departure time.
    - Confirm with engineering team of aircraft serviceability.
    - Keep the aircraft movement or network control center advised of flight handling status and if any assistance is required for follow-up or escalation when any issues that may impact punctual operational, commercial, or handling processes.
    - Confirm sufficient catering is on board.
    - Confirm cleaning has been completed as required by crew or airlines standards.
    - Ensure fueling of aircraft is underway on time.
    - If any flight spares are to be loaded, ensure the same is at the aircraft; otherwise, ask the loading team to follow up.
    - Brief the crew with all necessary commercial, operational, and handling aspects of the flight.
    - Get the boarding clearance and inform the boarding team.
    - Keep crew updated of the flight handling status periodically, also of any delays if anticipated.
2. Commercial responsibilities
    - Obtain briefing from load controller on the flight load specifics and brief the loading team as well.

- Check if any loads are on standby as well as the reasons and follow up for loading clearance with sufficient time for loading, or otherwise if there is any change to the load plan due to trim.
- Ensure all special shipment is at the aircraft for loading and arrival and special shipments have been sent to the appropriate section by the loading team.
- Obtain briefing from the boarding team regarding booked and checked figures, special needs passengers, etc. If there are any delays in check-in closure, then establish the reasons.
- If any loads are kept on standby, coordinate with the load controller to look at options for loading the same, if possible.
- Avoid any offloading without a justifiable reason.

3. Handling responsibilities
    - Ensure all the necessary equipment and manpower are available at the aircraft for handling as necessary.
    - Ensure the loading team checks the joining load at the aircraft and follows up for those missing. Monitor and ensure all are at the aircraft with sufficient time for them to load within the ground time.
    - For arrival, ensure all inbound loads are sent from aircraft to appropriate load processing areas within specified time frame.
    - Advise loading team about crew bags to be unloaded on arrival and sent to the appropriate area and joining to be loaded as per the LIRF. In regards to transit, check with crew on board and provide handling requirements to the loading team.
    - Monitor loading status and intervene if any delays or issues arise, as necessary to solve them and bring it back on track.
    - Monitor handling of special loads, transit, and transfer loads as well by checking with the loading teams or intervene if there are any issues and solve the same.
    - Ensure all the teams from various departments have completed the servicing of the flight, within the agreed time.
    - Coordinate with the boarding team, give clearance for boarding, and monitor boarding status.
    - Obtain missing passengers' details with their baggage position in the ULD or trolley in time to initiate the

Aircraft Ground Dispatch

baggage offloading process. This is to avoid delay or reduce delay if any.
- Ensure the loading team and the load controller coordinate closely with each other during flight loading and conduct necessary briefing before and debriefing after the flight.
- Confirm all handling documents, such as load sheet, trim sheet, passenger manifest, cargo manifest, etc. are on board before flight departure.

4. Safety responsibilities
   - Ensure all the safety checks have been done by individual teams, and constantly monitor any lapse and correct immediately. For example, that the engineering teams have done their damage checks, loading teams have checked the parking stand for any debris or equipment blocking the parking stand before aircraft parks and before pushback. If not, they have to ensure the same is done.
   - Ensure the loading team checks the loads are intended for the same flight. And also that they are following the loading instruction from load control.
   - Ensure deviations or changes in the loading, if necessary, are discussed with the load controller and confirmed, further advised to the loading team leader. And that the latest edition of loading instruction is used by the team.
   - Ensure LMCs are done correctly on the load sheet and the crew is aware of the same.
   - In some airports it is the dispatcher who operates the aero bridges. Only operate if you have completed sufficient training and are certified to do so. Ensure all safety checks are done.

5. Security responsibilities
   - Pass the baggage tags of missing passengers to the loading team for offloading from the aircraft. Once offloaded, recheck to ensure the same.
   - Same maybe required by the crew for reconfirming; hence, arrange to keep it at the agreed spot. Take necessary steps to avoid reloading by loading team by error.
   - If missing passengers bags are at the baggage build-up area, ensure written confirmation is received that the same has been offloaded there.
   - Ensure necessary steps are in place to avoid arriving passengers do not mix with departing passengers.

Aircraft Ground Dispatch

- Ensure necessary arrangements are in place to avoid any unauthorized entry into the aircraft cabin or aircraft holds.
- There must be clear understanding and valid reason for all personnel's presence and activity at the aircraft. If not, immediately seek clarity.
- Never board the aircraft before the crew does a security check of the cabin for any unaccompanied or dangerous items. Similarly, ask the loading team to check the holds before commencing the loading.
- Ensure the boarding over confirmation is received in writing from the boarding team leader and loading over confirmation from the loading team, before releasing the flight for departure.

As advised, the above are the most important of the many responsibilities and these may be different for different airport and airline set-ups. Some of the responsibilities may be shared or overlapped between the various teams at the aircraft. At some airports the dispatcher is only concerned with over the wing activity and has a casual monitoring role below the wing. However, it is desirable to have an overall responsibility and intervening power for a quick decisive role. Again, there are tendency to rely heavily on the dispatcher.

Precision Timing Schedule (PTS)

When there are a chain of interconnected and overlapping activities, meaning one to be completed for another to start and one activity to continue when another is starting etc. can be a confusing prospect. There will be lack of clarity, conflicts, loose direction, etc. Flight handling at the aircraft is a beehive of activities at times, all working towards the common goal of flight departure safely and punctually with the planned load. All these activities need to be coordinated, monitored, and times required standardized. For these airlines have devised the precision timing schedule (*See figure.IX.1*).

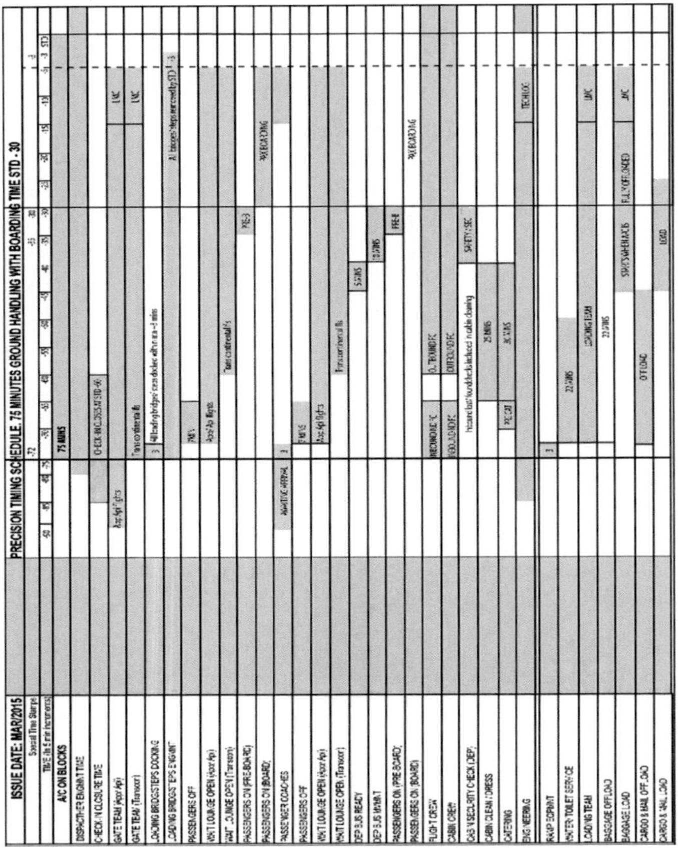

Fig. IX.1: Precision Timing Schedule.

It gives the exact time allotted for each activity, what are the interconnected activities, and which can be done with an overlapping. For example, first the cleaners need to clean the cabin, which is allotted 45mins before departure, then 10mins for crew to do their safety and security checks, and then can the boarding start. This is because if cleaners are in the cabin, crew cannot perform their checks, and if passengers board before crew complete their check, then there is no use of the checks. So if cleaning takes longer, then there will be knock-on effect. So then crew check will be delayed, which will delay the boarding and so on. There are other

Aircraft Ground Dispatch

activities that overlap but will not have an impact; for example, fueling can take place when boarding is going on, as long as there is crew are on board (due to safety and security requirements). Thus, as advised, every activity is measured in minutes and although each team is aware of their allocated time, it is the ground dispatcher's responsibility to ensure it is complied with, to prompt or escalate when not followed, and finally, guide toward the planned departure. The PTS acts as a tool for the dispatcher, it tells him which activity is not going as scheduled and can impact the flight schedule, when or where he needs to intervene or escalate, etc. It forms a guideline for all, especially the dispatcher, and helps to provide clarity, enables analysis, and assists is allocating delays if they happen.

There are other activities away from the aircraft that are as critical but have an earlier start and finish time, which are not included in the PTS. These will be too obvious to the dispatcher, and he may have sufficient time to intervene. Some of them are:

1) Cargo load finalization, which should ideally be done about 3 – 4 hours before departure, may get delays sometimes, so UWS is delayed, and the load controller will be unable to complete his load plan. Further, the ULDs or cargo load may reach late from the cargo build-up terminal to aircraft for loading. These need to be closely followed up and escalated to avoid impacts to schedule.

2) Baggage build-up: Although the first wave of baggage may be at the aircraft earlier than 1 hour to departure, the last baggage ULDs or last checked bags may come late to aircraft, between 30minutes to 10minutes or beyond, which can surely delay the flight. This can happen to various reasons, such as late check-in closure, bags stuck in the conveyor system, conveyor system malfunction, etc. The transfer bags are the most difficult at many airline hub airports. The inbound flight may come in late and thus, the transfer bags may need to be processed at the transfer baggage area (scanning or recording to confirm passenger is actually transferring on the outbound flight, then security screened, build-up, and transported to the intended departure flight). This can take time. Airlines authorize delays in these cases as it is a commercial requirement. Again, there can be delays further due to large volumes, congestion, etc. So it becomes necessary for the dispatcher and loading team to closely coordinate with baggage teams

to ensure all bags are at the aircraft with sufficient time for loading.
3) Passengers boarding delays: In some rare cases, the passenger check-in may be delayed due to various reasons, such a traffic congestion, industrial labor action, etc. Transfer passengers may arrive late from a delayed arrival flight. Here too the airline may allow for some delays, which will be advised in advance or otherwise allowed as a standard process with allocated connections times for accepting or boarding them.

In the above scenarios, the dispatcher will have sufficient knowledge of the same 01hr 10minutes or more before departure and thus, can take necessary action accordingly to solve the problem. Otherwise, if it is out of his control, he can escalate or otherwise establish the delay reasons with the owning section, keep all advised, and look for options to minimize the delay.

Dispatch Card and Checklist

The dispatcher needs a list of critical activities to be monitored and timing record for the same. It is a tool that corresponds with the list of activities and allocated time for each. So the most critical activities in flight handling (including operational) are grouped together for a flight on the dispatch card. It can be an integrated one, which includes or acts like a checklist as well. Here the flight number, date, route, type of aircraft, and each critical activity will be listed. Against each activity the actual timing is also to be updated. There will be columns to update commercial load details as well, such as bookings, transfer passenger and baggage details, etc. The rear page can be used for free text for report writing, suggest solutions to issue, etc. So the dispatcher card acts as a brief about the flight, analysis of delay, and a recording tool. Some dispatch cards have an included safety checklist as well.

Nowadays, with increased technological solutions, the manual dispatch cards have been replaced with automated handheld remote devices. They automatically get updated with allocated flight details, including commercial and operational data, prompt when critical activity's actual time is not updated when current time has crossed the PTS prescribed time limit, interact with other systems to update the dispatcher about boarding status, loading status, baggage

ULD list, etc. Some remote units even have messaging, scanning, or phone functions as well.

Functions of the Ground Dispatcher

The important functions of the dispatcher can be categorized into main three stages:

1) Pre-flight
2) Flight handling
3) Post-flight

Let us go into details regarding the role or functions of the dispatcher, with elaboration on the various teams involved in flight handling and who coordinates closely with him. These teams may be from different sections of the airport or handling company, etc., but they all come together as a single team with a single aim for handling that flight and ensuring it departs safely and punctually, with maximum possible convenience to the customer as possible. The timelines for each individual team activity may not be emphasized as it is covered by the PTS applicable for each airport or airline specification. To elaborate further each of the above stages based on a departure flight (consider using manual dispatch cards):

1) Pre-flight:
    i- Gather flight details from the flight allocator or the appropriate information system, such as flight number, date, route, aircraft type, and parking stand and update the dispatch card or record sheet or checklist as applicable. Check communication equipment is in good working condition, with sufficient battery power left.
    ii- Next, obtain briefing from load controller, obtain the passenger and other load booking, space allocation for baggage (priority, economy, transfer), cargo, etc. If any special loads, standbys, cargo offloads, their reasons and options. Verify the loading plan and based on the current ramp conditions (congestion, equipment shortage, etc.), look at options to adjust the loading plan accordingly without upsetting the other load planning factors, if possible. Discuss with the load controller and find amicable options, if necessary.

Aircraft Ground Dispatch

Collect a copy of loading instruction, UWS, latest baggage build-up list, and NOTOC (if any).
- iii- Brief the loading team, instruct to perform safety checks which should include checking the parking bay for any debris, making sure any dolly or trolley should be with brakes engaged, vehicles chocked, etc. Aircraft holds should not have any unaccounted loads or items, all loads are to be checked and verified with tags, etc. Obtain feedback on thoughts and requirements for smooth handling. Ensure they have made arrangements for the loading process manpower and equipment (hi-loaders, tractors/tugs for dollies with operators, etc.) which is sufficient based on the booked loads, aircraft type, and work involved.
- iv- Exchange communication contact details.

2) Flight handling:
- i- On arrival at the aircraft, reconfirm registration and parking stand, approximately 01hour and 15minutes to departure (can vary depending on airport airline or aircraft type. Basically, report before the most critical activity shown in the PTS that is applicable to that particular airport, airline, aircraft type.
- ii- Take an update from the loading team leader that safety checks have been completed, all loads other than baggage has been received, and how much of the baggage planned has been received, and if all equipment and manpower are available for loading and advise if any issues.
- iii- Check if aero bridge/steps and other equipment have been positioned safely as required against the aircraft.

Next, on board the aircraft:
- iv- Engineering team: There will be an engineer and mechanic allocated to the flight. They will perform serviceability checks before the crew report about 1hour 10minutes to departure time and also verify the technical log for any defects that were reported and cleared. There can be different engineers for different parts of the aircraft, such as avionics engineer, airframe engineer, in-flight entertainment engineer, etc. The allocated line maintenance engineer will be responsible to call out the appropriate engineer, if it is

beyond his scope of rectification and if the other required engineer is available. This option is only available at the base station of the aircraft, normally. Otherwise, it will only be a line maintenance engineer on the flight and no mechanics for assistance either. Sometimes there can be minor defects that can be cleared during the periodic service checks, rather than holding the aircraft, the flight can operate based on dispensation from the engineering department. There can also be defective equipment with which, if not serious, the aircraft can operate, as long as these equipment or components are not in the minimum equipment list (MEL). Sometimes defects can have an impact on the handling aspects as well; for example, carriage of additional fuel due to a component issue can reduce commercial load capacity availability. Or non-availability of netting in the bulk hold can cause engineering to stop any loading in that compartment, etc.

Further, the engineer will be advised by his office of the minimum or standby fuel required for the flight. As it happens, the flight may need a lot of fuel depending on the route. If we need to wait for the captain or his first officer to come, calculate the fuel required, and then start the fueling, this may delay the flight as it can take lot of time to fuel the aircraft. So based on the estimated fuel passed by the dispatcher, the engineer will fuel the aircraft up to a minimum amount from the total planned. Approximately, 10,000 to 5,000kg less than the total required. He will coordinate with fueling staff and start aircraft fueling even before the captain reports to the aircraft. Later, he will coordinate between the captain, the fueling staff, and aircraft tank readings to ensure the aircraft has been fuel as per the required quantity given to him by the captain operating the flight.

Depending on the airline and airport, the engineering team may also be involved in aircraft towing, pushback operation, and ground-to-flight deck communication. Sometimes the aircraft may need an after service check or may need to be repositioned to another parking stand. Here a qualified engineer needs to be in the flight deck to coordinate with the control tower, pushback tractor operator, and the headset man. In some airports it is the airline or handling agent mechanic who is the headset man performing the ground-to-flight deck communication. When the flight has come to a stop at its parking stand, the headset man will connect his headset to the internal communication system of the aircraft. He needs to inform the flight deck crew when the chocks have been placed at the tires (to stop it from rolling), so that the crew can shut off the engines and release the brakes. Similarly for departure, once the doors are closed, the mechanic or headset man will inform the crew if all servicing equipment has been removed and is clear of the aircraft, and the pushback tractor connected. The captain will inform to start the pushback operation, when he has got clearance from the control tower to do so. Before commencement, the headset man will inform that he is going to remove the chocks as well.

The engineering team also performs damage checks on the fuselage and engines on arrival and prior to departure as well. If any damages or defects are noticed by anyone, then immediately inform the engineer on duty.

Thus, the dispatcher on arrival at the aircraft needs to check if the engineer is available to check if the aircraft is serviceable and if the standby fuel amount has been received. If there is an issue reported, he needs to check if any handling functions needs to be held up and for how long, and accordingly inform the concerned team. For example, if the boarding cannot be initiated at the prescribed time due to a defect in the cabin, then the dispatcher must inform the boarding team accordingly with the estimated time, so that the passengers and others concerned are kept advised. Follow up closely with the engineer from time to time. Next, ensure the headset and pushback team arrangements are in place with concerned. The pushback team will be available approximately 20 to 15minutes to departure time for a departure flight and headset man for arrival flight will be on standby before the aircraft taxies in for parking. The headset man and or the engineering team also does a bay sweep to check if any equipment is blocking the bay for the aircraft to park or if any foreign object is on the ramp that can damage the tires or may be sucked into the engines. If any of this is noticed, the dispatcher or the control is to be advised and the foreign object removed, before the aircraft can be parked.

v- Catering team: Catering, including the catering trolleys from the inbound flight, will be replaced fully by the catering team If it is a departure flight, the airline planning department will advise the catering section of the booked load and the requirements well in advance (approximately 24hours in advance). The catering will be loaded closer to departure, about 1hour to 45minutes to departure time. This is because there are food safety and hygiene requirements. Only the crew are supposed to open the catering trolley to check if the amount of catering is as per requirement. The dispatcher needs to coordinate with the catering team to ensure flight is catered based on the bookings when he reports to the flight. The catering department of the airline would have given the specifications of the catering required for each sector well in advance. If any additional catering is requested by the crew, then this needs to be informed to the catering team and ensured that it is loaded before departure.

vi- Cabin cleaning team: When an aircraft arrives and after the inbound passengers disembark, its cabin is cleaned, headrests and blankets replaced with new, etc. by the cabin cleaning team. Once cleaning is completed, crew will check and give their approval. For a departure flight, where the aircraft has been on ground previously, the cleaning would have been done earlier, but the dispatcher needs to reconfirm this. If additional cleaning is requested by the crew, then he has to get the cleaning team to get it arranged.

vii- At the boarding gate, the boarding gate team will check the documents and boarding cards of the travelling passengers and if all are in order, collect the boarding gate portion of the boarding card and return the remaining to the passenger. The passenger is then guided to the holding lounge, where if there are any excess hand bags, they are tagged and taken for loading in the aircraft hold. The dispatcher on arrival at the aircraft will visit the boarding gate, to discuss with the boarding team about the flight specifics, bookings, if there are any special passengers, number of passengers boarding on wheel chairs till the aircraft door, medical passengers requiring special care, if there are any expectant mothers, etc. The boarding team will give a full briefing of all these special cases to the dispatcher and communication guidelines and time lines will be agreed upon for boarding and other aspects of handling. When the dispatcher gives the clearance for boarding the passengers into the aircraft, the boarding team will start the boarding accordingly, based on the class of travel. It is the boarding team who will initiate paging for the passengers for the flight, especially about 20 – 30 minutes to departure for those yet to report to the gate. For those still missing at 15minutes to departure, the boarding team leader will inform the terminal team to search for them and hand over a copy of the baggage details with loading position from the BRS to the dispatcher to initiate the offloading as required by the security. He will finalize the boarding after counting all boarded against those checked in, close the gates, confirm missing passenger is boarded if found and or if offloaded, then confirm the bags have been offloaded with the dispatcher and confirm boarding is over to the dispatcher. The boarding team will print the passenger manifest, special meal request list, class-wise distribution of the passengers with names and seat numbers, etc. and hand it over to the crew on board. In the terminal, there will be the terminal team who will guide the checked passengers to the boarding gates, search for missing passengers, and keep the boarding gate team advised. The dispatcher needs to at times ask them to advise missing passengers in the terminal for their flight, although this will normally be coordinated through the boarding gate staff.

viii- Crew: By crew it means flight deck crew (operating captain and his first officer) and cabin crew (the chief steward or purser and the remaining crew). The crew arrive at the aircraft for departure about 01hour to departure. Arrangements must be in place to load their bags in the allocated position, based on the loading instruction from the load controller. Re-check the aircraft serviceability with the flight deck crew and whether there are any concerns in regards to handling functions. The crew may in some cases ask dispatcher to hold boarding initiation or loading, etc. if there is an issue; thus, similar to earlier scenario, the dispatcher will coordinate with the engineer accordingly. Brief the flight deck crew of all the special loads and important aspects of the handling as well if they need to know. It will be the right time to also give a copy of the NOTOC provided by the load controller, so that they can verify if there are any restrictions or issues in carrying the shipment in the NOTOC. Next, brief the cabin crew of any special passengers or other requirements. And finally, obtain the boarding clearance from the cabin chief steward when they complete the catering check and safety and security check, and pass it to the boarding gate team leader.

Once the loading and boarding has started, then your role is monitoring of loading and boarding status, intervene if necessary or required if an issue is anticipated. Throughout the flight handling process, keep monitoring the activities and update the dispatch card accordingly.

ix- About 20 minutes from departure, get confirmation from loading team leader if all loads have been received, loaded as per loading instruction, and verified with UWS and baggage list. Instruct him to load the hand baggage collected by the boarding team in the allocated location as per the LIRF and to ensure no other load is remaining at the parking stand. Ensure the load controller has arrived at the aircraft and reconfirm if the same has been checked by him as well. Confirm pushback team with headset man is available at the aircraft. Give periodic update to the network control center of the flight status.

x- Check boarding status with boarding staff, if there are any missing passengers, obtain the details and pass them to the loading team leader to retrieve the bags of the missing passenger. Instruct him or her to position the bags after offloading towards the front starboard side of the aircraft, where the crew may be able see from the flight deck. Once the loading team has confirmed offloading, physically verify the tags against the printout given by the boarding team leader. Inform the boarding team leader of offloading completion.

xi- Once the boarding team leader provides confirmation of the boarding being over and that all passengers are on board, give clearance to the loading team leader to release all equipment. Ensure the passenger manifest, set list, etc. are put on board by the boarding team and other documents such as crew general declaration, cargo manifest, air waybill, etc. are also stowed in the documents bag. In some airports these documents are brought to aircraft by the load controller, while in others by dedicated documentation staff, while in still others by the cargo section staff, etc. Ensure the load controller has made the necessary LMC entries, if any, and the captain has signed the load sheet and other documents.

xii- Once all of this completed, get confirmation from crew that all airport staff have disembarked and give clearance to close doors. Once doors are closed, remove the aero bridge. Take the pushback time from the headset man, if aircraft communication system does not auto-send this to company monitoring system.

3) Post-flight:
   i- If there was a flight delay or an issue, then get an explanation or detailed report from the owning section on the causes or contributing factors, etc. and suggestions or steps to avoid recurrence.
   ii- Finalize the delay if any (decide the appropriate delay code and delay time allocated) and pass the off chocks or off blocks time to the network control or movement control center (inclusive of delay code and time allocated, if any).
   iii- Finalize the dispatcher card with full updates and reports, if any.

For an arrival flight

When the ground dispatcher is allocated for an arrival flight only and the aircraft will be operating a departure flight more than two hours later.

1) <u>Pre-flight:</u>
   i. Gather flight details from the flight allocator or the appropriate information system, such as flight number, date, origin route, aircraft type, and parking stand, and update the dispatch card or record sheet or checklist as applicable. Check communication equipment is in good working condition, with sufficient battery power left.
   ii. Next, obtain the CPM or the offloading instruction copy from the load controller. Check the same for the number of incoming passengers and amount of other loads such as baggage, cargo etc. This will give an idea of the resources and manpower required, e.g. if both high loaders required, number of dollies required, etc. If it is a bulk-loading aircraft, then the LDM will show the weight and number of baggage, and the weight of other load and the hold in which it is loaded, so accordingly the dispatcher can ascertain conveyors required, trolleys required for offloading the loads, manpower required for the offload, etc. Again, for ULD-version aircrafts, the number ULDs with different load types will give a clear indication of how many tugs will be required to send each train to the various load processing areas, such as baggage arrivals, transfer baggage processing area, cargo terminal, etc. The CPM will also advise of special loads such as dangerous goods, valuables, live animals, etc. Although it is more important for the offloading team to know and understand these, the dispatcher also must have sufficient knowledge of the same. He needs to verify that the offloading team has made sufficient arrangements. If an issue may cause delivery delay, he should be able to anticipate it and take corrective steps in advance; otherwise, if there is a delay in service delivery for incoming loads, then he should be able know the real reason. Annotate all the

       incoming commercial load details in the inbound column of the dispatch card.
- iii. Brief the loading team, instruct to perform safety checks which should include checking the parking bay for any debris, making sure any dolly or trolley should be with brakes engaged, vehicles chocked, etc. Ensure an aircraft pre-offloading damage check is done, both near the doors and in the holds. After full offloading is completed, there must not be any unaccounted loads or items, except for any flight spares that have been specifically informed to be kept on board as per the offloading instruction. All loads and or ULDs should be checked and verified with tags, etc. and dispatched to their respective processing areas within agreed timelines. Ensure they have made arrangements for manpower and equipment (hi-loaders, conveyors, dollies, trolleys, tractors/tugs for dollies with operators, etc.), which is based on the incoming loads, aircraft type, and work involved.
- iv. Exchange communication contact details.

2) Flight Handling:
- i. Confirm aircraft parking stand with movement control center, as flight parking can change due to delays and other last minute airport congestions, etc.
- ii. Verify safety checks, including parking stand debris check, etc. are carried out by the respective team.
- iii. Confirm sufficient resources are available, including the loading team.
- iv. Check if the aero bridge is serviceable and correctly in position. If it is remote parking, check that steps and sufficient buses/coaches are available.
- v. On arrival position the aero bridge, only after the beacons are turned off, chocks are in place, and clearance given by the head set man. Always allow the crew to open the door by giving the clearance through the door window. This is because only the crew will know if the emergency escape chute mechanism of the door has been armed or disarmed.
- vi. Do not allow anyone except the engineer to enter the aircraft till all passengers have disembarked, unless otherwise requested by the crew.

vii. Meet the crew after passengers have disembarked for anything they want to report. The incoming documents, like general declarations (few copies will be taken by the crew for immigration purposes at the arrival hall), cargo manifests, etc. will be collected by the appropriate sections concerned.
viii. Cleaners and catering should start their handling accordingly. The engineers will open the service doors for them on the starboard side, as necessary.
ix. Check with loading the team if all load has been dispatched as per prescribed the time and report if there are any discrepancies.

3) Post-flight:
   i. Report any discrepancy. If there are any incoming anomalies, send a report to the outstation concerned or to appropriate sections for corrective action.
   ii. Record and file.

For turnaround or transit flights:

It would be a combination of both arrival and departure together. However, the timelines need to be closely monitored for turnaround flights. There would be a full unloading and loading. Every activity will be critical as there is no luxury like starting early for a departure flight, since the aircraft in this case was not on ground earlier. Even the arrival passengers also need to be disembarked as quickly as possible. There would be a need for additional cleaners and other resources. Similar to a transit flight handling, there is added requirement for handling transit passengers and other loads, both above wings and below wings. Here if the transit passengers are disembarking and re-boarding, then arrangements must be made for them to carry all their handbags in the cabin with them, later when boarding to check their travel documents as well. Offloading missing transit passengers' baggage can be time consuming if the previous airport has not provided the baggage list. As then it will difficult to locate the same on board, unless all transit bags are removed and checked. Hence, there should be close monitoring and handling of transit passengers by the boarding and terminal teams.

Aircraft Ground Dispatch

Delay Analysis and Allocation

All airlines want their flights to operate on schedule as any delay can cost millions of dollars. For example, a delayed flight can miss the arrival slot at the next airport and may be asked to land at some other airport due to congestion or allowed to land but have no parking (burning fuel for keeping the engines on) or it may not be handled for a long time due airport congestion. Delays also can cause severe disruptions to the airline schedule as one delay can have a knock-on effect on other subsequent flights, since this aircraft after arrival may have been required to operate another flight. This would mean losing customers to competitors, etc. So any delay at an airport is analyzed closely for corrective measures.

A flight may be delayed to one or more reasons. There can be contributing delays from the same or different sections. And it is the dispatcher, who after careful analysis of all contributing factors will allocate he delay. There is a tendency by the owning department to argue, justify, or even take this as a blame or shortfall. The dispatcher thus will need to have all the facts to justify to his senior officer should it be questioned later. A delay will naturally point out an issue or shortfall or process flaw and thus, instead of taking it as a fault, appropriate steps should be taken to correct the same. It should be regarded as an opportunity for service improvement.

The dispatcher also must be impartial and work with high integrity. He must not hold any misguided or preconceived negative attitude towards an individual or section. He must understand that he is working around expensive and highly specialized equipment and highly skilled team members, in a very technologically advanced industry. A positive attitude, together with a professional approach, will assist the dispatcher to maintain his credibility and the approachability of all those around him. This will in turn assist him in flight handling by getting optimum support and reliable service.

The ground dispatcher is the final and important link in the chain of flight planning and handling. All the months of planning, coordination, and efforts culminate when the dispatcher dispatches the flight safely and punctually, with all the planned commercial load.

****

Chapter X
Aviation Safety and Security

Introduction

A book, manual, or article on airport handling is complete only with mention of the prominence of safety and security. That is the level of importance these two have in civil aviation industry, especially pertaining to today's airport operations environment. In an airport environment, safety and security is every airport user's responsibility and duty. It is not just for the security department or the airport police. If every person has a safety and security conscious mind, that could save lives, injuries, and costs. Creating the safety and security culture is a daunting task, but possible. The state, being a member of ICAO, is responsible for safeguarding civil aviation in the country against acts of unlawful interference. IATA also has recommended practices that the participating airlines can replicate or assimilate into their organizational framework and policies. These are then cascaded down to the employees of all organizations involved in airport operations. The necessity of a safe and secure environment cannot be overemphasized. It is important to build public confidence and sustain the unprecedented growth of the civil aviation industry. Therefore, everyone in civil aviation has an important role to play in ensuring safety and security is maintained. For every ramp staff, a highly focused safety attitude and security understanding is mandatory.

Chapter Contents

  Regulatory requirement and recommended practice
  Airport safety and security
  Organizational framework and programs
  Operational security requirements
  Operational safety requirements

****

Regulatory Requirement and Recommended Practice

ICAO has enacted regulations that require member states to safeguard civil aviation (passengers, crew, ground personnel, general public, and indirectly airline assets) against acts of unlawful interference. They are required to have appropriate agencies to enforce, protect, and also respond adequately to increased threats. ICAO and IATA have regulations and recommendations respectively in place for ensuring safety and security programs in each airline organization and country. There are standards and recommended practices provided by both these world bodies with guidelines to both the airline and the countries involved. ICAO annex 17 is one that deals with aviation security. These regulations and recommendations are incorporated into the organizational framework and procedures of every airline and handling company at the airport. In addition, the airport security agencies also enforce these on all other users as well. Hence, the rules are applicable to all airport users.

Various assistances are also provided by these world bodies to member states or airlines. For example,

1) Manuals with guidelines and procedures required
2) Training and inspections
3) Audits
4) Information-sharing assistance
5) Assistance with negotiations between members
6) Records and updates, etc.

The programs and assistance of these world bodies is paramount to the smooth operation of civil aviation and its development. The active involvement of both organizations is in itself a vast subject and the areas covered within safety and security are huge.

Airport Safety and Security

Why is it important to have an active safety and security climate at the airport? There are various reasons why an airport needs to enforce safety and secure procedures; some of them are:

- An airport nowadays has been converted into a commercial hub, where even non-flying general public comes for shopping, entertainment, food, etc. So there is a lot of public interest. So any act of violence or sabotage gets widespread media attention. These are targets for criminal intent.
- Further, the travelling public needs their travel to be safe and smooth. The fare-paying passengers are the greatest assets to both the airline and the airport.
- The airport employees, airline crew, general public, infrastructure, and equipment are highly specialized and expensive, which need to be protected.
- After an incident, it may take a lot of time to get the operation to normalcy, to get the public confidence back, etc.
- Employees must not misuse facilities and equipment, which can endanger them and others, and damage the equipment.
- The aircraft is one of the most expensive equipment, which needs to be protected against damages or unlawful interference.
- Any unlawful interference can have international implications.
- Lost man hours, repairs, bad publicity, etc. are costly in today's competitive atmosphere.
- When a customer is lost, it may take a lot more effort and money to bring in him back. In the process, he may even divert 10 others as well.

These just a few of the reasons why safety and security at the airport are important requirements.

The airport passenger terminal generally comprises of entrance area, general public area, security check area, check-in counters, immigration counters, security check area, boarding gate, aero bridge, or coach ramp area. There are various areas that are controlled, or in other words, sterile. These are normally areas after immigration counters or areas beyond the first security check point onwards. Some domestic airports may not have immigration counters. The general non-travelling public are not allowed in the sterile areas. In some airports the sterile areas start at the entrance area. These depend on the level of security alert for that airport. The sterile area of the airport extends from the terminal into the walled or fenced-off ramp area adjacent to it. The ramp area comprises of the aircraft parking stands, baggage areas, equipment, and ULD stowage area, etc. Similarly, at the cargo terminal, the areas beyond the cargo acceptance or security screening area on to the airport ramp area are considered as sterile. So all surrounding areas leading to and including the aircraft parking ramp area, that lay within effective security control mechanism are sterile areas. These sterile areas and their integrity are mandatory for airports, due to various reasons:

1) To stop the general public from interfering with airport operations or indulging in any criminal activity.
2) For effective control of people leaving the country and arriving (immigration).
3) To ensure passengers are not carrying on hand any dangerous items that can endanger other passengers, crew, airport employees, or damage equipment.
4) To stop any other forms of unlawful interference.

Movement of passengers is controlled within the sterile area. Also, inbound passengers are not allowed to mix with outbound passengers at an airport. This is due to the possibility of criminal actions or activity to perpetrate a crime or obtaining information or tools to cause harm. Each area within the sterile area may be accessed by passengers only based on their access requirement/authorization/travel program. Access to these areas is possible for employees based on their functions or job roles. For a ramp staff, he may not need to access the terminal. In that case he will only be given a ramp access pass.

It is necessary for all airport users to understand the importance of the safety and security personnel and appreciate their efforts in maintaining a safe and secure environment. There may be delays or irritating questions, but these are necessary and are part of their profiling requirements. Additional checks may be carried out, we may not know of the mode of action planned by criminals or the increased level of threat. It is therefore appropriate to agree to security personnel requests for checking belongings, etc. Some of the most important general security compliance measures for ramp staff are:

1) Never run in the terminal or on the ramp. There is a chance of getting injured or security team misunderstanding your intentions.
2) Answer questions truthfully and accurately when asked by security personnel.
3) Never smoke on the ramp and only at designated areas in the terminal.
4) Do not carry any weapons or items that can be used to endanger another person. If in doubt, clarify it with your immediate supervisor.
5) If an unattended bag or item that is out of place is noticed on the ramp or terminal, immediately inform security personnel.
6) Do not access areas not authorized or allowed to access.
7) Do not access the airport outside of official duty hours or for any personal needs.
8) Do not take part in commercial activity or any other activity outside of your job function.
9) If any incorrect security procedure or breach is noticed, immediately inform the supervisor, with clear details and description.
10) Be aware and keep up to date with latest security requirements and procedures applicable for your area of work and the airport.

These are just a few measures required. There are safety and security requirements that are incorporated into each ramp staff's role or function by his or her organization's standards and procedures section, which we will come to eventually.

Organizational Framework and Programs

The airport authorities, airlines, and handling companies will have their own safety and security departments. They will incorporate the standards and recommended practices of ICAO and IATA, but may also fine-tune them further to make them even more effective, depending on their local or international operational conditions or scenarios. Some organizations take additional security steps over and above the state or governing body requirements. For example, some airline security requires each bag to be screened from four angles. Changes, if any, will be based on security conditions at its area of operations, past experiences, recommendations of its own or state agency where the organization is registered, etc. Some of these standards and recommendations are then converted by establishing appropriate monitoring sections in the organization while others are incorporated into rules that are weaved into the job roles and functions, etc. Various methods are employed by the organizations spread awareness and emphasize the importance of the rules and requirements in regards to safety and security at the airport. For example,

1) Through media publications
2) Placards with instructions and signs boards
3) Charts and posters
4) Training programs, case studies
5) Audits and monitoring
6) Emergency or mock drills
7) Penalties or fines for offenders and appreciations or commendations for exemplary compliance etc.

The complete safety and security mechanism at the airport works like a chain of command, with the highest authority lying with the state agency responsible for airport safety and security. This can be a separate unit, airport police, army, etc. All others, like the airlines or other service provider's security department or security agencies will need to be aligned with the state security agency. However, for the complete requirement to function efficiently, there should be the participation of all airport users, especially the airport employees at all levels. To make this happen, the organizations operating in the airport must have an active policy of creating a healthy awareness in the employees. For this the organization must have an effective and active safety and security policy, which needs to be cascaded down to the lower levels. This can be done by establishing an active unit, by formulating the translation of the safety and security policies of the organization and incorporating it into every aspect of its area of operation. For the ramp staff there are safety and security factors interwoven with their job role, that are formulated by the standards and procedures section of the organization, with periodic monitoring, audit, and recurrent training programs, etc. These are specific and when all of the safety and security requirements or programs from various sections are taken into account, it will form a complete multilayered safety and security program that should align with the organizational safety and security policies. The organizational policies must complement those of the state, ICAO, and IATA.

Operational Security Requirements

Security of an area is when there are no elements or personnel that can cause any harm or danger through intentional interference. Then the area is said to secure. In addition, processes and activities must also be modeled to keep the area secure. Each area has its own operational security requirements and rules. For example, all areas of the baggage handling area are to be illuminated and visible. This is to avoid any pilferage or other criminal activity.

Similarly, each team in various areas or sections of the ramp will have necessary security requirements built into their job roles. A few are as follows:

1) Baggage without tags, torn, or not security screened cannot be loaded on a flight.
2) Passengers, baggage, and other load for a specific flight should travel as planned and this cannot be changed unless approved and security screened.
3) Baggage of a passenger not travelling on board the flight must not be loaded.
4) Checked baggage of passengers must not be accessed by passengers till collection at the destination arrival hall.
5) Passengers cannot board without cabin crew completing their safety and security check.
6) Loading staff must ensure the aircraft holds are empty of any unaccounted items after offloading and before loading.
7) Engineers must not leave behind any tools on board that can be used as a potential weapon or that can be used to cause damage.
8) Loading staff must not take any item not belonging to them. As sometimes it can be dangerous, such as radioactive or explosive items.
9) Boarding staff must verify travel documents, confirm the passengers are security cleared for travel, arrange to check suspicious looking handbags.
10) Ensure all passengers are boarded, by cross-checking the checked-in figures and actual boarding count and ensure no passengers are hiding in toilets or the holding lounge before boarding.

Aviation Safety and Security

11) Verify the correct missing baggage details are passed to the ground dispatcher.
12) The load controller must not plan any loads without proper and correct documentation.
13) The interline or transfer baggage staff must ensure to process bags of transfer passenger actually travelling on the correct flight by checking against the checking records and travel itinerary.
14) Ground dispatcher and loading team must reconfirm offloaded bags of a missing passenger before flight departure.

Thus, there are many security requirements within the job roles of each and every staff at the airport. And most of the backgrounds for these requirements arise from ICAO, IATA, or state or organizational security programs. Therefore, compliance is mandatory.

Operational Safety Requirements

There are risks involved in all activities and locations. Risk is actually the potential of a dangerous or unwanted outcome that can cause loss of life, injury, sense of loss in some way, etc. Hence, steps need to be taken or be in place to reduce the exposure to these risks. So the environment when steps are in place or processes are in place that can reduce considerably the threat level of risk factors or impair a risk from being realized is called a safe environment. Higher the risk, the greater is the need for applicable steps to reduce the risk factors or level.

The airport ramp is a beehive of activities. There are aircrafts, large equipment, personnel, and vehicles moving about, fueling taking place, high aircraft engines with huge suction power near staff work area, etc. So it is a high-risk area and so needs safety procedures and checks in place to increase the safety level comparatively than other areas. Even related areas like baggage and cargo build-up areas are no less risky. There too are huge machinery on the move, loads being moved overhead, heavy lifts, electric components, etc. Similar to the security requirements, safety requirements are also incorporated into each and every individual staff's job role. Adherence to the same can mean a matter of life and death, or injury to self and others around. Airlines and airports need highly qualified, experienced, and skilled staff to operate highly specialized and expensive equipment and also to perform specialized job functions in and around expensive aircrafts. It also takes lots of hours and money to train for achieving the required proficiency. So replacement of any of these valuable assets is not easy. Hence, appropriate and effective safety mechanisms should be on place to ensure the safety of all these assets. The safety mechanism can include:

1) Visual aids
2) Protective equipment
3) Clear directions or instructions
4) Training programs specific for each job role or areas
5) Audit and monitoring
6) Safety reports
7) Safety features (both general and built into job functions)

Let us expand the above a little:

1) Visual aids: Equipment need to have reflectors, must be brightly painted, mirrors installed on sharp bends, etc.
2) Protective equipment: Safety shoes, reflective/luminescent vests, noise mufflers, etc.
3) Directions and instructions: There must be markings on roads, boards, and labels to show low ceilings, electric cables, or machinery areas, equipment operating instructions, etc.
4) Training and certifications: Each section's training must include safety briefing and subjects. All equipment operations must be allowed only after proper training, certifications, and recurrent revalidation. Keep track of beneficial and applicable training methods, changes in safety procedures and requirements, newly developed safety equipment, etc. in the industry and try to assimilate same.
5) Audit and monitoring: Regular audit of job functions must include that of the safety process to avoid complacency. The supervisor must monitor and perform spot checks. Appropriate briefing must be given with correct procedures.
6) Safety reporting must be encouraged. All safety reports must be scrutinized, suggestions and feedbacks responded to quickly, and necessary steps taken to avoid recurrences.

7) Safety features: There are general safety requirements that are applicable for all ramp users and those that are specifically applicable for individual job functions are built into the standard operating procedure of the job.

General safety features or requirements for example are:
- All areas on the ramp are non-smoking areas, including baggage and cargo stowage areas as well.
- There are applicable speed limits on the ramp areas, which must be adhered to at all times by all operators and drivers.
- Do not ride on vacant spaces on open-top vehicles without a proper seat.
- Ensure all equipment are in good working condition and sufficiently fueled before and after use, otherwise report and tag accordingly.
- Do not access prohibited areas.
- Foreign object debris check and aircraft parking stand obstruction check is mandatory. And if any issues are noticed dispose them off immediately or report to supervisor as applicable.
- Do not walk on taxi ways, and if not authorized, trained, or accompanied by competent authorized personnel, never approach runways in any way.

There numerous general safety guidelines, requirements, etc., those listed above are just a few. Some airports display instructions and posters at prominent areas of the ramp offices and other areas to remind and emphasize on these.

As mentioned, all jobs will have the necessary safety requirements included in the standard operating procedures. A few from the ramp are as follows:
- Any loads transported on the ramp must be secured by the team dispatching the load.
- Safety briefing must be carried out by the loading team leader and dispatcher.
- All loose items or debris must be disposed of appropriately if noticed by any ramp staff.
- Verification of loads for loading in a flight is mandatory for loading team leaders due to safety implications.
- Load controller is supposed to check and ensure the actual weights are within the structural maximum limits. Also, the

CG of the aircraft must lie within the safe range of the aircraft trim allowed.
- Dispatcher must ensure all the necessary safety requirements, both general and specific, for individual functions are adhered to by all team members.
- Baggage build-up staff must not send tag-less, leaking, or suspicious bags to the aircraft, but must reported these immediately to their supervisor.
- Loading team leader must not load any item or ULDs that are leaking or without a tag or without proper covering documents in the aircraft.
- Hi-loader operators must check the height and side of the ULD for sufficient clearance between the ceiling and walls and the ULD surface, before attempting to load it into the aircraft hold. They must always ensure to align the hi-loader's platform with the aircraft doorsill.
- The loading team must check the serviceability of the ULDs and nets to confirm they are compatible with securing and lashing requirements. All aircraft locks must be checked prior to closing doors.
- Pushback tractor drivers must confirm all chocks under the tires have been removed before commencing the pushback operation of the aircraft.
- Engineers need to check the fuselage, engines, and other components on arrival and before aircraft departure.

Thus, these are just a few to list as examples only, but there can be many for each job role. These specific safety requirements in a way also have another importance. They enable the staff to perform their job functions completely. Safety checks complement actual job functions also.

An effective safety and security environment at the airport gives a sense of secure feeling for all airport users. A safe and secure attitude or the need to enforce and apply safety and security features give rise to positive habits that over time can be emulated by other team members and thus strengthen the required atmosphere.

This is important for such a dynamic and vibrant industry as the civil aviation for its prestigious march into the future.

****

References

IATA Station management.

IATA Standard ground handling manual.

Emirates basic aviation, ground handling and Weight & Balance training courses.

Aviation security and aviation ground handling diploma, Emirates Group security and Edith Cowen University.

Disclaimer

As we all know, aviation is at the forefront of adopting the latest technological advancements and efficient professional functioning. That is the way forward to ensure highest safety of operation, best industrial practices, maximizing profits, and minimizing costs. Therefore, kindly note that the content of the book is to explain the basic knowledge and requirement only, as the professional makeup, atmosphere, actual process, etc., at any airport depends on various influencing factors both in terms of the governmental directives and the local area or regional or business model of the set up. Also, the aviation industry is self-evolving continuously (which makes it interesting as there is always something new), so every effort has been made to capture the most essential at the time of writing this book. Again, this can vary in priority or application from airport to airport. This book in no way replaces any manuals, instructions (from any person or entity), processes nor is it challenging any rules or legislations, whatsoever. I have seen many students and colleagues trying to find the necessary knowledge or means of understanding the concepts or process, etc., in this industry. This book is only intended as a tool in enhancing and supporting that quest.

About the Author

The author, although academically marketing qualified, is also qualified in four different areas of the vast aviation industry—namely ground handling, aviation security, air cargo logistics, and flight operations. The book is a culmination of over 26 years of in-depth professional service in this industry. The author's airport handling experiences span several airports in the UAE, UK, India, and Sri Lanka under varying capacities and special projects. He has undertaken projects within UAE and international projects related to aviation, some for which he received international recognition from governments, airlines, and other authorities. The author had volunteered his expertise for humanitarian aid flights handling for an NGO at an airport. That was a reflection of his deep sense of responsibility towards other humans in need, using the knowledge he had gained from the aviation industry he admires and is a part of. He has vast airport handling agent experience with a multinational airport ground handling company and is currently part of a team in a major airline group.